Meeting the Challenges of Primary Schooling

Edited by Lloyd Logan
and Judyth Sachs

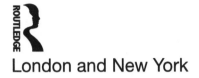
London and New York

First published 1997
by Routledge
11 New Fetter Lane, London EC4P 4EE

Simultaneously published in the USA and Canada
by Routledge
29 West 35th Street, New York, NY 10001

Typeset in Garamond by Routledge
Printed and bound in Great Britain by Creative Print and Design
(Wales), Ebbw Vale

British Library Cataloguing in Publication Data
A catalogue record for this book is available from the British Library

Library of Congress Cataloguing in Publication Data
Meeting the challenges of primary schooling / edited by
Lloyd Logan and Judyth Sachs.
(Educational management series)
Includes bibliographical references and index.
1. Education, Elementary–Australia. 2. Education, Elementary–
Australia–Administration. 3. Education, Elementary–Australia–
Curricula. 4. Elementary school teaching–Australia. I. Logan, Lloyd. II.
Sachs, Judyth, 1954– . III. Series.
LA2104.M44 1997
372.994–dc21
                                                        96–51866
                                                        CIP

ISBN 0–415–14655–0

Meeting the Challenges of Primary Schooling

Educational management series
Series editor: Cyril Poster

Contents

Illustrations

FIGURES

TABLES

Contributors

David Adams-Jones is a primary teacher at All Saints Anglican School, Gold Coast.

Carolyn Anderson is the Headmistress of Ipswich Girls' Grammar School, Queensland.

Dianne Andrewartha teaches at Oatlands School, Tasmania.

Stewart Bonser is a Senior Research Associate in the School of Education at Murdoch University, Western Australia.

Raymond A.J. Brown teaches at St Oliver Plunkett Primary School, Brisbane, Queeensland.

Kathy Davis teaches at Lilydale District High School, Tasmania.

Neil Dempster is an Associate Professor in the School of Education at Griffith University, Queensland.

Clive Dimmock holds appointments as Associate Professor in the Department of Educational Administration at the Chinese University of Hong Kong and Senior Lecturer in the Graduate School of Education at the University of Western Australia.

Belinda Eddy is an executive teacher in a small rural primary school in northern New South Wales.

Janice Flaherty is Manager of the Behaviour Support Unit at The Hub Learning Centre, Aberfoyle Park, South Australia.

Judith Gill is a Senior Lecturer at the Underdale Campus of the University of South Australia.

Miraca U.M. Gross is Associate Professor of Gifted Education, and Director of Gifted Education Programs, at The University of New South Wales, Sydney.

Susan Groundwater-Smith is Adjunct Professor of Education, Griffith University, Gold Coast.

Shirley Grundy is an Associate Professor in the School of Education at Murdoch University, Western Australia.

Elizabeth Hatton is an Associate Professor in the School of Teacher Education at Charles Sturt University in Bathurst.

Jill Heylen is Principal of Mylor Primary School, Adelaide.

Neville Highett is a senior officer in the Quality Assurance Directorate at the Department of Schooling, New South Wales.

Jacinta H. Howard is Assistant Principal of St Ives North Primary School in Sydney, and Coordinator of the Ku-ring-gai Unit for Gifted and Talented Students.

Lawrence Ingvarson is a Senior Lecturer in the School of Graduate Studies at Monash University, Melbourne, Victoria.

Andrew Laybourne is Coordinator at The Hub Learning Centre, Aberfoyle Park, South Australia.

Stephen Lewis is Head of Information Technology at All Saints Anglican School, Gold Coast.

Lloyd Logan is a Senior Lecturer in the Graduate School of Education at the University of Queensland.

Merrin Marett is Head of Science at St Leonard's School, Melbourne, Victoria.

Laurence Owens is Lecturer in Special Education at Flinders University.

Pamela Paton is currently seconded to the School Leadership Programme, Staff Development Unit of the Western Australian Education Department. Formerly she was a Deputy Principal in a Western Australian primary school.

Peter Renshaw is an Associate Professor in the Graduate School of Education at the University of Queensland.

Judyth Sachs is Professor of Education in the School of Teaching and Curriculum Studies, University of Sydney.

Larry Scott is the Senior Superintendent (Years 5–8) in the Department of Education and Arts, Tasmania.

Phillip Slee is Senior Lecturer in Education at Flinders University.

Richard Smith is Dean of the Faculty of Education and the Arts at Griffith University, Gold Coast.

Kathy Stewart is a teacher at Meadow Glen Primary School, Epping, Victoria.

Georgina Tsolidus is a member of the Faculty of Education at Monash University, Clayton, Victoria.

Christine Ure is a member of the Department of Early Childhood Studies at The University of Melbourne, Kew, Victoria.

Vivienne White is the National Co-ordinator of the National Schools Network, an Australia-wide school reform organisation.

Chapter 1

Challenges facing primary school administrators and teachers

Lloyd Logan and Judyth Sachs

Every day of the school year some 1.8 million children aged 4–12 years attend one of Australia's 8,000 primary schools. Schools range from an intimate group of 9 or 10 children to an institution of around 1,000 pupils, with a mean size varying from 167 in the Northern Territory to 329 in the Australian Capital Territory. Once at school, children will be taught by one or more of the nation's 125,000-plus primary school teachers assisted by some 30,000 administrative, specialist, clerical and general staff. The majority of the children (76 per cent) will attend a state or public school, the remainder a non-government school, apart from a small percentage undertaking home schooling or distance education. The vast majority of classroom teachers and ancillary staff (70–80 per cent) are women, and female principals and deputies are now common.

The school site might be a small inner-city block with asphalted playing areas; an area of 4–6 hectares in a suburb with gardens, outdoor teaching facilities, custom-built play areas and sports fields; a fenced section in a country town near the store and hotel; or a paddock cut out of the bush. The buildings might be solid red brick dating from the nineteenth century; high-set wooden structures designed to catch the breeze, provide shade and avoid flooding; or modern open-design complexes of glass and fibreboard. Almost invariably in the older, larger schools the architecture is a mixture of styles including the ubiquitous prefabricated temporary classrooms which became permanent long ago. The range and quality of facilities available to pupils and staff inside the buildings will be equally varied, reflecting the socioeconomic level of the neighbourhood, the school's history, the quality of past and present principals, the dedication and efficiency of the staff, and the capacity and interest of the parents to support the school. Also, many have a pre-school and provide after-school care.

Primary schooling is at once both the most common form of schooling in Australia and the most taken for granted. The majority of towns and suburbs either have their own school or have relatively easy access to one. Where access is difficult or denied due to distance or to a pupil's specific physical or emotional impairment, buses and alternative services such as schools of distance education guarantee every Australian child their right to primary schooling. However, despite its universality, a cursory examination of government policy, research and the educational literature shows that primary education is the poor cousin of the education family. It seems to have neither the social and emotional appeal of early childhood and special education, nor the economic significance attached to the secondary and tertiary sectors to attract funding. One consequence of this is that government policy tends to concentrate on young children and adolescents to the detriment of our primary-school-aged children. This does not mean that primary school has been exempt from the system-wide initiatives in curriculum, organisational restructuring, management and public accountability of the past two decades. However, few of those initiatives have been directly targeted at primary schools. In the main, in terms of government resourcing and attention, primary schooling is an educational fringe dweller.

This text looks at the ways that some of our primary schools are taking advantage of the opportunities that government initiatives and societal changes offer for educating children aged 4 or 5 to 11 or 12. It does this by focusing on two key questions:

1 What are the social and political pressures demanding attention from primary school administrators and teachers?
2 How have primary school administrators and teachers accommodated the pressures and utilised the opportunities that the changes offer?

Each chapter of this text documents how some of our primary school teachers are responding to these questions at the local neighbourhood level. Their overriding concern is not with the 'big picture' of national, social, cultural and economic reorientation but with the parochial and pressing issue of how best to cater for the current and future interests and welfare of their children in their school.

The accounts are grouped into three sections: the management of primary schools (Chapters 2–6), the curriculum and social justice (Chapters 7–10) and classroom practice (Chapters 11–16). The grouping is arbitrary and we recognise that each topic is related to, and impacts on, each and every one of the others. Also we acknowledge that in any school there are many initiatives and innovations going on at the same time. The accounts in this text concentrate on only one of these many developments. Finally, in addition to the energy and resources devoted to mounting and developing such initiatives, these teachers and their colleagues were expending considerable effort on maintaining and refining the best of their current practices. In fact, probably as much school and professional development come from refining current practice as from deliberate change interventions.

An inside–outside view of the practices given here is achieved in the main through chapters being co-authored by practising teachers working with academics or other personnel from outside the school. The result is a collection of narratives which give new insights into primary schooling.

This first chapter sets the general scene. It begins by outlining some of the major influences shaping the current context of primary schooling, beginning with the family. Attention is then focused on specific aspects of primary schooling including resourcing, management, learning outcomes, curriculum and classroom practice. This sets the scene for a brief discussion of the concerns of primary schooling and its reform.

THE SOCIAL CONTEXT OF PRIMARY SCHOOLING

The family is central to the quality of a primary-school-aged child's education. This is equally true for the pre-school and secondary years, but it is particularly so for the primary years for four reasons. First, this is the longest stage of compulsory education (six or seven years). Second, during these years the child grows from early childhood to late childhood and through to early adolescence. Third, throughout these years teachers figure large in children's lives. Fourth, family involvement tends to be higher in the primary than in the secondary years.

Today 'family' is defined as two or more people related by blood, marriage, adoption or a *de facto* relationship who live in the same household. Three major types of families are recognised: coupled families, one-parent families and families of related adults. Irrespective of the type of family, the need for close ties with the school are recognised and, in the main, are followed through in a variety of ways between teachers and parents. Given the importance of family to primary schooling, we begin by sketching out some of the general features of Australian families. While the data will not fit the context of any particular school, they provide a basis for thinking about a neighbourhood and the home life of the children who attend the school. Equally, they provide a basis for thinking about the backgrounds and home lives of the teachers, administrators and other adults who work in our schools or are voluntary helpers.

Australia has some 4.6 million families, the majority (53 per cent) being coupled families. Less than half of these families (43 per cent) are likely to have children under 15 years of age. The average Australian family size is 3.2 persons comprised of 2 adults and 2 children. Eighty-five per cent of children live in coupled families, and 80 per cent with their natural parents. Approximately 25 per cent of all births are outside marriage with about 80 per cent acknowledged by the father. About 15 per cent of children are in one-parent families, predominantly with their mother (90 per cent). The divorce rate is around 12.0 per 1,000, with 53 per cent of all divorces involving children. In the case of marriage breakdown, the median duration of marriage to separation is about 7.5 years.

In 45 per cent of cases both parents with children under 15 are likely to work full-time, with one partner working part-time in another 25 per cent of cases. At the other extreme, for some families social welfare is now inter-generational and no one in the household has ever been in regular employment. As children get older, the workforce participation of mothers increases.

Most children with parents in full or part-time work outside the home are cared for after school. However, for about one child in ten no after-school care is provided and a similar number are cared for by older children. Approximately 45 per cent of children at primary school will have been in kindergarten, pre-school or childcare. Mobility can be high, with more than 50 per cent of families changing their place of residence within a five-year period.

The health of Australia's children is cause for concern. Many are over-weight and register high cholesterol levels. Fast foods and prepared meals are part of the standard diet and account for around 25 per cent of expendi-ture on food. In some schools, a worrying number of children regularly arrive for the day without having had a satisfactory breakfast.

Only 40–5 per cent of boys and 35–40 per cent of girls aged 9–12 have sufficient aerobic exercise. Approximately 12 per cent are estimated to lose at least one day per fortnight of schooling due to sickness or injury. Asthma is the most prevalent chronic illness among children and adolescents with 23 per cent of 7 year olds having a history of wheezing at some time during a year. About 30 per cent of primary-school-aged children regularly take some form of medication.

Between 5 and 10 per cent of boys and girls aged 11 and 12 years use alcohol weekly. Thirty per cent of 10-year-old boys and 20 per cent of the girls have experimented with smoking and 5 per cent are regular smokers by the age of 12.

The immunisation profile of children aged 0–6 is: diphtheria and tetanus 90 per cent; measles 86 per cent; mumps 80 per cent; polio 72 per cent; and whooping cough 71 per cent. Considerable variation occurs between communities.

About 3 per cent of boys and 2 per cent of girls aged 0–14 are severely handicapped, 5 per cent are moderately handicapped and some 20 per cent are mildly handicapped. The World Health Organisation defines a handi-capped person as a disabled person aged 5 years or over who is limited to some degree by their ability to perform certain tasks in relation to one or more of the following five areas: self-care, mobility, verbal communication, schooling or employment (Jolly, 1992).

Most states and territories have implemented mandatory reporting by teachers of child abuse. Due to the sensitive nature of such cases, the vulnerability of children and the difficulty of substantiation in a signifi-cant number of incidences, the accurate situation with child abuse is difficult to ascertain. However, some general features are identifiable.

Girls are more likely to suffer from sexual abuse than boys. Physical, sexual and emotional abuse is most commonly perpetrated by family members or by close family friends.

The primary years for many families seem to be built around their children's out-of-school activities. Half of the children aged 5–14 regularly participate in sport organised by a club or association. In addition, for some, music and dancing lessons along with organisations such as scouts and guides, church groups and other such associations fill their out-of-school time. Cinemas are the most frequented cultural venue attended by families, followed by libraries, animal and marine parks and botanic gardens. Watching television is the most common home leisure pursuit of some 70 per cent of children aged 0–14 years followed by relaxing, visits from friends and reading newspapers. Indoor games, listening to music and crafts and hobbies are among the least common leisure activities.

Today's primary school pupils live in a multi-media, information-overload world. On average they watch over 20 hours of television per week, and have access to video and tape recorders, radio and electronic games. One in three homes has a computer. By the time some children arrive at school they might well have watched television, accessed the Internet, used a CD-ROM database, had radio as background noise, and solved a multitude of problems on an electronic game. In short, many primary school pupils are sophisticated users of information technology both for entertainment and learning purposes.

Finally, the population of children in primary school is projected to increase to 1.9 million pupils by the year 2002.

RESOURCING PRIMARY SCHOOLS

Annual federal and state expenditure on government schooling totals around $12 billion. In 1993–4 the Australia-wide expenditure per school pupil was $5,100, ranging from $4,800 in Queensland to $7,700 in the Northern Territory. Average expenditure on primary school pupils in round figures was $4,000, ranging from $3,900 in New South Wales to $5,900 in the Northern Territory. Comparable average expenditure on secondary school pupils per capita was $6,000, some 50 per cent higher than that for primary school pupils.

In a recent survey, primary schools were found to have an inferior level of provision on every indicator, from staffing to computers, compared with secondary schools (Schools Council, 1995). There is also resource disparity within primary schooling itself, with the upper primary stage arguably the least well resourced in a child's schooling (Schools Council, 1995a). However, the issue is not the disparity between sectors and within them. The real concern is whether or not every year of schooling is resourced at a level sufficient to guarantee the education required for individual and national development.

In addition to the direct cost to government, parents of pupils in government schools contributed on average in Victoria, through fees and fund-raising, some $255 per child annually, and in New South Wales $90–130. Moreover, the cost to families is likely to increase if the prediction of the Schools Council is correct.

> There was . . . widespread recognition that in an age of apparently decreasing support for the maintenance of a robust public education system, there will be limits on the extent to which governments are likely to increase their investment in government schools. If such limits are to be imposed, most of those consulted appeared to support the targeting of at least a proportion of the available resources on schools that are unable to generate revenue from their own efforts – an expectation that public schools seem increasingly to be facing.
>
> (Schools Council, 1995: xiii)

However, that picture is leavened somewhat by the same report stating that 78 per cent of taxpayers believe that public expenditure on education should be raised, with the increase met by additional taxes of up to $63 per head.

Recent developments that are likely to increase the demand for resources include:

- the adoption of participative forms of management which involve parents and staff in and out of teaching hours
- the greater awareness of rights and responsibilities and the need for documentation for public accountability and in case of litigation
- the expectation that every school will be inclusive and meet the learning needs of every child enrolled
- the greater emphasis on the welfare and care functions of the school
- the requirement to meet public sector policy and regulations such as health and workplace safety, audit procedures and staff appointment processes
- the demands for information technology hardware, software and recurrent costs
- the identification of Key Learning Areas and the associated curriculum readjustments
- the greater provision for children with special learning impairments and other conditions which inhibit their progress.

Developments such as these are designed to improve the effectiveness and efficiency of schooling in terms of student outcomes. Research studies on school effectiveness, with few exceptions, all but ignore the level of resourcing as a factor. Following their research into the impact of resources on schooling, Hill and Russell (1994) concluded that there was no simple, generic principles or formula to guide policy in this area. They concluded that the critical issue was resource use rather than the level of provision. This might be correct given that the schools are guaranteed sufficient resources to improve their current activities and to meet the demands associated with new priorities and programmes. However, the concern that a decline in expenditure will, in time, be deleterious to school effectiveness remains a real possibility (Marginson, 1993).

SCHOOL MANAGEMENT

Since the mid-1980s federal, state and local governments have reformed their public service sectors in the image of private enterprise. Consequently, every schooling system has been structurally reorganised during the last decade. Systems of governance and accountability, management styles, conditions of employment and promotion, and job descriptions have been redrawn. What it means to be a school principal and a school teacher have been radically reshaped by the changes of the last decade or so.

The structural reforms confirm central control over purposes, policy and finance and local responsibility for their implementation. Flat, collaborative styles of administration are promoted in place of power-coercive line-management approaches. The rights of parents and community participation are formalised rather than left to the discretion of the principal and teachers.

In general the moves to localise school management and to revise management processes have been well received by school administrators, teachers and parents (Caldwell, 1994; Logan et al., 1996). Benefits include better leadership, greater use of participative management, more opportunity for innovation and self-direction, stronger school community and teacher–parent linkages, and improved pupil outcomes. However, such gains come at the cost of considerable intensification of the teaching day, more bureaucratic accountability and the continual extension of school work into the teachers' personal time (Logan et al., 1996). Despite these side effects there is no strong call from the schools for a return to the old forms of administration.

The concepts of planning and review are central to the new management. The corporate or strategic plan developed by central office sets the parameters and priorities throughout the system for a given period, commonly of three years. This plan is translated into annual operational plans on the basis of yearly review. At the end of each three-year period the system's productivity is assessed in terms of the corporate plan. These requirements and practice also apply to schools. Therefore schools develop school development plans for periods of three to five years that are designed to implement central priorities in ways that accommodate specific local needs. Also, schools are expected to take their own initiatives. Some matters of school change, planning and review are dealt with in Chapters 2–6.

LEARNING OUTCOMES

The Common and Agreed National Goals for schooling in Australia, the so-called Hobart Declaration, emphasise the contribution of schooling to attitudinal development; the wellbeing of students; the preparation of students for participation in the workforce, further education and life-long learning; and for social responsibility and active citizenship. Measuring learning outcomes in most of these areas is extremely difficult, if not impossible. Where indicative national data do exist they can be neither aggregated nor compared. However, some general themes and trends are identifiable.

One general theme that emerges is that students on average have a higher level of general satisfaction with their primary than with their secondary schooling. A second theme refers to the state and territory data on performance testing programmes in literacy and numeracy. These suggest that there has not been any marked improvement or deterioration in student performance over the last few years. However, the absence of extensive time series information means that within the states and territories only partial analysis of trends is possible.

Some key examples of results are as follows:

- relatively stable scores in New South Wales over the past five years for Years 3 and 5 students' literacy and numeracy performance; whole non-English speaking background students have improved in both areas over this period
- improvements in Years 5 and 9 students' mathematics performance between 1991 and 1993 in Queensland, with a slight fall in the performance of Year 7 students over the same period
- slight improvements in mathematics performance for Year 3 and Year 10 students in Western Australia between 1990 and 1992, with improvement for Year 7 students
- in Tasmania, which has a relatively long record of reporting outcomes, numeracy levels have fallen over the last decade, while some literacy results have improved over the same period
- in the Northern Territory, improvements in mathematics and reading for Years 5 and 7 students between 1990 and 1994
- where they are recorded, the learning outcomes for Aboriginal and Torres Strait Islander students are lower than those recorded for the population as a whole.

(Steering Committee for the Review of
Commonwealth/State Service Provision, 1995: 200)

The data from the states and territories on equity objectives in Australian schooling carry no surprises.

An important set of objectives for school systems relates to meeting the needs of groups identified as facing educational disadvantage. These include, amongst others, students with learning disabilities, students from low socio-economic and non-English speaking backgrounds (NESB), and Aboriginal and Torres Strait Islander (ATSI) students.

Five jurisdictions provided disaggregated information showing results by target group for statewide tests. These show, for example, that Aboriginal and Torres Strait Islander students in Queensland, WA and the NT achieved below other students in those jurisdictions in all subjects and at all year levels tested. In Tasmania, students at low socio-economic status (SES) neighbourhood schools performed at lower levels than those from higher SES neighbourhood schools. Performance of other target groups shows similar, although not so pronounced, differences.

(Steering Committee for the Review of
Commonwealth/State Service Provision, 1995: 201)

The results of performance testing give a limited basis for making judge-ments about the quality, effectiveness and efficiency of the contribution that schools are making to their pupils and to the welfare of society. Some commentators and practitioners might deny that performance testing has any relevance in making such judgements. This might be true but the above data give reason for some disquiet. Where improvement in performance has been registered, it seems to be incommensurate with the human, financial and material costs involved.

CURRICULUM AND SOCIAL JUSTICE

The curriculum of the primary school is predicated on the school's respons-ibility to enrich the intellectual, emotional, cultural, social and physical development of every child within its care. Traditionally the curriculum consisted of arithmetic, reading, writing, English, social studies, science, physical and health education, music and art. Current moves for nation-wide recognition of Key Learning Areas has resulted in the identification of the arts, English, health and physical education, languages other than English, mathematics, science, studies of society and environment and technology as the curriculum for the compulsory years of schooling.

The development of the curriculum statements and profiles for each area is one of the most significant curriculum initiatives in Australian education (Reid, 1995). According to their advocates, the statements and profiles are no more than frameworks which stimulate diversity while acknowledging the need for commonality (Wilson, 1994). According to some commenta-tors (Randall and Kerr, 1994, Williamson and Cowley, 1994), the national statements and profiles are useful tools for teachers to use when creating their planned classroom learning experiences. The critics of the profiles and frameworks, such as Collins (1994), claim that they are based on false premises about knowledge, learning and development. These are: (1) that knowledge is divisible into discrete sections, in this instance eight key areas; (2) that such sections are coherent, and mapping coherency in strands improves the teaching learning process; (3) that children will typically follow the path of each strand; (4) that their development will be linear and continuous; and (5) that samples of work will be valid and reliable indicators of individual and collective progress. In Collins's view (1994: 48), the statements and profiles are anachronistic, 'a monument to the time lag of "common sense", a common sense which still believes in curriculum as a universal science for the universal child'. Other commentators, such as Reid (1995), see the development phase as an abject failure which can only be remediated by strong teacher consultation throughout the implementation phase.

However, as the authors of Chapter 7 point out, the main issues of curriculum are ideological rather than procedural. They identify the issues of quality and accountability as the driving concerns shaping contemporary educational policy and practice. Concentration on these issues reflect deeper concerns within the society over matters of human rights, social justice, and equality of access, opportunity and outcome. Chapters 8–10 deal with particular aspects of social justice such as extending options for gifted and talented pupils (Chapter 8), responding to the pupils' culture and language (Chapter 9) and the gender-responsive classroom (Chapter 10).

CLASSROOM PRACTICE

The pedagogy of the primary classroom since the late 1950s in Australia has been predicated on seven concerns:

- matching learning to children's individual differences
- activity and discovery methods of teaching and learning
- mastery of basic learning and thinking tools
- including parents in the child's schooling
- utilising the children's personal interests and social concerns in learning activities
- developing a sense of community
- tone, feeling, environment culture of the school.

These concerns were codified through the curriculum reforms from the late 1950s (e.g. new mathematics, new social studies, new science), and the open education movement. Both challenged the traditional view of the child as a receptive learner, didactic teaching styles, repressive forms of behaviour control and the validity of subject-based learning experiences. Bassett (1974) described the primary school of the early 1970s as a 'restless organisation' and the changes in its curriculum, organisation and practices as 'an expression of dissatisfaction with the adequacy of the traditional education for present and future needs' (p. 105). That dissatisfaction sponsored a catalogue of experimentation in Australian primary schooling which continued in various forms throughout the 1970s and 1980s. These include forms of: parent involvement; curriculum planning – integration, thematic planning; teacher deployment – team teaching, cooperative teaching specialisation; organising learning – small group work, pupil contracting, project work, activity corners, laboratories, resource-based learning, discovery learning, inquiry learning; grouping children – family grouping, non-grading, cross-grading, cross-setting; and reporting to parents – face-to-face, portfolio, class visits.

In 1992 the Schools Council identified two alternative models used by teachers to organise activities and experiences in Australian primary schools based on whether their orientation was mainly on children and learning or on teachers and teaching. The approaches reflect the tension between the traditional and experiential orientations to primary schooling identified by Bassett more than two decades ago (see Table 1.1).

Bassett's 'restless organisation' has continued to experiment and develop. Here, Chapters 11–15 describe how teachers who use a flexible approach to

Table 1.1   Alternative models of contemporary schooling

Focus	Element	Regulated models	Flexible models
Children and learning	Children Learning Grouping Assessment Progression	Dependent Predetermined Age/year Quantitative Lock-step	Enterprising Self-directed Multi-level Qualitative Individualised
Teachers and teaching	Teachers Teaching Curriculum Assessment Reporting Leadership Decision-making Innovation Administration Management Accountability	Directive Didactic Content-based Narrow Written Controlling Top-down Imposed Control-centred Rule-based System-based	Supportive Constructivist Student-based Broad Multi-dimensional Enabling Participatory Integrated Service-centred Principle-based Community-based

Source: Adapted from Schools Council, 1992: 9

teaching children are seeking to enhance pupil progress through assessment recording and reporting (Chapter 11), the use of technology (Chapter 12), managing pupil behaviour (Chapter 13), alternative approaches to children learning (Chapter 14) and different ways of grouping children for their schooling (Chapter 15).

CURRENT CONCERNS OF PRIMARY SCHOOLING

Two main ideas continue to underpin the philosophy and practice of primary schooling in Australia. One is the understanding that primary schooling is concerned with the total development of the child, intellectually, emotionally, physically, culturally, morally, economically and politically. The other is that teachers are concerned with assuring that every child's life is enriched by the level of care that they experience in the classroom, playground, family, neighbourhood and wider community. Providing these services is further complicated by the tension between conserving the best from the past and present, and preparing the nation's future citizens to control and shape their own destiny, and ours.

The tensions caused by the requirements for teachers to attend to the past, present and future in their teaching are neither new nor easy and the consequences of getting the balance wrong can be serious and far-reaching, as Bassett (1974: 3) warned some twenty years ago:

> Too great a concern with future goals may be self-defeating, partly because of the lowered vitality of a school that divorces its life from the present needs and interests of pupils. On the other hand, too great a preoccupation with what is familiar and limited to present interests may make the school too self-sufficient and inward looking, and dull its alertness to changing social needs.

How primary schools have interpreted and met this delicate balance during the 100 or so years of universal primary schooling in Australia have reflected the dominant beliefs of the wider community of the day. Today, fulfilling these are complicated by the rate, scope and intensity of social, cultural and economic change. During such periods in a nation's history, the comforts of certainty, predictability and confidence based on past practices and beliefs are replaced by the stimulation of insecurity, apprehension and opportunity.

In the emerging postmodern Australia the school remains one of the bastions of the modern state. As such it is expected to continue to meet the dual expectations of being at once a social museum and a virtual future reality. The first expectation requires schools to look backwards in order to conserve the 'best' of past and present human thought, activity and production. The second expectation requires the school to be futuristic in preparing children to shape their future world. The best way to do this, according to

Plowden (1966), is to ensure that children are living rich and challenging lives in the present. Achieving this requires reforming some of the policies, structures and practices that inhibit schools and their communities from doing so.

REFORM AND PRIMARY SCHOOLING

The catalysts for reforming primary schooling are threefold: (1) social, cultural and economic developments across the wider community; (2) initiatives stemming from government policies; and (3) new insights into the theory and practice of teaching developed by the teaching profession. Reform is notoriously slow in schooling and it is one thing for governments, employing authorities and school management, to mandate change, and another for it to become common practice. The current reforms, however, have two significant features which, while they might not guarantee successful implementation, increase its likelihood. One is that the reforms are part of a societal reform agenda which is not likely to go away. Second, they are comprehensive in so far as they address planning, management, performance, public accountability and conditions of work.

Social, cultural and economic developments impacting most directly on primary schooling include: an emphasis on human rights and social justice; a growing underclass dependent on social welfare concentrated in some neighbourhoods; the occurrence of intergenerational unemployment; greater tolerance of cultural and racial differences; recognition of alternative family structures; privatisation of government services; increased attention to litigation; more public accountability and surveillance; ready availability of multi-media goods and services; greater connectivity with the world through information technology; continual emphasis on materialism; high family mobility; an aging population; and the trend towards casual and fractional employment.

In response to such trends, governments have exerted significant influence on the purposes, policies and practices of Australian primary schooling during the last two decades. Intervention has been mainly by mandated change and resource-led change. State governments have the constitutional power to mandate their initiatives. Examples include the revisions to organisational structures, curriculum, pedagogy, assessment and reporting procedures, accountability requirements, and conditions of employment and work conditions. The federal government, since education is constitutionally a state matter, is required to adopt less direct, but equally effective, measures to promote its initiatives. It implements its policies mainly through tied grants and membership of national forums such as the Ministerial Council on Employment, Education, Training and Youth Affairs (MCEETYA). Examples include programmes addressing inclusivity, literacy, languages other than English, gender, multi-culturalism, information technology, national curriculum statements and profiles, and extending options for the gifted and talented.

While the changes sponsored by governments claim the most attention and publicity, we should not overlook developments pioneered by the profession. They include revisions to practice in the fields of curriculum, assessment and reporting, the application of information technology, and teacher–pupil relationships. Also revisions to school management, school review and working conditions, while due in part to wider public sector reform, have been shaped by the profession's contribution.

CONCLUSION

The purpose of this chapter was to paint a broad picture of the social and professional context of primary school life. Within this context there are many points of contention and concern. These include control over what is taught in schools, what counts as quality schooling, the role of the teacher in the curriculum, judging and comparing pupil performance, and school and teacher accountability processes. Running throughout such issues is the tension between teacher as professional and teacher as public servant. On the one hand, due to greater recognition of their professional status, it can be argued that teachers now exercise significant control over what and how they teach. On the other hand, due to organisational restructuring, accountability and legal requirements, the intensity of the teaching day and their involvement in management, they have restricted opportunity to exercise their professionality and are again being turned into functionaries of the state.

How some teachers resolve problems caused by such tensions and contradictions, and problems arising out of the context of their particular school community, is the subject of the following chapters culminating with our ruminations on these matters in Chapter 17.

REFERENCES

Bassett, G. (ed.) (1974) *Primary Education in Australia: Modern Developments*, Sydney: Angus & Robertson.

Caldwell, B. (1994) 'Australian perspectives on leadership: the principal's role in radical decentralisation in Victoria's schools of the future', *Australian Educational Researcher* 21, 2: 45–62.

Collins, C. (1994) 'Is the national curriculum profiles brief valid?', *Curriculum Perspectives* 14, 1: 45–8.

Grundy, S. (1994) 'The national curriculum debate in Australia: discordant discourses', *South Australian Educational Leader* 5, 3: 23–7.

Hadow, Sir William Henry (1931) *Report of the Consultative Committee on Primary School. London*, London: Great Britain Board of Education.

Hill, P. and Russell, V. (1994) *Resource Levels for Government Primary Schools*, Centre for Applied Education Research, Melbourne: The University of Melbourne.

Jolly, D. (Chair) (1992) *Health Goals and Targets for Australian Children and Youth: Project Report*, Canberra: AGPS.

Logan, L., Sachs, J. and Dempster, D. (eds) (1996) *School Planning Matters*, Deakin, Canberra: The Australian College of Education.

MacGilchrist, B., Mortimore, P., Savage, J. and Beresford, C. (1995) *Planning Matters: The Impact of Development Planning in Primary Schools*, London: Paul Chapman.

Marginson, S. (1993) *Education and Public Policy in Australia*, Cambridge: Cambridge University Press.

Plowden, J.P. (Chair) (1966) *Children and Their Primary Schools: A Report of the Central Advisory Council for Education (England)*, London: HMSO.

Randall, R. and Kerr, D. (1994) 'Trialing student outcome statements', *Curriculum Perspectives* 15, 3: 74–6.

Reid, A. (1995) 'Profiles: real problems or real gains – from whose perspective?', *Curriculum Perspectives* 15, 3: 76–80.

Schools Council (1992) *Developing Flexible Strategies in the Early Years of Schooling: Purposes and Possibilities*, Canberra: AGPS.

—— (1995) *Resources and Accountability: Commonwealth Funding Scenario for Government Primary Schools 1996–2000*, Canberra: AGPS.

—— (1995a) *Review of the Level of Commonwealth Recurrent Funding to Government Primary Schools: Report on the Consultations*, Canberra: AGPS.

Steering Committee for the Review of Commonwealth/State Service Provision (1995) *Report on Government Service Provision*, Canberra: AGPS.

Williamson, J. and Cowley, T. (1994) 'Case studies about implementing profiles', *Curriculum Perspectives* 15, 3: 69–71.

Wilson, B. (1994) 'Profiles meet poststructuralism', *Curriculum Perspectives* (newsletter edition) 14, 2: 20–1.

Theme I

School management

Chapter 2

Leading and managing restructuring at the school site
A Western Australian case study

Clive Dimmock and Pamela Paton

It was early March 1992. In a staff meeting at Greenslade Primary School, a challenge to the teachers rang out:

> So . . . what is it that's preventing you, the teaching staff, from rigorously exploring ways to do things better around here? What are the barriers to you making a difference – in the classroom, out in the yard, in the staffroom, in communication with the district or central office? Essentially – what stops you doing your job better?

The gauntlet was thrown down. Teachers sat silent; some stunned, others indifferent. In the words of one teacher who was anxious to break the silence: 'For heavens sake, just tell us what has to be done or give us some possibilities and we'll be off and running.' But the officers representing the National Project on the Quality of Teaching and Learning (NPQTL) – a teachers' union official and an administrator from the Education Department of Western Australia (EDWA) – chose not to provide any assistance. As one teacher commented: 'Slowly, it began to dawn on us that this was a challenge for *us* to reshape, rethink, restructure and reculture our workplace. An opportunity to stop and consider what we were doing and how we were doing it.' But first, the school had to decide whether it would accept the invitation to join the NPQTL.

This chapter is a case study of the progress of a Western Australian government primary school, henceforth known as Greenslade, as it undertook the task of major restructuring. It provides many insights into the realities of the local management of schools. The case study presents the trials, tribulations, successes and failures experienced by school personnel as they attempted to come to terms with the challenges of managing and implementing whole-school change. As with all case studies, an understanding of the context is important. Accordingly, a brief explanation is given of the broad education policy environment, largely shaped by the Western Australian government's attempt since the late 1980s to devolve more responsibility to schools. This description of the context includes

Greenslade's invitation in 1992 to join the NPQTL. This invitation is of particular importance in shaping the context within which Greenslade's reform efforts took place, since it was through membership of the Project that school reform was both initiated and subsequently shaped. Finally, the chapter addresses the processes and outcomes of change as well as the experiences of teachers and senior school administrators at Greenslade as they emerged from 1992 over the following three years. The account rendered in this case study is not intended to promote generalisation. Rather, it is hoped that the insights gained through the experiences of key personnel engaged in Greenslade's restructuring will enable readers to seek and recognise points of commonality and difference with their own situations, thereby furthering their understanding of the issues confronting school-site managers in attempting restructuring.

THE CONTEXT OF GREENSLADE'S RESTRUCTURING

The NPQTL was designed to promote school restructuring geared to improving the quality of teaching and learning. The Project's purpose and time of introduction are both significant. At varying times throughout the 1980s almost all Australian state governments formally introduced policies to dismantle the overly centralised bureaucracies that had characterised school systems throughout the century. Underpinning these new policies lay the clear intention to create more devolved and decentralised structures which would place much greater emphasis on school-based management.

In Western Australia, the decentralisation policy was heralded in a document called *Better Schools in Western Australia: A Programme for Improvement* (Western Australia Ministry of Education, 1988). The *Better Schools* report argued that devolving the management of responsibilities to schools would improve their effectiveness and increase their accountability to their communities. Central to the policy document were ideas now accepted as generic to the restructuring movement world-wide: schools were to receive a lump sum grant with more freedom over its allocation; school councils were to be set up so that parents and community could be more involved; and schools were to undertake development planning. However, the schools were to operate within more clearly specified system policy guidelines. The *Better Schools* report also advocated school-site appointment of staff, an idea that incurred the immediate wrath of the teachers' union and was quickly dropped.

It is important to clarify the origins of the *Better Schools* policy and others like it in Australian states during the 1980s. In contrast to the United States, where school-site management was advocated on the grounds of school effectiveness, school improvement, local ownership and the school being the most effective unit for managing educational change, school-site management in Australia had its origins in the drive to reform public sector management with the focus on efficiency and the better use of existing resources (Angus, 1995). As Angus states, 'The language used . . . has the resounding ring of corporate managerialism – audit, performance appraisal, corporate plan, performance indicators and so on.' Only a year before the *Better Schools* report, a Western Australian parliament White Paper, *Managing Change in the Public Sector* (1986), had recognised the difficulty of managing public services like education in financially constrained times. The need to continue to serve an increasingly demanding public with limited resources would require improved efficiency and effectiveness. In the same year, the Western Australian government introduced its Financial Administration and Audit Act, aimed at increasing the accountability of public sector institutions.

Yet, as Angus (1995) recognises, it would be wrong to conclude that the *Better Schools* report had no concern for the quality of schooling. Indeed, running through the document is a belief that the quality of schools and schooling would improve with the transfer of responsibility for problem solving from central bureaucracy to schools. However, herein lies the inherent weakness of devolution policies, like the *Better Schools* report. They were policies based on faith and belief. They manifestly failed to explain *how* the various elements of policy would or could lead to improved schooling. Most of the measures advocated were administrative in nature rather than pedagogic, and were always likely to affect the management of the school more than the classroom. No rationale was ever forthcoming as to how reconfiguring school management and administration would or could lead to improved schooling, a phenomenon that was dependent on teaching, learning and classroom-based activity. In the event, the drive to school-based management left teaching and learning relatively untouched. It should not be surprising therefore, that other restructuring initiatives, particularly those targeting the classroom-based activities of teaching and learning, were subsequently seen as necessary and complementary to the earlier wave of policies aimed at administrative restructuring. Such is the significance of the NPQTL. It sought to reconfigure teachers' work and to promote restructuring deep in the core technology of schools, in classrooms where teaching and learning take place – aspects of schooling long resistant to penetrating influences from outside, such as attempts to devolve administrative functions. Elsewhere, Dimmock (1995) has distinguished administrative forms of devolution (macro-restructuring) from restructuring initiatives aimed at curriculum, teaching and learning (micro-restructuring).

The following account of Greenslade's attempt to undertake whole-school restructuring captures some of the reflections of teachers and school administrators by quoting their own words for authenticity.

THE SCHOOL AND ITS DECISION TO RESTRUCTURE

The question had been posed and the challenge presented – was the school prepared to join the NPQTL and undertake major reform? Staff responses were wide ranging, from 'this doesn't concern me at all' and 'yes, let's go for it as long as it doesn't affect me' to 'let's get going now, why wait?' After numerous brief huddles in meetings, the staff voted, by show of hands, to join the NPQTL. Greenslade was one of seven foundation schools in Western Australia to participate in NPQTL. The schools were scattered throughout the state and collectively represented both primary and secondary, small and large, urban and country/isolated, as well as comfortable 'leafy' and more socioeconomically disadvantaged schools. Greenslade fitted the bill as a small primary school in an urban setting with students from a socioeconomically disadvantaged background. The school was nearly twenty years old. It had 260 students, ranging from 4 year olds, who attended part-time, to 12 year olds in Year 7. Many of the students came from one-parent families. For a large number of the parents, formal education had terminated at Year 10. Furthermore, unemployment among the parent group was high, as was the proportion of parents living in rented, publicly provided housing. Demographically, many students came from Aboriginal backgrounds and the school catered to a large section of ESL (English as a Second Language) students. Two classes were provided for education support students, some of whom were bused to the school. The staffing profile of the school comprised a teaching principal and a deputy, thirteen teachers, part-time specialist physical education and music teachers, part-time teaching assistants in the junior and education support classrooms, and a part-time librarian. The school had a registrar who had the assistance of a part-time clerical–administrative officer. Most of the teaching staff were very experienced, especially at working in this type of challenging, some might say difficult, school. Most of the teachers were female and more than half of the staff were on temporary contracts; that is, they were employed on a yearly basis according to student numbers.

Once the decision to join the Project had been taken, a small planning group of staff members was elected to explore the school's participation. The group included two teachers, the school's union representative, the deputy principal and the principal. The question on most people's minds at the first Project meeting was aptly summed up by one teacher, who asked: 'What are we going to get out of this?' Another commented, 'We were certainly in the bartering mode.' Most felt that the school's participation in what was seen as a unique cooperation between union and employer gave them the right to challenge existing EDWA policies and union industrial agreements that were perceived by some as barriers to restructuring. Staff had the clear understanding that existing rules, regulations and policies that were seen as obstructive were to be 'waived' while the school engaged in reform. A further benefit to the participating schools was the promise of quality professional development opportunities for individuals, whole-school groups and larger combined groups of schools, with the aim of exploring the critical elements contributing to and impeding the quality of teaching and learning. All seven foundation Project schools in Western Australia had access to state and national conferences in the form of summer and winter schools. By the end of 1994, most teaching staff had attended an NPQTL conference. In addition, communication links had been established, through meetings, e-mail, bulletins and video link-ups, with many other Project schools across Australia.

In the first place, the staff realised that before they could decide on a reform programme they needed to clarify the *status quo*. School structures and practices were typically traditional and conservative. For instance, the curriculum was delivered and learning settings organised through 'all-at-one-stage' student learning programmes, in single 'egg-box' classrooms. Students were isolated from each other, both physically and mentally. Although teachers were dedicated to their students, it was a form of dedication unrelated to the quality of teaching and learning. Existing school structures, in the words of one teacher, 'seemed to hinder and obstruct any efforts to secure long-term collaboration on matters such as planning, implementing, monitoring and evaluating whole-school improvement efforts'. Another teacher commented that the way the school was managed and organised seemed to render ineffective the attempts to achieve any notion of deep, continuous and connected learning – social as well as academic – for the students.

Early on in the process, Greenslade's staff were invited to attend a series of seminars provided for all of the Project schools in Western Australia. At that stage, they had only the haziest of notions about how, and even more importantly why, to restructure. The challenge to break rules and do things differently was for some teachers clouded by doubts about the importance of rules and their *de facto* influence on classroom practice. The NPQTL was officially launched in Western Australia by the Minister for Education. For three days the staff heard from leaders of business, unions and employers, all of whom gave their views on the state of the nation and the role of education in society. In the words of one of Greenslade's senior administrators:

We heard from the Employment and Skills Formation Council [The Carmichael Report, 1992] on proposals for an Australian vocational certificate training system, the Australian Education Council Review [The Finn Report, 1991] on proposals to increase young people's participation in post-compulsory education and training, and from the Mayer Committee [1992] on employment-related competencies. At the end, we were exhausted and distressingly full of anguish, self-doubt and confusion. This job, indeed the vocation of teaching we had long committed ourselves to, was under attack from without. Everybody seemed to be challenging us about how we did *our* business. It was said to be an antiquated system, not in tune with the world of work, lacking in learning connectedness, thereby offering no continuity or relevance for our students. It was attacked for being an isolated, separate enterprise acting as though it were in some way precious in an otherwise dynamic environment. Yet, critics claimed that it provided nothing of added value to the lives of kids!

All this was a revelation to the teachers at Greenslade. Surely, said one senior staff member:

> We had worked so hard on behalf of our students. Hadn't we changed curriculum, devised individual teaching and learning strategies, experimented with a variety of resources, implemented whole-school PSP [Priority Schools Program] plans and implemented everyone else's policies? But we had not examined ourselves, why we did some things one way and not another; we had not assessed our management structure; we couldn't even adequately describe what already existed and why it was like it was. That now seemed the best starting point – a careful examination of existing practice.

In these early days, the staff looked to lift themselves beyond the immediate and local environment of the school to a higher plane of issues to do with educational restructuring at the state level and to consider national agendas for schooling, industry and educational reform. As one teacher commented:

> We gave ourselves *permission* to look beyond the here and now and to dream of other possibilities, to describe and challenge and recognise the contribution we *could* make. We asked the 'what if' question. We were searching for a better match between the outcomes we sought for the students and the way this school was structured and managed to support those outcomes. There seemed to be huge dichotomies and dysfunctions between intentions and realities. We wanted collaborative learning for our students but rarely collaborated with each other; we wanted to promote risk-taking opportunities for our students, but we rarely engaged in any ourselves; we wanted student leadership and control of their own learning, but were guarded and unreflective about our own roles and responsibilities as teachers. We did not 'walk the talk' of local school management.

Like most schools, Greenslade had its mission or purpose statement, indicators of school performance and a plan for developing and improving that performance. But it was as though these 'new' management practices were undertaken more to satisfy central bureaucrats than out of staff conviction that they were beneficial for the quality of education in the school. What followed this initial 'search-and-destroy period' was an elaborate double act. Teachers maintained their isolated teaching behaviours and superficially indulged in whole-school planning to satisfy the terms of the union–employer *Memorandum of Agreement* (Western Australia Ministry of Education/State School Teachers' Union, 1991) targets. More importantly, however, they began to talk about what was going on in their classrooms. The real talk centred on pedagogy. Not all staff, however, chose to be involved in these discussions. Among those who were involved, the talk was often heated and disparaging of particular styles of teaching and learning. The quality of teacher interaction was not always professional nor of high intellectual integrity. It was often explicit, passionate and confrontational. But it was a healthy process of rethinking the core business – teaching and learning. There were fierce battles in the staff room, corridors and classrooms between teachers about the 'best' way to learn and therefore the 'best' way to teach. Was it direct instruction, or student-centred learning using a developmental continuum, that best served students?

Although staff did not 'come to blows', as one teacher put it, some deep and unresolved differences were exposed about learning theory and teaching practice. The key question centred around 'How do our students learn best?' Eventually, staff agreed on a balanced approach, deciding that differences of pedagogy would need to be accommodated at Greenslade school for at least three reasons. First, teachers recognised the importance of focusing on student differences in the way that they learn and on the range of learning experiences required, both of which meant that a variety of teaching methods needed to be accommodated. Secondly, teachers had their respective strengths and preferred styles of teaching and it seemed sensible to take cognisance of this fact. Thirdly, a centrally determined process of staffing schools still applied in Western Australia. Teachers were therefore assigned to Greenslade by the central office rather than being hired at the school site. In one way, this was perceived as bolstering the case for respecting individual teachers' rights to develop their own teaching strategies. The acceptance of diversity was considered quite a breakthrough. Ultimately, the challenge, after having identified the learning needs of the students, was how teachers, other staff and school administrators could support quality learning with appropriate resources and structures. A clearer reference point gradually began to emerge – the improvement of student learning outcomes – and with that, the real work of the school reform programme began.

GREENSLADE'S RESTRUCTURING AGENDA

In order to manage the balance between teaching and learning styles, a flexible, dynamic and purposeful approach was required. There was constant and ongoing questioning of the school's structures, pedagogy, appropriateness of resource allocation, professional development, communications, management and leadership in regard to whether they best supported the achievement of the agreed outcomes. Colleagues began to feel the need to tackle work together and to be more open to innovation and to celebrate the many admirable, value-added teaching and learning practices that already existed. A heightened sense of the need to have time to reflect about substantive issues of professional practice began to develop, the more so as the school became a challenging environment in which to work. Gradually, with a growing urge for action on the part of more and more staff, a further premium was placed on time. Meanwhile, with the growing impetus for reform, it was important not to lose sight of the central goal – the need to sustain and enhance the quality of relationships between teachers and learners.

Through June, July and August 1992, teachers sought diverse ways to give clarification and gain new insights to their thinking. They expressed their ideas visually, through diagrams; they read widely and spoke to colleagues across Australia. Some searched for articles on learning theories and made contacts with tertiary colleagues. Others investigated union work regulations and visited the central office department in search of clarification of policies, regulations, explanations and contacts. The process could be likened to outcome-based education planning. The starting point was the goal to improve the quality of learning for all students and from this goal the process backward mapped all the steps necessary to achieve the goal. It was a stage of looking outwards, exploring resources outside the school, and examining a wealth of educational philosophy. Many enduring and valued contacts and professional relationships were built during this period of exploration. Opportunities to talk, clarify, think, argue, read and reflect about new ways to work together were seized. In realising new roles as teacher leaders, the principal, deputy principal and union representative played key parts in modeling many of these behaviours.

It soon became apparent that most barriers to change were not rules or regulations, but negative perceptions and obsolete practices embedded in a school that was basically a loosely controlled and isolated organisation and enterprise. Moreover, a tradition of dependency had become embedded whereby staff relied on policy initiatives and interpretations from the central office. Such dependency on leadership and decision-making from outside the school suited well a staff of autonomous professionals. However, as 1992 progressed, leadership at the school level began to assert itself. Teacher leaders, with their colleagues, developed their own preferred learning theories, applications to practice and ways of monitoring student learning. With others in the school, they demonstrated a willingness to research, explore, articulate and defend their theories and the application of those theories. At the same time, they were ready to listen to others in finding better ways to operate. In the words of one teacher, 'We were renewed with a common energy towards schooling.'

One of the biggest barriers to school reform was the isolated and disconnected work that went on in classrooms. Teachers, it appeared, busily attended to their students' needs and taught in their well-accustomed ways. This 'egg-box' scenario resulted in an embedded social and functional culture of separateness among both teacher colleagues and students. Consequently, the curriculum was disconnected. Teachers taught and students learnt in ways quite unrelated to what others were doing in the school, and oblivious to what students had learnt in the past and might be expected to learn in the future. The need to plan together, to talk about student learning styles, to share resources, to monitor and evaluate more consistently across the school – all of these loomed as imperatives.

Mid-way through 1992, the organisation of school time at Greenslade was restructured to support reform. DOTT (duties other than teaching) time had previously been plotted neatly across the weekly timetable in discrete time blocks to suit the availability of specialist teachers and to satisfy administrative expedience. By reorganising these times, reconfiguring the timetable and putting the specialist teaching time back-to-back for classes, an extra period was found for both junior school and senior school teachers to meet for one hour each week. By creating time in this way, it was possible to give staff the opportunity to build professional relationships and to focus on the core business – teaching and learning.

One of the teacher teams, brought together at their own request, experienced considerable intra-group conflict. Professionals, so long isolated from each other, displayed all the characteristics of a dysfunctional group. At stake was who would wield power and control of the team. The central goal of a shared approach to student learning – planning, implementing, monitoring and evaluating – was quickly forgotten in meetings which were often trivialised with endless anecdotal and unreflective comments. The NPQTL leaders responded by offering a senior educational psychologist to address the tensions of the group and support its efforts to work successfully as a team. The efficacy of well-respected outside consultants in supporting school reform efforts is worth recognising.

However, despite occasional setbacks, as one senior school leader remarked, 'wonderful professional development opportunities resulted from these team meetings and were evident from mid-1992 onwards, peaking in 1993 and 1994'. Individual teacher strengths were shared with other team members. Teacher cooperation and collaboration took many forms – team teaching, resource sharing, information gathering, identifying and sharing student problems and their solutions. There were down sides, too. At times the team meetings were mere 'show-and-tell' sessions, others were full of 'administrivia', some were 'bandstanding', while still others were threatening and full of conflict. Importantly, however, previous autonomies were challenged. For example, the allocation of teaching assistants to particular groups of students was questioned. Closer links between classroom work and the work of specialists was demanded. One teacher commented, 'we learnt some hard lessons about a previously contrived culture of collegiality and what hard work being truly collaborative was'.

Work discussed in team meetings was taken to, and summarised at, larger whole-staff meetings. Each team of 6–8 teachers steadily gained control over their perceived 'patch'. As staff grew more adept at knowing how to collaborate, the larger staff meetings were given new meaning. They became slicker and more participatory. Words like 'loyalty' and 'trust' began to be used. A new culture of collaboration and improvement began to grow. The culture found visible expression in the modeling behaviours and language of school leaders, who would approach teachers with the response 'You seem to be clarifying a problem. How can I support you?'

Paradoxically, previous traditional teacher isolation had generated a strong dependency culture, whereas the new collaborative emphasis built a respect for the professionalism of the individual teacher. A great deal of decision-making was undertaken through trial and error. The intellectual and physical workload increased for everybody. Teaching and learning needed further examination; cross-curricular problems arose; moderation of student learning outcomes required attention; the question of whether and how improvements in student learning outcomes should be reported to parents and the community became an issue; and the need for support rather than direction, from the union, district and central office, warranted attention. After all, said a senior school administrator, 'Weren't we the centre of the world? Wasn't it our work that needed support?'

Greenslade staff recall some memorable moments as they became a learning community. The previous solid school boundaries evaporated and a more entrepreneurial, independent atmosphere pervaded the school. Problems became challenges that required collaborative solutions. Teachers actively sought interdependence with their colleagues. Problem solvers were revered. This is not to deny the difficulties. Greenslade was always, and will continue to be, a challenging school – the daily collection of syringes in the school sandpit, the condoms on the door knobs, weekend vandalism and graffiti – all continued. Also, conflicts and disputes between employer and teachers' union on matters outside the NPQTL pervaded the industrial relations climate.

Throughout these years the school continued its commitment to other initiatives. In particular, it was a core school for a large curriculum project called First Steps (Western Australia Ministry of Education, 1992), which was a primary school curriculum package based on student-centred learning principles. The school was also cooperating with the local secondary school in its attempts to introduce Stepping Out (Western Australia Ministry of Education, 1993), the secondary equivalent of First Steps, designed to introduce a concerted approach to the introduction of student-centred learning. Because of its catchment intake, Greenslade was also a member of the Priority Schools Program (PSP) experiential learning project.

As the reform agenda began to reshape some aspects of school management and organisation, it provoked a domino effect on areas hitherto left unattended. These now demanded attention. One such area concerned the induction of new staff, parents and students. The school lacked a well-thought-out induction programme. Consequently an experienced, recently appointed teacher was approached to highlight the difficulties that newly assigned staff, students and parents experienced. The teacher was an interesting appointment for this assignment, since she had experienced difficulty herself in settling in. On an agreed date, she presented to the staff a written draft document and oral presentation setting out the structural, management, curricular and social considerations that she deemed important in engaging new members to contribute effectively to the school community. Dissemination of information regarding the school's participation in various curricular and reform projects was considered important. The introduction of new formats and processes for induction were suggested, including 'buddy' and mentoring systems, formal and informal meetings, paired and larger group meetings. It was agreed that the induction process would be mostly self-paced after the initial welcome with support from an experienced colleague, fellow student or other parent. Parents were to be welcomed at two levels – first, by their parent groups, and second, by the staff, particularly the general staff, registrar, canteen manager and school nurse.

Students had always been informally welcomed into the school at the class level, but now more formal strategies were devised to achieve the best possible introduction for new students. The strategy relied on a build-up approach, starting with the student's home room, and progressing successively to class, team area, playground and whole school. The 'buddy' system was introduced for new students with the intention of providing early support to enable students to feel 'good' about the school.

One of the most deeply contested areas was accountability. In a more devolved, school-site managed system, the once 'all-knowing' central office was no longer seen as a source of ultimate power, or gatekeeper of all policy knowledge. Rather, central office staff were increasingly perceived by Greenslade teachers, and particularly the school registrar, as a resource for the school. In this new configuration of administrative and power relations, more responsibility was transferred to school-based personnel. Onus was placed on teachers, individually and collectively, to identify student needs, devise learning programmes, resource, implement and evaluate programmes, and report on the learning achieved by each student in individual, group and whole-school contexts. Topics of staff conversation focused on how each team member went about their business. Teacher talk centred on matters related to teaching, learning, curriculum and students. Accounts of students' performance were seen as ways of demonstrating accountability. One senior teacher became vitally interested in the notions of responsibility, accountability and performance management and, at the direction of her team, sought expertise and knowledge on these matters outside the school from tertiary and management institutions. This initiative, according to a senior school administrator, resulted in

> a stunning breakthrough in thinking and practice and signalled the depth of change in attitude towards demonstrating improved performance using documentary formats and processes which were trialed and checked for their degree of accessibility, equity and value for improvement in teaching and learning, before adoption.

Accountability for performance became accepted as professional practice. It was a shared and public notion of accountability, something to be undertaken with one's colleagues.

Significantly, the driving force behind Greenslade's reform was the desire to improve the quality of teaching and learning for all. The impetus for reform was the antithesis of top-down imposed change; it was not even principal-led. As a senior school administrator admitted, 'the school's management ebbed and flowed around the teacher-led reforms. It would be fair to say that sometimes the formal leaders felt the ground cut away from under them and were troubled and quite unsure as to what was appropriate leadership'. These were the moments when mentoring helped the principal and deputy to keep on track – it was, after all, about the shared and common goal of providing access to a quality education for all learners, students and staff. There was much talk and reading about effective curriculum leadership, best practices in leadership, effective schools, interpersonal skills and productive relationships. It always seemed to reduce to this – the building of the best relationships between students and teachers in support of learning. Such relationships needed to be built on trust, openness and the giving and receiving of feedback. School reform is inevitably about power and control relationships. It is fundamentally social and political. The interpersonal tensions which periodically surfaced enabled the school's leaders, in turn, to explore notions of leadership in a self-managing school. Developing from this exploration was a style of school leadership and management that emphasised MBWA (management by walking about); a style that relied on the curriculum credibility of both the principal and deputy, both of whom had proven teaching expertise, had been appointed on merit and had extensive experience of instructional leadership. However, whole-school reform required more than their expertise and these skills. Besides instructional leadership, it demanded transformational leadership, that is, the capacity to encourage and motivate others to become change agents, advocates and implementers of change. As transformational leaders, both the principal and deputy principal were on a steep learning curve.

Management practices underwent transformation in order to support the change efforts of others, particularly teachers. Although both the principal and deputy principal had long believed in building collaborative relationships, they now adopted a more 'open door' policy for improved communication, made key information on finance and professional development more accessible, introduced member-only status at most committee and working-party meetings in order to spread workloads, initiated reviews of communication methods and streamlined policy development. A more positive approach was adopted to 'selling the school' in the public arena; teachers and clerical staff were given training to enable them to assume certain budgetary control; and regular school planning and review sessions were introduced. All the time, the focus on curriculum development was maintained. The observed language and behaviour of all teacher leaders became more assertive, participative and confident. School administrators and key teachers also learnt to handle the continual questioning from parents, and the seeking of information from other schools, the community, the district and central office education officers, unions and NPQTL project personnel.

Teachers' practices and approaches were also reconfigured. There was more freedom and support to experiment in their classrooms. Teachers developed a balanced sense of autonomy combined with team and larger staff responsibilities. They actively sought forums for discussing such issues as effective teaching and learning. Teachers displayed a more open and public commitment to their work in classrooms and took greater cognisance of the diversity of individual students and their learning styles. They undertook team curriculum projects, questioned almost everything, including reporting to parents, standardised testing, integration and transition programmes, and moderation of the First Steps learning indicators. They thought about ways that they could manage the many individual projects to create a more coherent and holistic learning programme across the school.

Membership of the NPQTL project placed great emphasis on professional development, particularly that geared to improving teaching expertise in the classroom and school. Two teachers, in particular, took the self-managing school principles deep into their classrooms and instituted radical social changes based on shared power with their students. They introduced interesting strategies including daily and weekly goal setting, class meetings about programmes, joint planning and feedback, and held regular debriefing sessions with students about learning. Emphasis was put on shifting the locus of control to students. These classroom environments became models of social justice and teachers were often invited to speak about their so-called 'reformed classroom structures'. In the longer term their success highlighted the need for a whole-school approach and in due course the school became involved in student-centred learning professional development. In 1993–4 a Year 1 teacher, long discontented with the school's reporting system to parents based on reports at the middle and end of year, embarked on an individual profiling system which relied on intensive observation of small groups of students over 5–6 weekly intervals. She began to profile the learning of her young students more closely through observing and monitoring their progress. The process received the ongoing support of her team, other specialist teachers, the administrators and, overwhelmingly, the parents. The overall effect of these changes, based on a belief in the power and potential of self-managing schools, gave the school a vitality, a dynamism, a collective energy and a momentum that led to its total transformation. The energy and excitement spread to all groups of stakeholders in the school community. However, in the words of one former senior administrator, 'it would be nonsense to imagine that this school was always a "caring, sharing" place at all times and for all people during the reform period'. Some of the teachers, general staff, students and parents were inevitably marginalised during the school's involvement with the Project. There was always active debate, argument, disagreement, dissension and continual disruption. 'But', she continued, 'no one could ever doubt that we were alive and thinking.'

That staff felt their professional lives enhanced is a startling testament to the creative power of the NPQTL project. The school's union representative successfully stood for election to the State School Teachers' Union, where her leadership strongly reflected her commitment to teaching and learning within social justice and industrial frameworks. Another teacher's curriculum expertise helped her to apply successfully to work and to model her leadership of learning at the district education office. One teacher applied for a leadership role at the school when a temporary vacancy occurred and duly became, by a process of merit selection over the course of one year, a key teacher, the deputy principal and, finally, the principal! She filled all roles with distinction. Others successfully sought promotion and job enhancement outside Greenslade. Many staff returned to formal study or conducted action research projects or sought active membership of professional associations. It was remarkable how, from a small teaching staff, so many were invited to deliver presentations and workshops at district and state level on curriculum leadership and management. The professional networks made during this period served all the school's participants well in terms of their own professional development.

In 1994, the Project was interrupted by state industrial action by the teachers' union. Consequently, the school decided to maintain existing, rather than institute new, reform initiatives. Although in one sense this could have been viewed as a major interruption, as yet another example of industrial action leading to the abortion of a school reform effort, in reality it proved to be a year of consolidation which was appreciated by all, particularly the parents who had found the breadth and scope of school change and the promotion and spotlighting of the school bewildering.

By the end of 1994, the senior leadership of the school had substantially changed. Many of the key reform personnel had moved on, leaving only a depleted number of key reformers still in place at the school. NPQTL came to the end of its life and was replaced by a National Schools Network (NSN) whose aim was to continue promoting school reform across Australia. As 1995 progressed, however, the industrial relations climate in Western Australia grew steadily worse. The NPQTL and, to a lesser extent, its successor, the NSN, were projects that relied on cooperation between the state government and the teachers' union. These school reform initiatives became entangled in other, more immediate and politically pressing disputes between the state government and teachers' union concerning the state government's desire to restructure teachers' work and working conditions and the union's determined effort to seek substantial pay awards for its members. By the end of the first term of 1995, it was clear that – in spite of the school's efforts over the period since 1992 to document the policy and framework required to support reform, irrespective of the changes already accomplished in both managment and teaching structures, and regardless of an emergent professional culture of continuous school improvement and of the benefits to students which had been so publicly advertised and acknowledged – the school had lost its momentum for reform and had begun to lose the focus and direction so essential for reform to continue.

WHY GREENSLADE'S REFORM FALTERED

Why did Greenslade's reform falter? First, the school hitched its reform effort to a national Project; indeed, it would probably not have embarked on reform in the first place if it had not received an invitation to join the Project. While membership of the Project gave the school reform process early support and extra resources, once the life of the Project began to expire, membership became something of a drawback. External support from outside is generally regarded as beneficial for within-school change, as long as the initiatives, responsibilities and ownership reside with the school. In this case, the school probably relied too heavily on the external support that came from Project membership. Secondly, many of the reform initiatives were not fully embedded and institutionalised in the day-to-day operation of the school. This is hardly surprising. Whole-school reform of this magnitude is generally regarded as requiring a minimum of three to five years (Fullan, 1991). Greenslade was barely approaching the three-year mark, one year of which had been characterised by industrial dispute. Herein lies a third important factor, one that again centres on its participation in the Project. An initial strength and appeal of the Project in regard to school restructuring was the joint collaboration of employer (the state government) and teachers' union as equal partners in the scheme. This initial benefit, however, turned out to be its eventual undoing. When the industrial relations climate subsequently soured, the reform initiative fell victim to wider political and industrial hostilities. Fourthly, the change of key personnel, particularly senior administrators in the form of principal and deputy principal, was bound to weaken the restructuring initiative, especially so early in the process. Not only did Greenslade lose some of its most senior administrators within the first three years of the reform programme, it had more than one change in both the principal and deputy principal positions during that time!

Furthermore, while Greenslade staff, like those in other Project schools, were appreciative of the 'quarantine' allowing existing rules and regulations to be broken, in reality few were ever seriously challenged. It may be that the benefits experienced by schools offered special 'quarantine' conditions are more psychological than real. They feel 'special' and 'different' and this, in turn, promotes the change effort. On the other hand, as Murphy (1991) has recognised, the problem with 'quarantining' schools to support change is that the impetus may stop when the 'prop' is subsequently removed, and that the message delivered to other schools interested in reform may be that restructuring is only possible when special privileges are offered. In fact, the real barriers to change, as recorded by one senior staff member, 'were not bureaucratic rules and regulations, but were intrinsic to the nature of teaching and learning itself'. Hence, a further factor explaining Greenslade's difficulty to secure embedded reform relates to issues such as how to assess learning in a student-centred classroom and how to overcome barriers resulting from traditional, time-honoured work practices related to the use of spatial structures. The adverse effects on teaching and learning of operating in an open-plan school, where teachers constructed improvised barricades to provide partial separation of classrooms, became embedded in the cultural life of the school.

History seems to be littered with examples of schools like Greenslade, which embark on adventurous and challenging whole-school restructuring programmes, achieve remarkable change within a relatively short time, then fail, for various reasons, to institutionalise the reform effort. At the end of the three-year period, what reflections remain? They are best expressed in the telling words of one teacher:

> The way we were . . . so focused, so energised, so keen about improvement, for ourselves, our students, our teaching, our learning. So much more in control. We will never be the same again.

REFERENCES

Angus, M. (1995) 'Devolution of school governance in an Australian state school system: third time lucky?', in D.S.G. Carter and M.H. O'Neill (eds) *Case Studies in Educational Change: An International Perspective*, London: Falmer Press.

Australian Education Council (Finn Report) (1991) *Young People's Participation in Post-compulsory Education and Training: Report of the Australian Education Council Review Committee*, Canberra: Australian Education Council.

Dimmock, C. (1995) 'Reconceptualising restructuring for school effectiveness and school improvement', *International Journal for Educational Reform* 4, 3: 285–300.

Employment and Skills Formation Council (Carmichael Report) (1992) *The Australian Vocational Certificate Training System*, Canberra: National Board of Employment, Education and Training.

Fullan, M.G. (1991) *The New Meaning of Educational Change*, London: Cassell.

Mayer Committee (1992) *Employment-related Key Competencies for Post-compulsory Education and Training: A Discussion Paper – Executive Summary*, Melbourne: Mayer Committee.

Murphy, J. (1991) *Restructuring Schools*, New York: Teachers' College Press.

Western Australia Ministry of Education (1988) *Better Schools in Western Australia: A Programme for Improvement*, Perth: Government Printer.

—— (1992) *First Steps* Perth: Government Printer.

—— (1993) *Stepping Out*, Perth: Government Printer.

Western Australia Ministry of Education and State School Teachers' Union (1991) *Memorandum of Agreement*, East Perth: Ministry of Education and State School Teachers' Union.

Western Australian Parliament (1986) *Managing Change in the Public Sector: A Statement of the Government's Position* (White Paper), Perth: Government Printer.

Chapter 3

Strategic planning in schools

Neil Dempster and Carolyn Anderson

INTRODUCTION

This chapter is about the use and effects of strategic planning in schools. Strategic planning is a term that was unheard of in education only a decade ago. Most teachers would have been forgiven for believing that strategic planning was something that was important during wars or that was undertaken by big multi-national business corporations. This 'naivety' among teachers has been transformed in the 1990s because strategic planning has become one of the processes commanding attention from all engaged in school activity. Strategic planning as a phenomenon is the result of developments in the worlds of business, industry and commerce where it has been common practice for over a decade. Governments of the 1980s, moved by the successes of the private sector, implemented reforms in the public sector which mirrored practices in private enterprise.

In this chapter we make the point that strategic planning and review are twin processes central to effective school management. Contrary to the view that schools must be kept under surveillance to ensure that these processes are carried out, we argue that schools are seeing benefits in their use to help regain control over an agenda of, often, forced change, but more importantly schools are seeing these processes as tools for the kind of continuous improvement necessary in developing learning communities.

To make our case, we structure the chapter in six sections. In the first section we provide a brief background to strategic planning as a phenomenon in public sector management, to set the scene for our discussion of it in schools. In the second section we outline what we mean by a learning organisation. The third section explains what we mean by strategic planning in schools. The fourth section draws on our practical experience to examine how strategic planning can be accomplished in schools. In the fifth section we examine some of the effects, benefits and problems encountered in strategic planning in primary schools in particular. The sixth section discusses how strategic planning and review can contribute to the development of a learning organisation.

CHANGES IN PUBLIC SECTOR MANAGEMENT

Since the mid-1980s, there have been significant shifts in approaches by governments in many Western democracies to public sector management. Sir William Taylor (1992) argues that these shifts have been dominated by economic imperatives and that they carry the hallmarks of an underpinning faith in market theory. Market theory espouses principles such as competition, consumer choice, user payment, efficiency in productivity and cost-effectiveness. At the same time accountability is essential.

A raft of public sector restructuring has accompanied the shifts in thinking outlined above, in many of the countries with which Australia usually compares itself. In summary, restructuring has tended to move public sector organisations in the direction of their private sector counterparts. This is most evident in approaches to management which Knight (1992) and Dempster et al. (1994) characterise as corporate managerialist in style.

Education as a public sector enterprise has not been immune from the shifts implicit in market theory nor from restructuring towards corporate managerialism. The signals that such a restructuring has been taking place are evident in the following changes in school systems:

- from public control towards market and consumer control
- from management by civil servants towards governance by councillors
- from public institutional monopoly towards open competition between institutions
- from centralisation towards increased decentralisation and decision-making at local work sites
- from predominantly top-down leadership and administrative management towards shared leadership and collaborative management
- from management by regulation towards goal- and performance-oriented management
- from implicit quality control towards explicit quality specification and public accountability.

Among these trends there are several that signal the importance of strategic planning and review processes in schools. Goal- and performance-oriented management indicates that systematic planning processes are now expected of schools. These planning processes are meant to be the result of local decision-making of a collaborative kind. The resultant plans are the means by which school quality is specified and against which systematic reviews and evaluations are conducted for accountability and improvement purposes.

Given these 'big picture' trends, it might appear that strategic planning is a 'blunt' instrument used by education systems to mask surveillance of what happens in schools. Although this is true in part, we argue that there are many positive aspects for schools when they use it as one of the tools that can help them in developing a learning organisation.

LEARNING ORGANISATIONS

The concept of the learning organisation has entered the discourse of theorists in organisational development in recent years. Although the focus of discussion has centred on the world of business and industry, the concept offers much for those engaged in the service sector. Even in public sector environments, learning is essential for continuous improvement and for survival in an increasingly competitive marketplace. Stata suggests that 'the rate at which individuals and organisations learn may become the only sustainable competitive advantage, especially in knowledge-intensive industries' (Stata, 1989: 64).

How do organisations learn? Simon (1991: 125) argues that organisations learn in two distinct ways: (1) individual members of an organisation gain new knowledge and skills through access to internal think tanks, external learning programmes and benchmarking best practice; or (2) organisations bring in new people with knowledge and skills considered valuable in transforming existing practices. Both of these strategies, however, demand attention to spreading the new knowledge and skills throughout the organisation. Without dissemination and subsequent change in behaviour no organisational learning will be evident. This view suggests that for an enterprise to be called a 'learning organisation' it must pay attention to all the strategies mentioned above. Garvin (1993: 80) endorses the idea that these strategies are essential by asserting that 'a learning organisation is an organisation skilled in creating, acquiring, and transferring knowledge, and at modifying its behaviour to reflect new knowledge and insights'.

Senge's definition adds a social dimension to organisational learning, arguing that collective action is critical:

> [a learning organisation is one] where people continually expand their capacity to create the results they truly desire, where new and expansive patterns of thinking are nurtured, where collective aspiration is set free, and where people are continually learning how to learn together.
>
> (Senge, 1990: 3)

Other characteristics of the learning organisation are its capacity to respond to changes in the external environment, to grasp 'cutting edge' opportunities without entrenched interests blocking the flexibilities needed to move into new fields. Above all, for an organisation to learn it must be constantly adaptive.

The key activities of learning organisations, according to Garvin (1993: 81–90), are fivefold:

1 systematic problem-solving
2 experimentation with new approaches
3 learning from past experience
4 learning from the experiences and practices of others
5 transferring knowledge quickly and efficiently throughout the organisation.

The themes embedded in these key activities include using systematic methods to diagnose problems rather than relying on instinct alone, creating a culture that enjoys risk-taking in the search for new horizons, entrenching critical review procedures as normal practice in the organisation, actively seeking external views about performance from clients, stakeholders and leading competitors, and using a wide and effective array of learning strategies for employees.

Each of these activities and themes is applicable in the school setting. In fact, wherever there are people engaged in the pursuit of common goals, the key activities and themes of the learning organisation provide the foundation for the development of an ethos that values strengthening what is best, improving what is worst and embracing innovation. This ethos is the cornerstone of strategic planning, to an explanation of which we now turn.

WHAT IS STRATEGIC PLANNING IN SCHOOLS?

Strategic planning is a process designed to set down the longer-term view of where a school is heading. In the Australian states and territories various titles are used as covers for strategic planning – e.g. school renewal planning, school development planning and school improvement planning, to name but three. Recent national research (Logan *et al.*, 1994) shows that all schools claim to be involved in strategic planning and by 'longer-term' they mean from three to five years. The strategic planning process enables school management and school communities to establish agreed ends to endorse the values on which the school wants to build its reputation, to develop the operational principles that inform its work, to determine the means to attain nominated ends and to set outcome targets.

Strategic planning is distinguished from operational planning which is usually carried out on an annual basis. The operational planning process takes up specific priorities for the year in question and adds an explicit action dimension to them. This 'action plan' details objectives, tasks, responsibilities, timelines, resources required and performance indicators to facilitate monitoring during implementation.

When considering the focus of strategic and operational plans, it is helpful to use the maintenance vs. development distinction established by Hopkins (Hopkins and Hargreaves, 1994). Figure 3.1 shows this distinction in an extension of Hopkins' work.

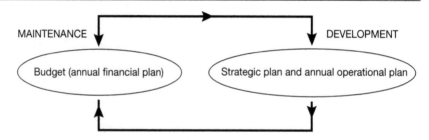

Figure 3.1   The relationship between maintenance and development
in strategic planning

Figure 3.1 illustrates the point that schools face a myriad of maintenance issues. These are the kinds of things that they have to do as well as they can all of the time, come what may. Because the scope of these maintenance activities is so large, strategic plans should draw important issues from the maintenance pool and place them in a development pool for the life of a strategic plan. The year's operational plan should then be constructed around selected priorities on which the school is prepared to expend time, energy, effort and resources. Such an approach recognises that strategic and operational plans are never sufficiently comprehensive to cover all of the activities in which schools engage. These can normally be recognised in the budget or financial plan. What Figure 3.1 emphasises is the place of strategic planning in building a learning organisation by concentrating on realistic improvement issues year by year.

We have said that strategic and operational planning are processes. This begs the question 'What kind of processes are used in these types of planning?' Generally, schools in Australia say that they use either consultative and/or collaborative processes (Logan *et al.*, 1994). By 'consultative processes' we mean management-initiated planning to which contributions are sought from interested stakeholders before plans are finalised, implemented and ultimately reviewed within the school. By 'collaborative processes' we mean planning in working parties through which decision-making is shared and where responsibility for implementation and review is distributed among stakeholders. McGilchrist *et al.* (1995), drawing on research in English primary schools, highlight four types of planning processes – rhetorical, singular, cooperative and corporate.[1] It is the latter two types that use consultative and collaborative processes and that, they argue, are most effective in schools.

HOW IS STRATEGIC PLANNING ACCOMPLISHED?

There are usually two entry points to the strategic planning process. Some schools choose to begin by reviewing existing practice for strengths, weaknesses and potential priorities for development. We say that this approach is retrospective in style (or review-led planning). Others begin by looking forward to where they want to go without reliance on systematic assessment of where they have been. We say that this approach is prospective in style (or futures-led planning). Review-led planning is inherently more cautious than futures-led planning. The latter is more risky, setting directions and taking initiatives largely based on a common-sense feel for the school. To illustrate our argument we provide brief examples of processes used in both approaches to strategic planning.

Review-led strategic planning

The example of review-led strategic planning that we describe is consistent with the McGilchrist *et al.* (1995) corporate approach. It relies on whole-school collaborative activity to assess where the school is performing well and where it should be directing improvement efforts. Collaboration in planning activity extends beyond school staff, students and parents to include external influences on review and planning activity.

What is essential for review-led planning?

The essential elements for review-led strategic planning are a reference group, working parties and external monitoring. The *reference group*, chaired by the principal, is composed of convenors of working parties and school management, to provide leadership, coordination, support and monitoring during the process.

Working parties are made up of stakeholders who are responsible for the review of a particular area of the school's operation and the development of proposals for planning action. Working parties provide the opportunity for all staff members to be involved and to take ownership of the process. Generally, working parties are formed around focus areas such as curriculum (e.g. English, mathematics, science, the arts, etc.), cross-curriculum issues (e.g. assessment, special needs students, behaviour management) and infra-structural support (e.g. information technology, library and teaching resources, assets and grounds, etc.). The number of working parties may be large or small, depending upon the scope of the review and where the school is located in its strategic planning cycle.

External monitoring involves agents and agencies from outside the school who provide criticism and advocacy, benchmarking and facilitation. *Critical advocates* are people with known and respected expertise, accepted by management and staff as able to provide advice that is both theoretically and practically credible. They challenge, probe, question, interrogate, doubt and inquire in order to ensure that every facet of a working party's brief is considered seriously and credibly. In short, critical advocates have the dual task of offering both critique and advice about present realities and possible futures. *Benchmarking* aspects of school performance with that of schools with reputations for best practice encourages the critical examination of current school practices in the light of comparisons with schools recognised for their achievements in nominated areas. Finally, the assistance of an outside *facilitator* is recommended for review-led strategic planning to add motivation to the carriage of the process, to provide dispassionate guidance and expertise, to free the school principal to dedicate leadership time to the task and to expose staff to the range of skills required in the process.

How is review-led planning conducted?

Our experience of review-led strategic planning has enabled us to distil a number of important steps in the process. Figure 3.2 illustrates ten steps into which external monitoring (represented by the shaded boxes) is injected at appropriate points. Initially a full meeting of staff is required to establish the aim of the strategic planning process, to outline the role of the various groups, particularly the working parties, to establish the context and any constraints on the process, to emphasise the commitment of school

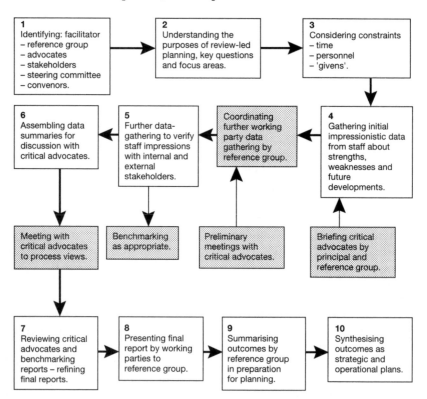

Figure 3.2 An approach to review-led strategic planning

authorities to the outcomes of the strategic plan and to undertake necessary training in the issues and techniques of evaluation and planning.

A time-line needs to be developed around the steps outlined in the diagram. Since all staff are participants, the time-line must take into account existing workloads without unnecessarily prolonging the process. We suggest a maximum six-month period to allow for flexibility and rigour in the process. The reference group needs to monitor the working parties' progress with regular meetings of convenors to ensure that the knowledge and skill required for each step are available among the participants.

The outcomes of the approach we have described are a strategic plan outlining broad goal directions and general strategies for a set period, an operational plan for the first year and amendments to the school's over-arching mission statement, values and aspirations in the light of what is learnt during the planning process. These plans and amendments are returned to the participants for comment before final adoption.

Futures-led strategic planning

The example of futures-led strategic planning that we explain is consistent with the cooperative approach identified by McGilchrist *et al.* (1995). It relies on consultative approaches to planning activity, initiated by school management working in partnership with a selected representative consultative group drawn from the staff and the school community. Futures-led planning can be tackled in a number of ways but, whatever the approach, there are several essential prerequisites.

What is essential for futures-led planning?

To carry out effective futures-led planning requires the following:

- a dedicated facilitator
- a small writing group committed to producing a draft plan
- concentrated discussion with representatives of the school community
- a balance in the representation of internal and external views of the school's performance
- time for consulting with staff and school community on the plan
- time for revision and confirmation.

Most important among these conditions is the balance between internal and external views of the school. Therefore the composition of the group to take part in planning sessions must be given careful consideration.

How is futures-led planning conducted?

The five-step sequence we outline below provides a typical example of futures-led strategic planning. It is possible to conduct this sequence with groups that range in size from 10 to 100, depending on the skills of the facilitator.

Step 1: Developing a vision for the school

PURPOSE :   The purpose of Step 1 is to gather views about the kind ofinstitution that the school should be trying to become.

PROCESS :   Participants work in heterogeneous groups (of about six people) with a nominated convenor. First, they are asked as individuals to note on stickers (computer labels or Post-It notes) their personal responses to the following driving question:

What big or key purposes do you want this institution to serve in this community if it is to be regarded as a great school?

Participants should restrict their responses to three or four purposes, one per sticker. In their groups, participants table their stickers and, where necessary, explain what it is they are seeking in the school. Similar ideas are clustered together to form groups to which 'cover terms' are attached. The cover term should clearly identify the key purpose contained in the grouped ideas. When this has been completed for all stickers held, the group should use the cover terms to produce two or three sentences that give a concise answer to the driving question. Convenors of each group report their cover terms and their sentences at the plenary gathering which concludes this step.

OUTCOME : The outcome of this step is a series of statements which is used later by the planning group to form the basis for the preparation of a draft vision/mission statement for the institution following the intensive planning period.

Step 2: Clarifying values

PURPOSE :   The purpose of the second step is to clarify the values on which the institution's vision/mission is based.

PROCESS: Participants work in groups as for Step 1.
Groups are provided with a list of the terms that identify the values used in the vision/mission statements produced in Step 1. The planning group and the facilitator need to

extract the list of values prior to the commencement of this step. Groups are asked to discuss the values terms and to settle on what each means.

Groups record their responses to this task using the following stems:

Our school values . . .
By this we mean . . .

Convenors of each group report their values statements at a plenary gathering which concludes the step.

OUTCOME: The outcomes of this step are multiple value statements from which an aggregated set, to complement the vision/mission, can be constructed by the planning group following the planning session.

Step 3: Developing strategic goals

PURPOSE: The purpose of Step 3 is to develop strategic goals in areas of importance to the school's operations.

PROCESS: Participants work in homogeneous groups based on interest in one of a number of nominated goal areas identified by the planning group prior to the planning session. Examples of goal areas include curriculum, staff and student welfare, management and administration, finance and resources, school facilities and environment, parent and community relations. All groups are asked to address the same driving question:

For this area, what would you want the school to achieve over the next three/five years?

Group convenors chair discussions which encourage participants to develop up to five strategic goals. Goals should be framed in terms that are observable, namely, to increase, to reduce, to build, to improve, to maintain, to establish, to attract, to balance, and so on.

To aid discussion, some consideration of how particular goals might be achieved can help to clarify understanding. However, it is emphasised that this is not a discussion of strategies. Emphasis should be on realistic achievements over the 3–5-year period. If a goal looks far too ambitious, the group should revise it so that it becomes feasible.

Finally, group convenors record the four or five strategic goals using the following stem:

In the area of . . . , the following strategic goals commit the school:

to reduce . . .
to establish . . .
to build . . .

Convenors of each group report their strategic goals at a plenary gathering which concludes the step.

> OUTCOME: The outcome of this step is a collection of 'first pass' strategic goals for each nominated area from which the planning group can refine a draft set consistent with the school's vision/mission following the planning sessions.

Step 4: Projecting the future

> PURPOSE: The fourth step focuses on gaining an understanding of hoped-for achievements for the institution in ten years' time.

> PROCESS: Participants work in heterogeneous groups. Convenors manage a brainstorming-style discussion in which equal time is given to responding to the following driving question from four perspectives:

If you returned to the school in 2010 and it was clear that it had become a great school, what would you expect to see

1   *in its students?*
2   *in its teachers?*
3   *in its parents?*
4   *in its local community?*

This step encourages participants to lift their horizons beyond the present by seeking to identify high but reachable expectations. A summary statement of expectations is produced on a prepared proforma and this is reported by convenors at the final plenary gathering which concludes the planning sessions.

> OUTCOME: The outcome of this step is a data set from which a long-term expectations profile can be produced by the planning

group. These expectations can be used to write a statement of aspirations – or targets – to accompany the values identified earlier in the process.

Step 5: Consultation

PURPOSE: The purpose of the last step is to seek feedback on a prepared draft strategic plan and to expand ownership beyond the participants involved in the planning sessions.

PROCESS: A variety of processes are available to ensure that plausible consultation takes place. School leaders working with the planning group should try to include as wide a body of the school's stakeholders as possible. Information nights to discuss a draft document prepared by the planning group, staff meetings, discussion groups among senior students and circulation of the draft document among the school community are some of the strategies that might be employed. Whatever the choice, sufficient time should be given to the exercise so that amendments and new ideas can be gathered. However, given the fact that a strategic plan is a concise document, a reasonably short consultation period is recommended.

OUTCOME: The outcome of the consultation period is a set of comments from a wider community of: stakeholders which the planning group can incorporate in the official final draft of the school's strategic plan.

Summary

Review-led planning carries some significant benefits over futures-led planning. It results in evidence that can be utilised in meeting accountability requirements. It must be said that both review-led and futures-led strategic planning produce committed constituencies as well as documents. However, the widespread collaborative approach of the former carries a higher in-built ownership potential than does the latter. On the other hand, futures-led planning, because of its controlled number of sessions with a representative group, can be accomplished in a much shorter time frame than review-led planning. The choice of which approach to take is a judgement that is best made by school leaders in the full knowledge of their local contexts.

WHAT ARE SOME OF THE EFFECTS OF STRATEGIC PLANNING?

Our experience of strategic planning using either of the two approaches indicates a number of positive and negative effects, at the point of initiation, while planning is being carried out and during implementation. Research conducted in Australia by Logan *et al.* (1994) into development planning in schools is used to substantiate some of the effects that we have encountered during the process.

On initiation   Strategic planning challenges a school management and staff to commence a process to make change an integral part of the working environment and this is often viewed with trepidation. Overcoming initial fears requires a clear definition of the purposes of strategic planning, and a philosophical and practical commitment by the school principal to continuous improvement, to reduce possible anxieties about exposing school weaknesses through review.

Overcoming the negative effects of past experience may also be essential at the point of initiation. 'Nothing ever comes of staff and community input' is a cry sometimes heard in schools where previous planning journeys have been undertaken. Responses to understandable scepticism must be considered, consistent and convincing. Successful initiation is assured when clarification of, and common commitment to, the purposes of the strategic planning process have been achieved.

During the process   It is possible for all participants to develop a sense of personal contribution. There is the opportunity for a sharing of opinion which can increase respect for co-workers. This is particularly advantageous when teaching, support staff, parents and others outside the school combine to clarify their opinions or to prepare planning reports.

If dedicated training is provided during the planning process, teachers and parents are able to develop the capacity to support the continuous improvement philosophy that is intrinsic to strategic planning and essential in a learning organisation.

Reference to outside standards through the use of external monitoring and widely representative planning groups can contribute to overcoming doubts about the rigour and reliability of the process. The opportunity to work with experts in a particular field gives a less insular perspective and provides professional stimulation. Working parties and planning groups establish a level of communication that endures beyond the planning period and teachers articulate their ideas in a way unlikely to happen within the day-to-day business of the school.

When working well, the planning process develops a high degree of staff commitment to, and ownership of, the ideas and reports developed. Completion of the task within an agreed time frame provides a sense of achievement for all.

Throughout the process, however, staff workloads and workplace stress are considerably increased. Constant monitoring of progress and willingness to build flexibility into time-lines is essential. Thought must be given to the support that can be offered to staff through administrative assistance and reduced commitments elsewhere.

Our experience of the process is supported in recent research undertaken by Logan *et al.* (1994) into the effects of development planning in primary schools. This work reported that principals, associate administrators, teachers and parents felt that involvement in strategic planning enabled them:

1 to focus on the 'big picture'
2 to emphasise points of accountability
3 to increase involvement and shared responsibility among school community members
4 to enhance staff professionalism
5 to develop a broader knowledge base about the school
6 to strengthen participative decision-making
7 to identify and celebrate successes
8 to open up parent and student input.

On the other side of the ledger, Logan *et al.* (1994) found that there were significant negative effects accompanying the strategic planning process. These included:

1 increased workload for all
2 increased stress
3 a greater time commitment from parents, teachers and administrators
4 drawing teachers away from the 'real' work of teaching.

During implementation   Annual operational planning provides a forum for reaffirming school philosophy and ensuring that chosen priorities are designed to enhance school achievements in line with that philosophy. Treating the strategic plan as flexible allows unforseen circumstances and new conditions to be taken into account. Annual operation plans give wider voice to resource implications to achieve priority outcomes. School community involvement in funding discussions can result in less conflict over scarce resources, given agreement on annual priorities drawn from the strategic plan.

To sum up, we suggest that there are five important issues that must be faced by those engaged in strategic planning if they are to ensure positive outcomes and to overcome the negative effects revealed by the research:

1 how to keep the process manageable within the school's resources and competing demands
2 how to deal with different stakeholder perceptions of and attitudes towards the school

3 how to accommodate the additional demands on people's time
4 how to spread ownership of and commitment to the outcomes sought in the plan
5 how to manage unanticipated external requirements placed on schools by their employing authorities.

Given that Logan *et al.*'s (1994) research showed overwhelmingly that schools did not want to return to centralised forms of planning, the issues identified above must figure prominently in preparation for strategic planning. It is clear to us that the process needs to be owned by those who participate in it; it needs to produce local results of significance, allowing participants to be fully involved with appropriate support in terms of time and resources, with effective leadership being a taken-for-granted imperative in strategic planning that counts.

In the final section of the chapter we return to our central theme – that strategic planning can be a significant tool in developing a learning organisation.

HOW CAN STRATEGIC PLANNING AND REVIEW CONTRIBUTE TO THE DEVELOPMENT OF A LEARNING ORGANISATION?

As well as a concrete plan to guide action and resource allocation, the strategic planning process can establish some of the essential conditions for developing a learning organisation. We cc ⁄ ⋅de the chapter with the elaboration of some of those conditions and three operating principles to inform school planners.

Earlier we argued that activities and themes essential in a learning organisation included systematic use of past experience, learning from the experience of others, transferring knowledge quickly throughout the organisation, and seeking new horizons by using the views of a wide array of stakeholders to improve what is worst, to strengthen what is best and to embrace innovation. We asserted that strategic planning was one of the means through which some of these activities and themes could be realised. More specifically we now suggest that strategic planning assists in developing a learning organisation by:

1 helping to structure the change process
2 focusing on a nominated period and the change priorities for that period
3 enabling immediate problems to be addressed through annual operational planning
4 developing a mind set or understanding of both the need for accountability and the need for improvement
5 making the linkage with continuous improvement transparent
6 providing a systematic use of external views of the organisation
7 enhancing internal organisational communication and learning

8 improving shared knowledge about long-term goals, immediate objectives and strategies.

To conclude the chapter we offer three operating principles to guide school-based strategic planning. These principles pick up the leadership imperative that we mentioned earlier.

Principle 1   For effective strategic planning, there should be a balance between top-down and bottom-up management control. Stakeholders should participate in the process and must accept responsibility for it.

Principle 2   For effective strategic planning, the process used must be in harmony with leadership style, organisational politics, school culture and educational philosophy.

Principle 3   For effective strategic planning, leadership needs to be committed to the concept of ongoing improvement and must provide the framework within which others can be empowered to respond. Leaders must act as catalysts and sustainers, providing both pressure and support for the activity.

Finally, real success as a learning organisation is achieved when strategic planning has retreated as the focus and when improvement in the outcomes from the process commands attention. If this occurs, everyday activity in schools is harnessed to the achievement of shared values and directions.

NOTE

1 The following characteristics of rhetorical, singular, cooperative and corporate plans are taken from McGilchrist *et al.* (1995: 120).

The rhetorical plan

- No ownership either by the head teacher or the teaching staff.
- Lack of clarity of purpose.
- No leadership or management of the process.
- Negative impact.

The singular plan

- Owned by head teacher only.
- Used as a management tool by the head teacher.
- Limited leadership and management of the process.
- Limited impact.

The cooperative plan

- Partial ownership by the teaching staff but willingness to participate.
- Used to improve both efficiency and effectiveness.
- Led by head teacher but management of process shared among some teaching staff.
- Positive impact across the school and in classrooms.

The corporate plan

- Shared ownership and involvement of all teaching staff and of some others connected with the school.
- Shared sense of purpose to improve efficiency and effectiveness.
- Shared leadership and management of the process by the teaching staff.
- Significant impact on school development, teacher development and pupil learning.

REFERENCES

Dempster, N., Kruchov, K. and Distant, G. (1994) 'Development planning in primary schools: an international perspective', in D. Hopkins and D. Hargreaves (eds) *Development Planning for School Improvement* (pp. 25–36), London: Cassell.

Garvin, D.A. (1993) 'Building a learning organisation', *Harvard Business Review* 71, 4: 78–91.

Hopkins, D. and Hargreaves, D. (eds) (1994) *Development Planing for School Improvement*, London: Cassell

Knight, J. (1992) 'The political economy of industrial relations in the Australian education industry, 1987–1991', *Unicorn* 18, 4: 27–38.

Logan, L., Dempster, N. and Sachs, J. (1994) 'School development planning in primary schools', *Ensuring Quality in Education*, selected papers from the 1994 Australian College of Education National Conference held in Launceston, 28–30 September, pp. 75–88.

McGilchrist, B., Mortimore, P., Savage, J. and Beresford, C. (1995) *Planning Matters*, London: Paul Chapman.

Senge, P. (1990) *The Fifth Discipline: The Art and Practice of the Learning Organisation*, Sydney: Random House.

Simon, H.A. (1991) 'Bounded rationality and organisational learning', *Organisation Science* 2, 1: 125–34.

Stata, R. (1989) 'Organisational learning: the key to management innovation', *Sloan Management Review* 30, 3: 63–74.

Taylor, W. (1992) 'Educational administration in a post-modern world: economic, political and ethical dimensions', in F. Crowther and D. Ogilvie (eds) *The New Political World of Educational Administration*, Victoria: Australian Council for Educational Administration Inc.

Chapter 4

Managing school development
A case study

Elizabeth Hatton and Belinda Eddy

School development planning (SDP) is planning that is typified by the identification of long-term goals and shorter-term objectives and strategies to
achieve them within set budgetary constraints. SDP is a product of the
implementation of corporate managerialist approaches to educational
management and has become a common practice in almost every primary
school in Australia (Logan *et al.*, 1994: 6). To be more precise, in Australian
educational systems, a hybrid form (Macpherson, 1991) of corporate
managerialism has been most commonly implemented. Under devolved
structures, this form leaves schools responsible for interpreting and enacting
policy within the framework of centralised guidelines (Seddon, 1994: 3).

SDP provides the means for schools to make explicit how they plan to
implement, monitor and review central policy and priorities effectively, efficiently and with high fidelity (Logan *et al.*, 1994: 11–12). Logan *et al.* note
that, in Australia, employing authorities documentation indicates that
expected benefits include

> increasing staff and community creativity, commitment and involvement
> in the school; more economic and efficient management; more focussed
> and supported leadership; more informed and shared decision-making;
> lessening the impact on school administrators and teachers of bureau-
> cratic rules and procedures; strengthening school–community interaction;
> improving teachers' professional development; and improving classroom
> work and outcomes for students.
>
> (Logan *et al.*, 1994: 6–7)

However, until a recent national study utilising surveys and case studies
(Logan *et al.*, 1994), these claims lacked empirical support. One of the case
studies in this national study was conducted in Meiki, a small, rural,
working-class primary school in the state system in northern New South
Wales (Hatton, 1994). New South Wales (NSW) is a paradigm instance of
the hybrid approach to corporate managerialism.

The case study depicts both how staff managed SDP and to what effects.
Significantly, the case-study data reveal that, in this particular context, SDP

realises many of its presumed benefits (see Logan *et al.*, 1994, for a broader view across a range of schools). This outcome appears largely attributable to the collegial, collaborative way in which SDP has been managed most recently in the school. Interestingly, teachers are committed to SDP despite some serious reservations about the way that it impacts on their lives. There are clear grounds for these reservations since managing SDP in this small, rural school makes extensive time demands on teachers and consequently blurs boundaries between the teachers' personal and professional lives through the intensification of their work. Indeed, it is evident that managing SDP in this school has personal and professional costs for teachers which are unanticipated in the policy literature. These material effects on teachers' lives and practices are sufficiently significant that they may, in the long term, undermine teachers' enthusiasm for SDP and make it less successful as an approach to school development. A second significant finding to emerge from the study is that managing SDP in this small, rural, racially divided working-class community provides unique problems which would not necessarily be evident in larger urban or regional middle-class settings.

MANAGING SDP AT MEIKI PRIMARY SCHOOL

At Meiki, there is a teaching staff of nine including the teaching principal. There are also three aides. The staff is mainly female and Anglo-Australian, while the pupils are one-third Aboriginal and two-thirds non-Aboriginal. Few of the staff have been in the school very long. Two groups currently contribute to the affairs of the school: the Parents and Citizens Committee (P&C), which tends to be exclusively non-Aboriginal, and the Aboriginal Education Consultative Group (AECG), which the principal treats as a *de facto* P&C since Aboriginal people see the P&C as a 'white' organisation. Consonant with the schools renewal strategy, a school council will soon be functioning in the school.

Although the current principal is well regarded by Aboriginal and Anglo-Australian groups within the community, there is still considerable variation in the school community relationship. Those who are actively involved in the school claim that parents are always welcome there. Other parents are thoroughly intimidated by the school, rarely visit and see it as a hostile environment. Teachers are treated with suspicion by these parents.

The principal of this small school faces extensive time demands. Despite teaching full-time, he has a staff of fifteen to supervise, responsibility for the administration of the school and minimal time release for the increased administrative burden brought by devolution. Racial divisions in the town also make time demands as the AECG and the P&C operate, according to the principal, very independently of each other . . . and they are both very sensitive.

The form of SDP has changed and developed yearly at Meiki. Under a previous principal, SDP was managed hierarchically with the principal taking major responsibility and control. Teachers talk of this phase as one in which they felt disempowered and disenchanted. They describe extensive written documentation which they felt no responsibility to implement. They viewed the SDP documents as show-pieces rather than guides to the school's practice.

The current principal, by contrast, works collaboratively with teachers, devolving work to committees. Devolution to committees is supported by the principal on three grounds: if they are involved in it, they are likely to do it; getting many people involved enables more ideas in planning; and the complexity of the school mitigates against him taking sole responsibility. The planning process in 1992 and 1993–4 were almost identical. There were two significant differences which were subsequently partially or totally addressed in 1993–4. In 1992 planning proceeded without prior knowledge of budgetary constraints which subsequently created extra work for some committees if they had overspent. Second, all planning was undertaken out of class time. Consequently, although the school set out to work collaboratively across programme and curriculum teams, constraints of time subverted this process. As Watkins (1993: 131) indicates, difficulty in finding time for meetings is a result of the inherent contradictions in imposing a time/space administrative structure of representative, collaborative committee systems over the traditional timetabled structure of teachers' work. And in a small school where the teachers have obligations to a number of committees, this problem is exacerbated.

Planning the 1994 strategic plan began in 1993 and extended into 1994. Priority initiatives taken from the principal's performance management statement were first discussed at staff meetings. In late 1993 a pupil-free School Development Day (SDD) was held for which a written invitation was extended to parents to participate in one or more sessions on designing a new report card, options for class allocations for 1994 and budget allocations for 1994.

When the committees, including coopted parents, met early in 1994, they did so in classroom release time. At this time, committees extended their long-term plan to cover the period 1994–8 and developed and devised a detailed plan for 1994, taking into account their budgetary constraints. The process began with a review of the 1993 detailed year plan and a review of the programme plan for 1994, so that, as the principal commented, 'it's just a matter of sitting down with the team and working out what you are going to do with the money you've got, and what has to be done'. Committee responsibility for plans is so total that when they are written, there is no further debate. Plans are taken to a staff meeting merely to familiarise staff; 'otherwise', said the principal, 'you'd be chasing your tail forever'. The principal simply collected finished planning from each committee and put it into a booklet. From that point on, the committees 'are responsible for making sure that they do what they said they were going to do, within reason, you know, unless there's some extenuating circumstances'. The principal cautioned his staff not to overcommit themselves because part of 'their performance management [evaluation] . . . is that they must do what they said they were going to do'.

The extent of participation is captured in this remark from a teacher who was previously an executive teacher. When asked if she missed being part of the executive team, she said, 'No, I don't, because everything that I was involved in as an executive I do here. In fact I think I do more here. . . . [The principal] puts everything at a staff meeting that we ever had at an executive meeting.'

A major innovation in this phase was the involvement of parents in both the SDD and on committees. A group of eight parents attended the full day; others came for one or two sessions. The school is conscious that this aspect of the SDP, currently being emphasised at regional level, poses special difficulties for them, as these comments from an executive teacher illustrate: 'we've got very reluctant parents, because they feel inadequate, you know. School to them is a horrible place.' Differences in class and ethnic resources and dispositions showed clearly during the SDD. The principal noted:

> We had a [professional person based at Meiki] . . . he was very confident. He got up and expressed his opinions. . . . [And] on the other end of the scale there were several there [including two Aboriginal parents] that you hardly heard boo out of for the whole day.

According to teachers, parents felt 'daunted' by the agenda: 'The [school development] plan, you know, sorting out the curriculum teams and what needs to be in each area. That sort of thing is fairly foreign to parents, so they didn't have a lot of say in that.'

Impacts and effects of SDP on pupils at Meiki

Meiki's school-based initiatives developed through SDP are all aimed at redressing educational disadvantage. Teachers have taken a school-wide perspective on this issue and have supported initiatives to ensure that literacy and numeracy gain adequate attention in early years of schooling so that teachers in middle and upper grades do not find themselves overwhelmed by large numbers of students who are unable to cope with curricula (Hatton et al., 1996). This endeavour is proving successful. Recent basic skills results indicate that academic performance in the school is improving. The Year 3 1993 and 1994 results have been above the state average. This is a significant achievement since, typically, results in disadvantaged schools generally are well below state averages. These results provide some indication that the school is effectively working through SDP towards meeting the educational needs of its pupils.

Impacts and effects of SDP on teachers at Meiki

Teachers preferred the latest form of SDP to any that had preceded it. The implementation of an SDD and the use of classroom release time for planning meetings are significant in shaping this perception. To the extent that they express concerns, these relate to time demands. To get to the point of writing the SDP, the principal estimates that, aside from the SDD,

> it took three full days of meetings . . . to nut out what was done, then of course you've got your clerical hours. . . . I suppose on average each person would have probably put four working days into it, so four times – probably forty working days, I guess that is. That's just for the curriculum areas. . . . Then on the management, etc. . . . I've done that in my own time, so that's independent of that.

The collaborative approach to SDP at Meiki surprised some teachers:

> I remember being floored. . . . Because I'd been involved in it on an executive level, not on a staff level . . . in my mind that sort of . . . plan was executive stuff. And it [is usually] imposed on the rest of the staff. I remember . . . spending hours as an executive doing it and then saying, 'Here you go, staff.' And all of a sudden I sit down at a staff meeting and [the principal] says, you know, 'These curriculum teams, you get together and do this and, you know, all work together, and here's a budget.'

The teacher was sufficiently disoriented initially to feel uncertain about contributing adequately. Her initial discomfort has since disappeared. She says, 'I feel a lot more confident. And it meant more too because I was involved . . . there's a lot of pride.' She adds:

> I can't see how the school could run without its [school development] . . . plan. Because that's what we do. [Moreover, it] makes it a really happy school because it runs and when it doesn't run it's because something has fallen down in the management plan, and you can pick it up.

While some staff members were, and remain, reluctant to be involved, they concede that involvement in SDP is a positive feature of their work. Their major concern is that SDP is time-consuming: 'I think a lot of times, you know, we'd wish that [the principal] would do it in the office. Just go in and tell us what we've got to do and get it over and done with.' However, this position is usually qualified: 'I think the ownership that it gives is really worthwhile. You know, people feel that they're not having it done to them. It's a decision that we're all making and we're all having a say.' While being on many committees means that 'everyone has got lots of hats to wear', and that is 'exhausting', it is also 'good because everyone knows what's going on because you're involved in most things'.

Teachers appreciate the principal's emphasis on streamlined planning which contrasts with the previous principal's preoccupation with 'making everything look good on paper' to the neglect of practice:

> whereas now . . . what's happening is impressive and blow the paperwork, sort of thing. . . . Do what you have to do . . . what people are asking for. . . . But . . . there's none of this spend[ing] week after week sort of presenting and binding and [so on]. . . . That isn't user friendly anyway.

The principal also questions the time–cost dimension of SDP while acknowledging the positive outcomes of staff and community ownership of school-wide planning. He says that wide ownership, at a practical level, 'slows [planning] down. . . . I reckon I could knock that up in–oh, probably a week, which is a lot less than forty days'. He concedes, however, that the plan is unlikely to 'mean as much' if written by him, so 'you're weighing the two things'.

Another concern is that aspects of devolved planning are uneconomical:

> I think it's window dressing. . . . A lot of the things that I'm saying in [it] would be very similar to things that have been said in other schools and a lot of it's put there to fill up space, if you like. I think that the process could be shortened a great deal without having any real influence in what's going on in schools. . . . I know that I say a lot of things that I said . . . other schools would have said similar things.

These concerns are serious, given the rhetoric of efficiency and effectiveness which provides the justification for SDP. In Meiki, it is clear that doing SDP under devolved structures has significantly intensified the principal's work. Importantly, the principal claims, much of the new work is trivial and diverts him from more important educational work:

> Like the budget business . . . a lot of principals have said it, that they really *feel like a bill-paying service for the Department.* . . . I mean, I'm now paying the electricity bill that used to be paid by regional office and I'm now paying the rates that used to be [done by a clerk]. And yet I've got to sit down and come up with these plans . . . I mean, you look at most of the administration things that I do . . . energy, that's gas and electricity, should have been – should be looked after by regional office. Ah, maintenance – regional office. Equipment service – regional office. Postage – regional office. Short-term relief – regional office. Phone – regional office. Waste disposal . . . all that stuff . . . [was done] by regional office, so . . . they cleaned out regional office and . . . there's not the same wage

bill involved down there, but they put the workload onto us and we're not getting the compensation for it in time. See, what they've done is save quite small [clerk's] wages . . . and then they're squeezing more, for the same amount of money, out of principals . . . and taking away from what we're actually meant to be doing. They just kept on . . . piling things on us and they say, 'yeah, we're saving the money out of education budget', and I guess they are but . . . they're doing that at the expense of the time of principals that have been taken away from what they were meant to be doing.

Views such as these are accumulating in the research literature (Thody, 1994: 38).

A pattern of intensification is evident for all members of the staff. The distinctive nature of Meiki school also makes its own contribution to intensification. Even without devolution and SDP, Meiki would be a busy place, given the work involved in preparing submissions for and monitoring social justice funding. So the unique nature of the school and its clientele, its small size and the fact that the principal is a teaching principal with time-consuming responsibilities under devolved governance, make SDP especially demanding in this site. It is not surprising therefore that SDP is seen as a mixed blessing by the principal and the staff.

One negative outcome arising from the intensification of teachers' work is that there are implications for the quality of classroom practice. For example, the principal expresses concern that his classroom preparation suffers. He worries about the effect of this on his pupils. Some teachers also admit that occasionally attention and energy may be displaced from teaching to SDP paperwork. Since this is a school in which the students are almost totally dependent on their teachers for access to academic knowledge, loss of teaching time is important.

In addition to these costs, there are other significant ones. Take, for example, the case of the principal and his wife who also teaches at Meiki. She finds that her personal life and professional life are shaped by her partner's work:

he's over [at school] quite often till midnight. He'll come home and have tea at about six, and then he's back over again . . . which means looking after the kids in the afternoon, getting all that dreadful time of bath and all that sort of thing . . . left to me, which is difficult because . . . I've always got [planning] that I have to do at home.

The principal is also affected since his participation in family life is limited. It is plausible to assume that hidden, personal costs such as these were not taken into account when the school's renewal strategy was devised. Efficiency and effectiveness are being achieved at considerable personal cost in Meiki. And this is not explained by suggesting that this is merely the result of personal choice. The complex dynamic that motivates teachers to work so hard at Meiki is a result of teachers responding positively to the challenge of SDP which, in turn, has given them an increased sense of control and achievement in their work. This has created its own dynamic of commitment. Moreover, the feeling of being appreciated and respected motivates staff and executive alike to 'put out' for each other. This, too, adds to the momentum within the school. So the coincidence of these circumstances encourages the staff at Meiki to participate willingly in the intensification of their work and thereby perhaps in their own exploitation.

Impacts and effects of SDP on the community

As yet, parents are involved to a limited degree in SDP despite the endeavours of the school. Parents offered some explanations of poor parental attendance at the SDD which point to particular difficulties in managing SDP at Meiki. One parent claims that traditional written invitations are ineffective in Meiki since 'if you want [Meiki] people to come you have to go and knock on their door and give them a personal invitation'. Moreover, because many working-class parents view formal situations negatively, he suggests, to understand what people think 'you've personally got to go and sit down with that person in their house'. Another notes that the small size of the town makes the pool of committee attendees small: 'I mean, you can have one meeting and just change the name every half hour and you could go through all the meetings in one afternoon, without anyone coming or leaving.' Therefore it becomes difficult 'to get people who actually come to meetings to another meeting, you know, they just throw their hands in the air — "I've had enough of those bloody meetings".'

Personal invitation was subsequently used successfully to coopt parents onto planning committees. Indeed, one parent says that she participated only because of the personal approach. Parents claimed that they were initially nervous, even 'terrified', about participating; however, they discovered that in small groups, and subsequently on in-service courses, teachers were supportive and inclusive. Parents note that one outcome of this involvement is a positive change in their perception of teachers. One parent says now, contrary to a common community perception, that she sees 'teachers as human people, not stuck-ups'. She claims that many parents refuse to even approach the staff room, so strong is this negative perception: 'it's just the way Meiki is really . . . . You know, that's the way they were brought up.'

DISCUSSION

If measured against the list of presumed benefits identified by Logan *et al.* (1994: 6–7) it is evident that a number of positive outcomes have emerged at Meiki, not the least of which is enhanced educational outcomes for pupils, greater commitment and involvement of teachers despite their concerns about the time demands of SDP and the fact that where parents have been encouraged into participation, negative feelings about teachers have been overcome. There are some claims for which the case study did not yield suitable or sufficient data. For example, whether staff and community creativity has increased or decreased remains open for speculation. This case study of managing SDP does, however, reveal two distinctive problems relating to the impact of intensification on teachers' work and personal lives and the suitability of this approach to small, rural, working-class, racially stratified contexts like Meiki. Each is discussed in turn.

Intensification and teachers' work and personal lives

A significant claim made for SDP is that it results in more economic and efficient management. From a system perspective, it is likely that SDP has brought with it significant economies and efficiencies. Given the data, there are some doubts about whether, in this small rural school, this view also holds true. Recall the principal's characterisation of himself as a 'bill-paying service for the department'. These extra tasks simply have to be absorbed into the principal's role whose working conditions are in no way modified to accommodate this additional level of work. This situation holds true for all principals working under devolved structures; however, at Meiki the situation is more difficult, given that the principal teaches full-time. While he is funded for some classroom release time, the allowance is meagre in relation to the administrative tasks required of him.

Moreover, the work of teachers is likewise similarly changed without accommodating changes in working conditions. Consider, for example, the number of committees on which teachers in this small school must serve to plan and monitor SDP in the school. One outcome of enhanced work demands associated with doing SDP under devolved structures is that the work of teachers at Meiki is significantly intensified. And ironically, all involved indicate that, despite their preferences, this has negative impacts on classroom practice since both the time that teachers have available to teach their classes and the quality of the preparation that they are able to do is inevitably affected. Consider, too, the way in which intensification of trivial work diverts attention from the tasks that the principal considers more appropriate to his role. Clearly economies at system level have an alarming potential to thwart educational leadership (Hatton, 1995). That teachers are able to achieve enhanced educational outcomes at Meiki despite these constraints on their practice is a credit to their dedication and efficacy.

It is not only teachers' professional lives that are affected by the intensification brought about by responding to the demands of SDP in this small school. This impact spills over into teachers' personal lives. This is perhaps illustrated most poignantly by the difficulties encountered by the principal and his partner in managing the dual concerns of career and childcare. Shortly after the conclusion of the case study, the principal sought and gained promotion to a larger school because of the negative effects on his family of his intensified work situation. Without this concern, he claims that he would have stayed longer at Meiki. While the principal has been the first to seek a new position as a result of intensification in this small rural school, it is quite possible that teachers could judge the impact on their personal lives to be exerting too high a toll and also seek other, less demanding positions. The principal's move has not been as destructive as it might have been. Historically, it appears that incoming principals arrived at Meiki, with its difficult, disadvantaged pupils, more concerned with implementing idiosyncratically conceived changes to make their 'mark', to maximise their chances of moving on quickly to another, more desirable, position. Ensuring continuity has apparently played a comparatively insignificant role (see Hatton, 1994). In this case, however, the incumbent executive teacher became principal, so continuity of initiatives and philosophy has been possible. In other circumstances, there was a real potential for a negative impact on a school in which continuity of successful initiatives is imperative.

Suitability of SDP to the context

Given the data, questions could and should be asked about the suitability of SDP to this particular context. At every point in the management of SDP at Meiki it seemed that the context threw up peculiar problems. These related to both the size of the school and community and the distinctive difficulty of involving parents in this racially divided, working-class community in SDP. Aside from the workload difficulties posed for teachers, the small rural context posed particular difficulties for parental involvement since the pool of people in the community willing and able to attend committees is limited. Consider, in this context, that SDP demands a school council as the mechanism for giving the community a say in the management of the school. At the completion of the study, the constitution for the school council had been ratified and an election was soon to be held. It is worth speculating about whether the community has the resources for this mechanism, given that there is a struggle to get adequate attendance at the P&C and the AECG, and given the class-based community perception that membership of organisations like the P&C is appropriate for 'nobs', rather than for people like themselves. The fact that the combined meeting of the

AECG and the P&C held to ratify the constitution attracted very few community members is indicative of the difficulties brought about by both the size of the community and its stratified nature.

It is hard to imagine how the school might encourage enhanced parental involvement without extra financial resources being made available to it. Extra resources could perhaps be used to test out whether personal visits could be employed usefully to enhance parental involvement and participation. This school has set about managing school development planning in very productive and positive ways. Despite this, it has encountered difficulties. It appears there is prima-facie evidence that the managerialist approach to SDP is less easy to implement in working-class settings than, for example, in middle-class, urban or regional settings. In the latter contexts, not only is the pool of available committee attendees greater, but parents are also less likely to hold views about membership of committees being inappropriate for them.

The lack of match of SDP to the specific context is also evident when parents become members of curriculum committees. Meiki's parents, unlike many middle-class parents, do not come to curriculum committees with ready-made knowledge about curriculum. To involve parents effectively in these committees, the school is sponsoring them to acquire an adequate knowledge base through in-service courses. The school does not receive supplementary funding for this. Parents are enjoying this experience, and it is having the effect of making some parents more comfortable about their relationships with teachers. However, in an impoverished community where fund-raising is difficult, it is placing a burden on the school which would not be evident in middle-class schools. Indeed, questions could be asked about whether this constitutes the most efficient use of scarce resources. This is not a criticism of the *modus operandi* of the school. Rather, it is arguably the case that since forms of behaviour required by SDP are not context- or class-sensitive (Hatton, 1995), they inevitably generate practices that might be questionable on grounds of efficiency and economics.

CONCLUSION

On balance, SDP appears to be a success at Meiki. School management has become a more open, inclusive practice which has significantly enhanced teachers' sense of control and ownership in their work. In this context, SDP has achieved one of the most significant of its intended outcomes, namely, enhanced academic outcomes. The whole-school perspective, developed through collaborative SDP under devolved structures, has enabled the school to develop thoughtful, effective, classroom-level initiatives (see Hatton, 1995). These initiatives have ensured that students in the K-3 area of the school are achieving well in mathematics and literacy rather than falling steadily behind, as typifies the schooling experiences of many disadvantaged students (Nicklin Dent and Hatton, 1996).

Two areas remain problematic. First, there is the unanticipated impact on teachers' professional and personal lives which is a product of managing SDP effectively and collaboratively at Meiki. It is possible that teachers will find it increasingly difficult to sustain the level at which they are currently working. Should conditions change in the school (for example, should a new principal arrive), and should teachers feel consequently less appreciated and supported, it is arguably the case that the work dynamic in this school would change and SDP might well become less effective. Second, given the size of the community and its particular social and cultural dimensions, parental involvement in SDP has proved particularly difficult to achieve in Meiki. Both of these issues are unanticipated in the policy literature and both have the potential to undermine SDP in this setting.

REFERENCES

Hatton, E.J. (1994) *Strategic and Management Planning at Meiki Primary School: A Contextualised Case Study in NSW*, Case Study for the Primary School Planning Project, forwarded to the School's Council, NBEET, Faculty of Education, Griffith University, Nathan, Queensland.

—— (1995) 'Corporate managerialism, intensification and the rural primary principal', *Education in Rural Australia* 5, 2: 25–32.

—— (1996) 'Corporate managerialism in a rural setting', *Journal of Research in Rural Education* 12, 1: 1–13.

Hatton, E.J., Munns, G. and Nicklin Dent, J. (1996) 'Teaching children in poverty: three Australian primary school responses', *British Journal of Sociology of Education* 17, 1: 39–52.

Logan, L. Sachs, J. and Dempster, N. (1994) *Who Said Planning Was Good For Us? School Development Planning in Australian Primary Schools*, Report for the School's Council of NBEET from the Primary School Planning Project, Faculty of Education, Griffith University, Nathan, Queensland.

Macpherson, R.J.S. (1991) 'Restructuring of administrative policies in Australian and New Zealand state school systems: implications for practice, theory and research', *Journal of Educational Administration* 29, 4: 51–64.

Nicklin Dent, J. and Hatton, E.J. (1996) 'Education and poverty: an Australian primary school case study', *Australian Journal of Education* 40, 1: 42–60.

Seddon, T. (1994) 'Assessing the institutional context of decentralised school management: schools of the future in Victoria', *Discourse* 15, 1: 1–15.

Thody, A. (1994) 'Abroad thoughts from home: reflections on an academic visit to Australia', *Journal of Educational Administration* 32, 2: 45–53.

Watkins, P. (1993) 'Finding time: temporal considerations in the operation of school committees', *British Journal of Sociology of Education,* 14, 2: 131–46.

Chapter 5

School review for improved student learning

Neville Highett[1]

INTRODUCTION

This chapter discusses the programme of Quality Assurance (QA) reviews that were introduced within the New South Wales government school system in early 1993 and explores some of the lessons learned since then.

The New South Wales government school system is the largest school system in Australia with approximately 34 per cent of the Australian student population. There are 2,222 schools with a total enrolment of over 750,000 students, 46,000 teachers and 12,500 ancillary staff. It is the fourth largest enterprise in Australia.

THE NSW SCHOOL REVIEW PROCESS 1993–5

Schools in the New South Wales government system operate in a system that has devolved much authority and responsibility to the individual school. The QA programme of reviews was established to provide a system of accountability for schools that was independent of management and administrative structures. However, in addition to an accountability function, the QA programme has always maintained a strong focus on school development and improvement. It seeks to support the establishment of quality practices in all stages of the work of schools and aims to ensure that schools are highly effective in achieving the best possible learning outcomes – cognitive and non cognitive – for students.

The guiding principles for the QA school review process have been outlined in a policy document which states:

1 School reviews support schools in evaluating and assessing their practices and outcomes to improve student learning.
2 School reviews contribute to the evaluation and assessment of services and programmes which support schools.
3 School reviews strengthen accountability for the quality of education in individual schools.

4 School reviews are undertaken through the participation of school staff, students, parents and the review team. Reviews provide opportunities for input from all those interested in the school's performance and development.

5 School reviews are planned and constructed to take account of the context of each school.

6 School review teams have the necessary knowledge and skills to ensure reviews are of direct benefit to schools.

7 School review team members are bound by ethical and professional standards.

8 School review teams use methods which are consistent with established best practices in school reviews and evaluation.

(New South Wales Department of School Education, 1995: 4–5).

Once every four years each school in the state is provided with an external school review. Over the three-year period 1993–5, 1,482 school reviews of between two and five days were undertaken by school review teams. The time that a team spends at a school is determined by the nature and size of the school. Teams typically have a membership that includes the host school principal, a local community member, an executive member, at least one teacher and a team leader from the QA office. The executive member and the teacher are seconded to the QA directorate for periods of time that range from one to four school terms.

There are three clearly defined yet closely linked stages in the school review process: pre-review, the review and post-review activity.

Stage 1: The pre-review process

The first stage occurs up to six months prior to the visit by the review team and commences with a meeting between the leader of the review team and key stakeholders in that school's community. This meeting has three major purposes. The leader of the review team provides information on the major steps and aspects of the school review process. The team leader asks the school to check the accuracy of a statistical profile of the school which has been drawn from administrative records, and seeks additional detail in preparation for the review. A most significant purpose of this meeting is to establish the basis on which to negotiate the focus areas to be addressed during the quality review.

Focus areas are identified collaboratively by the school, the community and the team leader. To identify the foci for each review, the team leader and school community undertake an analysis of the school development plan, available student outcome data and school performance judged against a school review framework which has been developed collaboratively by the directorate. The basic purpose of using student learning outcome data in this process is to organise the data so that the relevant stakeholders can analyse and use it to improve opportunities for students, while at the same time being aware of possible misinterpretations and misuses.

In essence, this analysis and the subsequent school review assesses four key aspects of performance:[2]

- Factors *enabling* current successful programmes.
- Factors *impeding* current performance.
- Key areas for development necessary to meet emergent community needs over the next three to five years.
- The effectiveness of services and programmes delivered by other parts of the school system to schools.

Once the focus areas have been agreed upon, specific data gathering processes are organised and the review team returns several weeks later to undertake the review.

Stage 2: The school review and review methodology

The school reviews draw on a range of methodologies that have been developed in the educational evaluation and social science literature. Reviews follow the basic methodology of establishing the evaluation questions (this is done as part of the pre-review process), collecting data, processing information, and interpreting and giving meaning to the information in the process of clarifying and generating the findings.

Data are collected by interview, document analysis and observations. Interviews are scheduled with random samples of each of the stakeholder groups. Interviews are also available, if requested, for any other stakeholders not formally selected into the samples. A typical review of a 400-student primary school would speak to about 80 persons in total.

Students meet in groups of two to five with a member of the review team, while all other interviews are normally held on a one-to-one basis. In addition, interviews are held with each member of the school executive, individuals who have specific responsibilities or others who have been central to the development of the areas that are the focus of the review.

The observations of classrooms and other aspects of the school's work and the analysis of documents is strategically directed to the focus areas and evaluation questions negotiated with the school prior to the review. The analysis of information obtained from students, staff and parents, plus the perusal of documents and observation in classrooms and elsewhere in the school, form the evidence base for the review. The reviews have developed procedures to safeguard the anonymity and confidentiality of its sources of information on each issue.

The methodology of a review can be compared with the process used in judicial decision-making. In general, issues are analysed through cross-examination until a consistent interpretation is available from corroborating evidence. 'There is a constant interplay between the observations or realities and the formation of concepts, between research and theorising, between perception and explanation' (Blumer, 1982: 35). While this may involve triangulation of evidence from a range of sources by a range of methods, the principle of corroboration overrides that of triangulation. The reviews seek to determine whether the particular issue indicates an important aspect of the school's functioning and operation that would benefit substantially from focused improvement efforts.

The visit by the review team concludes with a presentation of a preliminary oral report to the school staff, invited parents, students and members of the community. This report covers the major strengths and achievements identified during the review, significant findings and an indication of the directions for the school's future development.

Stage 3: Post-review

The team leader writes the formal report, consulting with the principal who checks the report for accuracy. The findings highlight school achievements and identify areas for further development. The report contains evaluative assessments of the primary development issues addressed by the review and future directions to assist the further improvement of student learning. The statements of best practices contained in the school review framework are used as the backdrop for writing the recommendations for ongoing school change and development.

Recommendations are written in terms of the outcomes to be achieved but do not discuss the strategies that the school will need to implement to achieve these outcomes. The recommendations are clearly delineated as being targeted at either incremental improvement – for example, the extension of a programme to other groups of students – or at fundamental development. Fundamental development refers to changes that will require structural or cultural changes to the way that the school operates.

School reports are public documents. Following the release of the report the school principal is accountable for implementing the improvements contained in the recommendations. Schools report progress against the review recommendations in their public annual reports.

THE SCHOOL REVIEW FRAMEWORK

As soon as review teams become involved in the analysis of data and the meanings contained within those data sources, it is important to state explicitly the underlying assumptions about the values associated with success, goodness, high performance, etc. The QA Directorate has endeavoured to do this by publishing the School Review Framework (SRF).

The SRF sets out the major dimensions of a school's operation. Within these dimensions the major areas of operation and aspects that define the scope of an area are made explicit. The SRF indicates how teachers and other practising professionals would describe best practices in that area and sets out descriptors which indicate whether best practices are part of a school's operation.

The best practices achievement statements within the SRF serve four purposes. First, they provide a framework for determining the foci for school reviews. Second, they provide the parameters for professional judgements and debate during school reviews. As such they are the landscape against which school review findings are analysed and against which recommendations are written. Third, the achievement statements provide a framework for ongoing debate about best practice at the school level. They can be used by schools to assess aspects of their performance and to plan for their ongoing development. Fourth, they provide a basis for assessing and reporting the performance of the system.

The best practice achievement statements represent what the profession agrees are the parameters for highly effective operation, both at the school and classroom level. The development of these statements was a challenge, for as Murnane and Raizen (cited in Porter, 1993: 18) have demonstrated, experts do not always agree on what constitutes good teaching. Practitioners' views of best practice may be limited by their own teaching experience and sphere of understanding. However, the writing teams were chosen from a group of persons acknowledged by their peers to be excellent in the application of their craft. The writing teams constantly tested their work with networks of colleagues and documented the research used to support the statements.

The achievement statements require the application of connoisseurship (see Eisner, 1991) or professional judgements to determine performance level. As Eisner explains, connoisseurship – the art of appreciation – is a means for educators to understand what is occurring in schools and through those understandings improve practice and policy. Eisner defines connoisseurship as 'the ability to make fine-grained discriminations among complex and subtle qualities' (p. 63). This requires detailed understanding of the context, and is best known by the practitioners at the local level.

Given that qualitative achievement statements are meaning-laden, they must proffer explicit statements of what is best practice. Hence, associated with each achievement statement is a series of descriptors. They point to the best practice and what is observable if the best practice is in operation within the school's context. During a review it is necessary for team members to determine whether or not it is appropriate to expect a particular practice to be present or not in the situation that is being observed. Hence, the observers need to be context-sensitive as the 'interpretation of such data can never be unequivocal and direct but depends on a communication and on the standpoint of the listener or observer' (Ashworth, 1986: 8).

Table 5.1 School Review Framework

Learning and teaching		Leadership and culture		School development and management	
Area	Aspect	Area	Aspect	Area	Aspect
Learning	Learning environment	Leader-ship	Contextual leadership	Development	School purpose
	Student learning		Leadership for change		Setting priorities
	Teacher learning		Inclusive leadership		Planning
			Leadership for learning		
Teaching	Planning and implementation	Culture	Cultural context	Management	Managing incremental improve-ment
	Assessment and reporting		Developing ownership		
			Culture of learning		
	Reflection and evaluation		Integrated culture		Managing fundamental change
			Culture of improve-ment		

The statements were developed to take into account different school contexts and differing phases of development. The dialogue that occurred while the descriptors were being developed focused the statements on the fundamental issues associated with best practice in schools and classrooms. Many descriptors were discarded as the focus on critical aspects of school functioning was sharpened. The achievement statements specify the 'whats' desired or to be achieved. They do not say how to achieve an outcome. Determination of how to achieve an outcome is the professional domain of school staff. The mix of professional expertise, resources and local context have a significant impact on determining the appropriate strategies to use in any development initiative.

The organisation of the review framework statements is shown in Table 5.1. The critical aspects of a school's operation have been defined in terms of practice in three dimensions of schooling:

- teaching and learning
- leadership and culture
- school development and management.

The SRF is used to make judgements about performance. Respondents decide whether the practice described in an achievement statement is consistently in operation, is evident, whether there is awareness of the practice or whether the practice does not operate. The judgements are entered into a computer and the results displayed for analysis.

The School Review Framework as a tool for school development

The achievement statements are predicated on agreement about best practice. The context in which schools operate means that not all schools are at the same stage on the journey to the goals and it needs to be recognised that there are multiple paths to achieving the same goals. However, articulation of the goals and the measurement of performance against the goals can clearly indicate the direction of journey that remains. Clearly articulated but locally developed strategies can then be put in place to continue the improvement process and measurements over time can provide feedback about the success of strategies being implemented to improve student learning. As the American Quality Foundation Report (1992) graphically indicated, applying the same treatments to all organisations is counterproductive. Knowledge of the context and stage of development of any organisation is crucial when planning strategies for ongoing improvement efforts.

The statements can be used by schools to challenge assumptions and organisational myths that are embedded as part of operational practice. Given that dramatic change is occurring in educational organisations, many myths and associated folklore that underpin a range of practices in education need to undergo intense scrutiny.

Computer software that assists with the recording and analysis of judgements against the achievement statements has been developed. Judgements can be collected from staff, students and parents and then compared and presented graphically. The variation of assessments across respondent groups assists with the generation of dialogue about the relative importance of various descriptors for targeted school development. Teaching is a very oral profession and the generation of dialogue against the framework provides opportunities for teachers to reflect on and critique their own and others' thinking and practices.

LESSONS LEARNED FROM SCHOOL REVIEWS

Evaluations undertaken by Henry (1995) and Eagleton (1994) indicate that support was widely given to the development of school reviews. The QA process was seen as an 'open, consultative and developmental model' (Henry, 1995: 6).

Initially the introduction of school reviews was helped by the nature of the reviews themselves. Monitoring by QA has found that:

- schools have assessed the conduct of review teams as professional and ethical
- school community members, particularly non-school-based members such as parents, welcomed the opportunity for reflection about their school which the review provided
- review reports have acknowledged strengths and achievements and the review process as a whole has been an affirming experience for school community members
- review recommendations have set directions for school development and for improved student learning in a context appropriate to the school's capacity for change and with relevance to focus areas chosen by the school.

School review and school planning

The pre-review process, the actual review and the resultant public report all provide the pressure to initiate change within a school. The challenge for schools and the school system is the provision of effective support to effect the required changes. Planning competence in schools grows with experience, support from the system and increased opportunities for the inclusion of all sectors of the school community in the structures in which it is undertaken. Given that all sectors of the school community are involved in the review, the reports provide readily established information about why changes are needed and the review recommendations provide the required focus for school planning processes.

However, a recent QA evaluation has shown that

the perceived effectiveness/internal condition of the school was a reasonable predictor of the level of impact of the review. Put another way the more ready the school was for a review the more the school got out of it. The poorer the organisational condition of the school the less impact the review had. Below a certain level of effectiveness the review had no impact at all.

(Hopkins, 1995: 13)

The 'readiness' of which Hopkins writes is indicated in part by the kinds of structures and processes that schools use to plan, implement, monitor and evaluate effective development. Schools that approach best practice in these matters will be influenced most by reviews. This presents a problem in terms of systemic improvement of schools because the schools most able to cope with implementing fundamental change recommendations are those with higher performance levels. Schools at the lower end of performance continuum are those that most need to undertake fundamental change initiatives.

Irrespective of the above, ongoing monitoring and feedback from stakeholders has indicated that pre-review processes are critical to both the success of the actual review and the implementation of report recommendations.

Reviews where the pre-review processes have identified focus areas that were 'developmental' have had a greater impact. Schools that are challenged to increase their capacity for meeting best practice benchmarks and for enhancing cognitive and non-cognitive student learning outcomes, as well as being applauded for their achievements, react more positively to review processes. The foci need to provide schools with the capacity to both praise and challenge. Since the improvement of student learning outcomes is a crucial purpose of reviews, at least one focus area needs to be concerned specifically with learning and teaching. Focus areas need to be selected in a collaborative manner and be based upon sophisticated data and their analysis and evaluation.

In an attempt to enhance the developmental capacity of the school a range of data is now presented and analysed as part of the pre-review process. Generally schools are data-rich but information-poor. QA team leaders assist schools to seek out their data sources and use technology to display them in a range of formats. This includes information about student achievement in state-wide tests, attendance data, classroom records, records of student behaviour, involvement in external competitions, etc.

Once the information is tabled, it is then possible to ask a series of questions. Three effective discussion starters are: 'Why is it so?', 'What does it mean?' and 'What patterns or connections exist?' When the information is displayed it becomes the 'pressure' component as used by Michael Fullan (1991) in his conception of pressure and support, both of which are required for school change. Once acknowledged, it is harder to ignore the messages being conveyed by the data and staff generally wish to tackle the issues behind the data. The process of tabling a range of data and the analysis of those data converges opinion on the required focus areas for a review. It enhances commitment to finding out 'why it is so' during the review and increases the desire to act on recommendations.

School review and classroom practice

The internal developmental capacity of a school is a reflection of the culture of the school – the degree of shared beliefs and assumptions about the school's purposes, ethos and values. When there is significant social capital (to use Ramsay and Clarke's [1990] phrase) or agreement about these aspects, a school can respond positively to a review. Evaluation has revealed, however, that there is a divergence between the responses of school leaders, community representatives and directors on the one hand, and classroom teachers on the other. This divergence influences the level of impact of school reviews and the commitment with which recommendations intended to enhance student learning are implemented.

The attitudes of classroom teachers as a group represent a major challenge to the proponents of school reviews as a QA device. There is increasing acceptance of school planning as a legitimate process but monitoring and evaluative expertise may take longer to acquire and to embed as part of school culture. The factors of time, opportunity and practice will be important, but there appears to be a greater reluctance in schools to accept that monitoring is an integral part of change. Many commentators have made that kind of remark (e.g. Caldwell and Spinks, 1992; Fullan, 1991; Huberman, 1993; Mortimore, 1995). The actions of teacher unions suggests that teachers do not welcome contemporary evaluative and monitoring measures focused on the outcomes of their work. The closer that QA school reviews move to direct intervention in the classroom, the more difficult it may be to foster attitudinal change towards newer techniques for monitoring student learning.

Until the significant minority of these practitioners who presently reject them are convinced that school reviews have benefits for their work, they will be tempted to dismiss reviews as unnecessary disruptions to routine, and build those walls around their present practices and classrooms of which Huberman (1993) writes so insightfully. If their judgements of reviews can be aligned more with the majority of their colleagues who express varying levels of satisfaction with the review process and its outcomes, then the potential for school reviews to have meaningful impact on school operations and on student learning will be enhanced significantly.

One should not deny the importance of using the whole school as the focus of change, which is the perspective of the teaching staff. Such a 'classroom exceeding' view has been proposed by experienced researchers (Van Velzen, 1985; Hopkins, 1987). However, there are good grounds for asserting that the key factors in enhancing learning are classroom behaviour and relationships. As Hill argues:

Most reforms in education are directed at the pre-conditions for learning rather than at influencing behaviours within the classroom .... Many reforms stop short of changing what happens beyond the classroom door and thus fail to deliver improved learning outcomes.

(Hill, 1995: 12–13)

Unless schools can be brought to measure and evaluate changes in student learning as a result of changed staff activity resulting from the impact of school reviews, 'we will have to admit ... that we are essentially investing in staff development rather than in the improvement in pupils' abilities' (Huberman, 1992: 11).

School review and student perception of quality teaching

The research literature into what constitutes effective teaching offers insights into what we should strive for in the search for excellence (see Hosford, 1984, for an earlier but succinct summary). Students who talk to school review teams consistently indicate that good teaching occurs when:

- there is no barrier between the student and teacher based on authority
- the expected learning outcomes are known
- discussion occurs about the information in textbooks, materials and notes being presented to the class; this is seen as assisting with the under-standing of and finding relevance for the material presented
- a variety of presentation methods are used, including group work and hands-on activities
- the students respect the teacher and the teacher respects the students
- personal attention is given to individual students and students are allowed to learn from their mistakes
- classroom behaviour is controlled because disruptive students hinder other students' learning and this leads to dull and boring lessons
- all students are treated fairly.

While there is a degree of consistency in students' perceptions of their needs, those who speak to review team members indicate that they are not always having their needs met. The challenge is to address these issues within all classrooms. Changing teacher classroom performance is essential for improved student outcomes and needs to be the focus of school develop-ment initiatives. Student judgements about the quality of their classroom life provide powerful information to teachers reflecting on their practice.

School improvement and improved student learning

Acceptance and commitment to a commonly held vision is a prerequisite to an effective and highly achieving organisation. Schools that encourage staff reflection on the core business of teaching and learning are able to enhance commitment to the central vision of the school (Schon, 1987).

From schools where staff engage in frequent and precise conversations about teaching practice and learning outcomes, will emerge leaders (not necessarily correlated to hierarchical position) with an ability to 'infuse the work of institutions with those meanings, and thus draw the allegiance of other members of the organisation towards those meanings and purpose' (Starratt, 1993: 63).

'Language cloaks power and has power' (Hodgkinson, 1978: 204). The power in these cases (teachers talking about student learning) is the power of active professionals mastering and continuously improving their craft. It impacts on the culture of the school and demonstrates to all the importance of the central purpose of school development – improving learning outcomes for all students.

The SRF statements developed by the QA Directorate provide a focus and shared language for the development of a school vision. It is a vision of what is possible and defines the parameters of what can be achieved. The statements provide a focus for the activities of school staff as they learn, converse together and plan for the development of student learning outcomes within their school. The shared learning increases collegiality.

Work by Lieberman and Miller (1984) clearly indicates that support and close collegial relationships are essential if teachers are to change their classroom practice to focus on student learning. Mentoring has been shown to be effective for assisting less experienced colleagues to establish and consolidate their operational practice. However, it takes a great deal of support to change practices that are central to one's understanding of the teaching learning process. The quality of working relationships among teachers strongly influences implementation of such fundamental change (Fullan, 1991). Collegiality, trust, support to answer questions as they arise, learning on the job, getting results, job satisfaction and morale are all closely interrelated. Rosenholtz (1989) found that such schools could be classified as 'learning enriched'. They provide powerful models of learning environments that stimulate continuous improvement.

To be highly effective, school reviews require well-developed structures within a school. These processes need to focus on the development of shared understandings of school purpose, collegial staff development focusing on changed classroom practice for improved learning outcomes. This requires a commitment of all to life-long learning to assist in discharging moral, professional and contractual accountability.

NOTES

1   The views expressed in this chapter are those of the author and may not be those of the New South Wales Department of School Education. However, I wish to

acknowledge the critical comments and suggestions provided by Graham Kahabka, Principal of Fairy Meadow Demonstration School, and Dr John Manefield, Chief Education Officer, Quality Assurance Directorate.
2 For a more detailed discussion see Cuttance (1994).

REFERENCES

American Quality Foundation (1992) *The International Quality Study: Best Practices Report. An Analysis of Management Practices that Impact Performance*, Victoria: Platypus Oz.

Ashworth, P. (1986) *Adequacy of Description: The Validity of Qualitative Findings*, Sheffield: Sheffield City Polytechnic.

Blumer, M. (1982) *The Uses of Social Research: Social Investigations in Public Policy Making*, Oxford: Allen & Unwin.

Caldwell, B. and Spinks, J. (1992) *Leading the Self-Managing School*, London: Falmer Press.

Cuttance, P. (1994) 'Quality systems for the performance development cycle of schools', paper presented at the Seventh International Congress for School Effectiveness and Improvement, 3–5 January, Melbourne.

Eagleton, H. (1994) 'Operational review of school reviews', *Quality Assurance Directorate*, Sydney: NSW Department of School Education.

Eisner, E.W. (1991) *The Enlightened Eye: Qualitative Inquiry and the Enhancement of Educational Practice*, New York: Macmillan.

Fullan, M. (1991) *The New Meaning of Educational Change*, London: Cassell.

Henry, D. (1995) 'Key factors enabling or impeding the quality assurance initiative for New South Wales, Australia', paper presented at the Eighth International Congress for School Effectiveness and Improvement, 3–5 January, Leeuwardin, Netherlands.

Hill, P. (1995) 'School effectiveness and improvement', Inaugural Professorial Lecture, University of Melbourne.

Hodgkinson, C. (1978) *Towards a Philosophy of Administration*, London: Basil Blackwell.

Hopkins, D. (1987) *Improving the Quality of Schooling*, Lewes: Falmer Press.

—— (1995) 'The impact of New South Wales quality assurance processes on school development', draft paper presented to Quality Assurance Directorate, unpublished, NSW Department of School Education.

Hosford, P.L. (ed.) (1984) *Using What We Know About Teaching*, Alexandria: Association for Supervision and Curriculum Development.

Huberman, M. (1992) 'Critical introduction', in M. Fullan (ed.) *Successful School Improvement: The Implementation Perspective and Beyond* (pp. 1–20), Buckingham: Open University Press.

——(1993) *The Lives of Teachers*, London: Cassell.

Lieberman, A. and Miller, L. (1984) *Teachers, Their World and Their Work: Implications for School Improvement*, Alexandria: Association for Supervision and Curriculum Development.

Mortimore, P. (1995) 'Effective schools: current impact and future potential', director's inaugural lecture delivered at the Institute of Education, University of London.

New South Wales Department of School Education (1995) *Quality Assurance School Reviews: Principles and Processes*, Sydney: New South Wales Department of School Education.

Porter, A.C. (1993) 'School delivery standards', *Educational Researcher* 22, 5: 24–30.

Ramsay, W. and Clarke, E. (1990) *New Ideas for Effective School Improvement: Vision, Social Capital, Evaluation*, London: Falmer Press.

Rosenholtz, S. (1989) *Teachers' Workplace: The Social Organisation of Schools*, New York: Longman.

Schon, D. (1987) *Educating the Reflective Practitioner*, San Francisco: Jossey-Bass.

Starratt, R.J. (1993) *The Drama of Leadership*, London: Falmer Press.

Van Velzen, W. G. (1985) *Making School Improvement Work: A Conceptual Guide to Practice*, Brussels: Leuven.

Chapter 6

The middle years of schooling

Larry Scott, Kathy Davis and Dianne Andrewartha

Most state education systems are structured around traditional primary, secondary and post-compulsory divides, and the existing cultures within these bureaucracies see little point in creating a new organisational tier. Yet support among educators, at both primary and secondary levels, for the concept of middle schooling is increasing rapidly.

Ironically this lack of recognition at a systemic level has had a positive effect on developing middle schooling initiatives, allowing individual schools the freedom to develop their own action research models of change, rather than adopt centrally imposed change policies. Although reform in these circumstances is often idiosyncratic and unlikely to have universal application, there exist enough similarities for some studies to be undertaken.

In contrast to the states, the federal government, through the Department of Employment, Education and Training (DEET), has provided conceptual leadership and financial input to the middle school reform movement. Projects such as the Schools Council, *In the Middle* (NBEET, 1993) and the more recent report on opportunities for reform in the middle years of schooling, *From Alienation to Engagement* (ACSA, 1996), have given the movement a national focus by identifying good practice and recommending key strategies.

In the preface to this latter report, the then Minister for Schools, Vocational Education and Training, Ross Free, noted:

> There is increasing evidence to suggest that not all students are achieving their potential within the traditional structure of primary and secondary education. A common theme emerging from recent research is the need for the middle years to be viewed as a designated stage of schooling that is more responsive to the developmental needs of young adolescents. The focus is now on developing a new philosophy or culture of schooling, which will fully engage young people, rather than the 'bricks and mortar' issues associated with creating middle schools.
>
> (ACSA, 1996: vi)

New philosophies and cultures rarely owe their genesis to system policy initiatives. Instead, they are more likely to originate as 'percolate-up' models of change in which teachers focus upon a significant issue that needs addressing. Initial success increases the momentum and often diverges to encompass associated problems and their solutions.

Free's comments identify an essential difference between Australian and British or American concepts of middle school reform. In Australia the reform is less concerned with creating new policies or schooling sectors, tending more to focus on practices of good schools in developing pedagogies, structures and curricula that cater better for the learning needs of young adolescents. Usually such reform takes place *within* the current structures of schooling.

Most Australian initiatives have started with the identification of the needs of young adolescents. They seek to align the turbulent and dramatic social, physical, emotional and intellectual changes accompanying adolescence with more appropriate strategies for successful learning. As a result, the term 'middle schooling' takes on a new meaning. The focus shifts from the organisation (school) to the subject (young adolescent). It is the child who is in the middle – not his or her grade group.

This shift in focus forces educators to consider the change from child to adult as the reason for being 'in the middle', rather than adopt any simplistic notion of the young person being in the 'middle grades'. In such a paradigm, solutions are generated from the needs of young adolescents, rather than from the more abstract needs of structures and systems. Hence, in order to conduct successful reform, prominence needs to be given to understanding the nature of adolescence, its various constructs, and the social milieu within which our young people are immersed.

THE SOCIAL CONTEXT OF ADOLESCENCE

Every generation says of the next, 'It wasn't like that in my day!' and of course they are right. Today's world is changing so fast that it is hard to make social comparisons between generations. Parents who say to their child 'When I was your age . . . ' can rightfully expect the answer 'You were never my age!' from a recalcitrant offspring. The dramatic changes of adolescence are so intertwined with the social and cultural influences of the day, that any relative comparisons of teenage culture between generations is, at best, tenuous and, at worst, dangerous. Times and technology have changed so much as to render such comparisons redundant.

Consider the following societal changes that have occurred over the last twenty years.

	1970s	*1990s*
Life expectancy, males	68.2 yrs	74.5 yrs
Life expectancy, females	75 yrs	80.4 yrs
Unemployment	2.5%	10.4%
Households with colour TVs	49%	99%
Households with videos	0.1%	80%
Households with microwaves	0%	62%
Female participation in workforce	40.6%	51.7%
Male participation in workforce	82.5%	73.9%
Membership of trade unions	55%	39.6%
Higher education eligibility	6%	13.7%
Telephone connections per 1,000 people	230	520

These statistics paint a picture of a new generation in which people live longer, are less likely to be employed (especially full-time) and have access to technologies that did not exist twenty years ago. In addition, workplaces have a higher proportion of female workers and are less union-oriented. More than twice the number of people qualify to enter tertiary education institutions. All this comes before the most recent technological and social changes are taken into account!

A recent issues paper from the Queensland Board of Teacher Registration, *Preparing Teachers for Working with Young Adolescents* (1994), highlights these changing social conditions. The paper argues that many aspects of social life in the 1990s pose particular challenges for young adolescents, not simply because of the rapidly changing society, but also because of an inability or reluctance of an ageing teaching force to keep abreast of popular teenage subcultures. Simple misinformation on the part of teachers and planners often militates against the best use of opportunities to develop more effective teaching and learning strategies.

The Queensland paper provides a good framework for teacher discussion and deliberation. It includes:

- *demographic changes* reflected in inter-state and overseas migration, as well as rapid urbanisation and rural poverty
- *declining sense of community belonging*, with fewer community-based clubs, declining church attendance and increased fears for personal safety
- *breakdown and disruption of the family* or social unit
- *youth homelessness* and disaffection with family relationships
- *economic problems* of unemployment, retrenchment, lack of public transport and infrastructure
- *influence of print media*, TV, radio and video games on the values of adolescents
- *peer pressure* and the influence of subcultures
- *changing sexual mores*, earlier commencement of sexual activity, 'safer sex'

- *emerging health issues* such as drug and alcohol abuse, HIV/AIDS, obsessive dieting
- *varying parental expectations*, and conflicting values from different family members.

A cursory examination of this list reveals that for young people today, life's experiences are significantly different from those of earlier generations. Parents or teachers who draw only upon their own teenage experiences when discussing solutions for today's youth can rightly be accused of living in the past. Failure to acknowledge these changes is a potential source of conflict that can lead to increased estrangement or alienation of many young people.

There is an expectation in society that schooling should be an integral part of a student's life, rather than abstracted from it, and therefore the discourse in schools should more closely resemble the way in which communities and families function. Greater understanding of the societal demands placed upon our young people is the pre-eminent condition for realistic middle school reform. While some practices in schools may be a current source of adolescent alienation, schools also represent a significant locus through which the problem can be addressed.

Cormack (1991, 1996) provides a rich source of information about adolescents from a number of different perspectives, including health and sexuality as well as intellectual, personal and social development. Students, teachers, parents, academics, social workers and others who live and work with adolescents, view them thro ᵒ ᵢ different lenses. They think of them in quite different ways, drawing upon their own experiences and training, and basing their observations on different theoretical and philosophical assumptions. It is thus difficult to obtain a coherent view of adolescence, and naive to assume that such a view can be easily achieved.

Indeed, the ways in which young adolescents interact with society and their environment is quite complex and varied. At different times students feel estranged or alienated from school, parents, police, peers and the like. They do so for different reasons and under differing circumstances. Alienation is manifested in many forms; it is multi-faceted and multi-dimensional. It is also compounded when teachers and parents fail to detect deep-seated problems or leave them unattended for long periods of time.

Cumming (1994) makes a strong case for the inclusion of other agencies in addressing the issues of concern to young adolescents. He claims that since schools are only one source of alienation, other agencies such as health, welfare, justice and youth affairs need to develop more pragmatic partnerships in producing eclectic solutions. For instance, combined inter-agency efforts, with on-campus facilities, are more likely to provide universal and lasting solutions.

DIFFERING CONSTRUCTS OF ALIENATION

The literature on student alienation teems with different theoretical perspectives, all of which prescribe varying panaceas. It is difficult to classify these theories, as they overlap at times, and in some cases are conflicting and contradictory. At the risk of over-simplification, Cormack (1996: 7–20) attempts to outline four different philosophical constructs commonly used by researchers in the field. They serve as a good reference point for investigation, challenging workers and researchers to examine their own opinions, and to assign some philosophical construct to their *modus operandi*.

Critical theory views of alienation

Critical theorists tend to work in a neo-Marxist paradigm which focuses on social class and economic factors as the basis for social alienation. They identify as a cause of alienation the concentration of power in the hands of a few, who control the outcomes of society for their own benefit. Power is usually the major issue, with the most alienated in our society being those with least power. Young adolescents are seen as exercising little power over the education system and school outcomes, and schools are seen as institutions that reproduce the inequalities of the past.

Critical theorists are therefore concerned with the 'social construction' of phenomena, and conclude that very little of what occurs in society is 'natural'. Rather it is controlled by the powerful and influential in our society. They see the growth of youth subcultures as a response to powerlessness, as an outward expression of resistance to the oppression imposed by the powerful. Critical theorists highlight voluntary choice, active participation in the decision-making processes, cooperation and clearly defined and agreed goals as ingredients for successful schooling.

Psychological views

Researchers in this field tend to concentrate on the individual or an identifiable group, for example the poor, immigrants, indigenous and NESB (non-English-speaking background) minorities. The locus of alienation is perceived as an internal state, usually manifesting in two main forms.

Frustration – self-esteem model

Failure at school lowers the self-esteem of students, which often leads them to reject the institution (school) that causes them to fail. In this model, teachers tend to blame the student for a lack of ability or interest, and label them as uncooperative, unwilling to participate, disruptive, or poor attenders.

Participation – identification model

Students who are achieving well at school identify strongly with the institution, becoming attached to its daily routines and having a sense of belonging. They value the success that it gives them, and this success generates greater participation. On the other hand, students who do not experience this success, or who come from homes where such success is not so highly regarded, are often alienated by the rituals of schooling.

Most psychological views on alienation blame the individual and his or her circumstance: they are deficit models. Alienation is linked to factors such as socioeconomic status, culture, gender, behaviour and mental health. There is a tendency to see the cause of the alienation as external, and provide technical solutions such as supplementary or complementary educational programmes, and to assume that the young adolescent will eventually mature or 'grow out' of the particular cause of the estrangement.

Postmodern views

Postmodernism arises from a concern that society has changed so dramatically that traditional totalitarian neo-Marxist theories of power and control no longer adequately explain the attitudes and values of young people. Recent writers in the field claim that the influence of the 'third wave' society (Toffler, 1990), such as the information revolution generated by new technologies, has produced new agents of control. The power-broking dominance of the influential few has been replaced by more individual and networked forms of control. In their view, the influence of telecommunications and mass media is pervasive and needs to be understood in coming to grips with the dilemmas that young adolescents currently face.

At the school level, postmodernists believe that schooling has become increasingly irrelevant to students' lives. They contend that the structure of education is caught in the time warp of a print-bound culture that is increasingly irrelevant to a student cohort nurtured in a telecommunication and multi-media world. The electronic information revolution, coupled with increasing cynicism about politics and economics, has made many young adolescents seriously question the traditional values of schooling.

Educational writers who adopt the postmodernist stance make cases for the dissolution of traditional subject boundaries, greater use of the electronic technologies as a learning tool (rather than a separate subject or skill), more hybridised or integrated fields of study, and for teachers to be the public intellectuals who promote a more negotiated and student-determined curriculum.

Feminist views

Feminists have highlighted how schooling is alienating for girls. Schools reinforce inequity through their organisational, pedagogical and curricular practices. Schooling 'naturalises' traditional gender roles, thus enhancing the environment in which boys are able to practice and assert power over girls, and often denies opportunities for the development of more positive gender relations. Equitable outcomes become even more difficult to achieve, since the dominant male paradigm is supported and reinforced by the intransigent structures in schools.

Feminist writers have shown a more eclectic approach, incorporating, for instance, a strong element of classical neo-Marxist power and dominant culture theory; a recognition of the importance of 'third wave' informational and technological revolution upon the educational outcomes of boys and girls; and a vestige of psychological and physiological explanations. Perhaps, more than any other perspective, the feminist view highlights the importance of avoiding a simplistic single category model in describing alienation.

These four constructs show how alienation is multi-faceted and multi-dimensional. It is an issue for primary and secondary teachers alike. For many students it is more obviously manifested during secondary schooling, but its effect begins in the primary years. At different times in their lives young adolescents will feel powerless, will consider much of schooling irrelevant, will believe that the very nature of their gender is a factor causing alienation and estrangement. The culture in which teachers work will continue to reinforce success by some students at the expense of the self-esteem of others, and teachers will continue to label students by socioeconomic status, behavioural attributes, gender, intellectual ability and classroom performance.

The challenge is to change this culture. Taking the time to identify causes of alienation can provide us with the impetus to re-examine our own assumptions about schooling and the implications of our current practice.

RECENT AUSTRALIAN DEVELOPMENTS IN MIDDLE SCHOOLING

Middle school reform is littered with unsuccessful enterprises. One reason for the lack of success may be that the reform goals were purely extrinsic, too distant, and based on false premises. Telling a 15-year-old student, for example, that she should work hard to ensure a good job in three years is no longer a powerful motivator, and is treated by many teenagers with great scepticism. In today's politico-economic world of high youth unemployment and restricted tertiary placements, such extrinsic motivators lose their value.

Middle schooling must be intrinsically valuable to students. Reforms simply focused upon preparation for secondary schooling and perhaps preparation for later work or tertiary studies are of little appeal. For young adolescents schooling must have immediate value, not just longer-term promises.

Early successful junior secondary reform borrowed heavily from good primary school practice in attempting to provide more immediate, intrinsic worth to the learning enterprise. This reform included:

- reducing the number of teacher contacts for each student
- reducing the number of student contacts for each teacher
- increasing pastoral care roles for teachers
- including more integrated or thematic approaches to learning across traditional subject boundaries
- placing emphasis on the development of literacy, numeracy and social skills
- developing a more child-centred curriculum model.

Such changes were rarely made in isolation, usually affecting curriculum and pedagogy as well as structural or organisational elements.

A watershed in the development of middle schooling was the commissioning of Viv Eyers by the Education Department of South Australia to review junior secondary education. The initial brief was solely for secondary education, but along with his colleagues Phil Cormack and Robyn Barratt, Eyers chose to focus upon the nature of young adolescence as the framework for the review. In so doing, the committee rapidly came to the conclusion that the education of young adolescents was not confined to secondary schools and teachers. Their report, *The Report of the Junior Secondary Review* (Eyers *et al.*, 1992), argues for reform and restructure of upper primary and lower secondary schooling as the best means of delivering a more appropriate learning culture and environment for students in Years 6–9. It recommended a three-phase developmental concept of schooling, namely, R–5, 6–9, 10–12.

The review was accompanied by Cormack's (1991) literature review on the nature of adolescence. It is a rich source of information regarding the physical, psychological, social, emotional and intellectual development of 10–15-year-olds. It highlighted the differential development occurring during these turbulent years and reinforced earlier studies that the level of diversity in this age group tends to be greater than in other age groups. Issues such as the nature of different learning communities, the need for a core curriculum, different pedagogical styles and appropriate professional development for teachers received added emphasis and a new direction. In addition, the study stressed the need for genuine family and community partnerships in schooling.

The South Australian Review also had wider, national implications. It

was the first system-sponsored report that questioned whether the traditional primary–secondary sector model of schooling was the best means of
providing appropriate learning environments and strategies for young
adolescents. Another major project conducted in Australia at the time
reached similar conclusions.

The Compulsory Years of Schooling Project, *In the Middle*, conducted
during 1992/3 by the Schools Council of Australia, became the first national
body to give 'detailed attention to the vital segment which lies between the
early and post-compulsory years – that of the middle years of schooling'
(NBEET, 1993: iii).

The Schools Council report reaffirmed that this sector of schooling
needed to be recognised by state systems as having intrinsic value in its own
right. It strongly recommended that new directions and innovative strategies be designed to improve learning outcomes for all adolescents. The
Schools Council concluded that there was no 'preferred model' for middle
schooling, but that exemplars of best practice contained in their report
might provide practical support for the increasing numbers of teachers and
schools undertaking reform in the middle years.

Two other important players took up the challenge of middle years'
reform. The first, the National Schools Network (NSN) links together
schools, education unions, university colleagues and government and non-
government employers. There are over 300 Australian schools in the
network, with a significant number rethinking ways in which schools can
improve the learning opportunities that assist young adolescents to cope
with increasingly complex social change and rapidly changing technologies.
Within this framework, the NSN has made middle schooling a priority
target for reform.

In conjunction with the Australian Teaching Council the NSN (1995)
has conducted numerous workshops across the nation that focus on curricular and pedagogical reform. Of particular interest are the partnerships
established with American colleagues, Ted Sizer (Coalition of Essential
Schools) and James Beane (Middle Schools Association of the United
States). Beane's work on an integrated curriculum, designed and owned by
the students, is gaining popularity and acceptance in a number of
Australian states.

The second, and more recent, contribution to the middle schooling movement has been the DEET-sponsored project of national significance, Student
Alienation in the Middle Years (SAMY). This project was undertaken as
field studies in three states – Victoria, South Australia and Western
Australia. Seventeen schools representing primary and secondary sectors in
both state and private systems were involved in partnerships with universities and education centres. The key findings were presented at a national
workshop in July 1995.

Teams of teachers worked in partnership with external researchers to identify ways in which alienation and adolescence were constructed by young people themselves and those who worked with them. Using an action research model, teachers identified a specific local issue or problem the dimensions of which were informed by data collection and analysis. They then identified an alternative approach or modified work practice to solve the problem or at least improve the situation. Finally, teachers reflected critically on the strategies and outcomes that were generated with a view to gauging their effectiveness and formulating new directions.

(ACSA, 1996, Vol. 1: 2)

SAMY was released as a three-volume report, *From Alienation to Engagement: Opportunities for Reform in the Middle Years of Schooling*. Volume 1 contains key findings and recommendations, volume 2 is an issues paper outlining the theoretical constructions of alienation, and volume 3 is a synthesis of contemporary perspectives and teacher actions aimed at reform in upper primary and junior secondary levels. It highlights strategies employed by field studies teachers in very differing circumstances.

This project used an action research model and was a joint venture between classroom teachers and university researchers:

teachers as the investigators adopted an action research model in an attempt to investigate [issues]. They collected data by surveying and talking with students, then analysed it, reflected with colleagues, made findings and suggested implications.

The most important aspect of this process was the need for teachers to 'unpack' their assumptions.

(Hudson and Carr, 1995)

The participants were continually kept informed by university field studies, contemporary research findings, and theories and models of good practice. These theoretical dimensions helped to ensure that the specific, locally identified problems or difficulties were seen in a wider educational context. Many of the participants found this valuable, and indicated that they would pursue similar models in future.

SAMY also brought together many of the earlier researchers and practitioners in the field, such as Cumming, Barratt and Cormack, with significant stakeholders in the learning enterprise (unions, state and private systems, NSN). This consortium became an important forum for discussion of research findings and for sharing good practices with stakeholders. The forum also became a catalyst for future development in middle schooling. DEET has already agreed to fund a joint national middle schools curriculum development project during 1996/7. The project has been contracted to ACSA and Barratt appointed as project officer.

KEY ISSUES IN THE EDUCATION OF YOUNG ADOLESCENTS

The work of Hargreaves and Earl, *Rights of Passage* (1990), has had a significant effect on recent middle schooling initiatives in Australia. They identified
ten developmental tasks that need to be accomplished by young adolescents
in order to participate meaningfully in today's society. Eyers *et al.* (1992) drew
heavily upon these in developing a framework for middle school organisation
in South Australia, stating that young adolescents need to:

1 adjust to some profound changes: physical, social, emotional and intellectual;
2 grow toward independence (while still needing security in many
 personal relationships);
3 gain experience in decision making, and in accepting responsibility for
 these decisions;
4 develop a positive self-confidence through achieving success in significant events;
5 progressively develop a sense of 'Who am I?', and of personal and social
 values which become part of that person's life;
6 establish their own sexual identity;
7 experience social acceptance, and gain affection and support among
 peers of the opposite sex;
8 think in ways that become progressively more abstract and reflective;
9 become more aware of the social and political world about them, and
 gain skill in coping and interacting with that world; and
10 establish or maintain relationships with particular adults who can
 provide advice and act as role models.

(Eyers *et al.*, 1992: 9)

This list is hard to disagree with, and may seem rather trite and obvious. Its
significance, however, lies in its recognition of the need to develop a range of
intelligences when teaching young people. In keeping with the multiple
intelligences model of Howard Gardner (1983), Hargreaves identified
aesthetic, physical, rational, linguistic and social intelligence as also requiring
development. This is not to devalue the importance of cognitive development,
rather to recognise that in the turbulent adolescent years a more holistic
development of intelligence is required.

To say that something is required is one thing, but to provide for it is a
vastly different proposition. Much of the rest of this chapter is dedicated to
suggesting practical actions that schools can take to improve education in
the middle years of schooling.

Hargreaves, Gardner and Eyers suggest that a more personalised culture
in schools (where quality relationships and development of multiple intelligences are key features) requires a major restructure of curriculum and
pedagogy as well as significant organisational changes. Ames and Miller, in

Changing Middle Schools (1994), addressed the issue of holistic change and suggested nine principles for restructuring middle schools. They propound that changing middle schools

1 begins with personalising adult–child relationships. Reaching a child's mind begins with reaching his or her heart;
2 requires personalising adult relationships. School structures must support collaboration and shared decision making;
3 requires transformational leadership (vision, risk taking, accessibility);
4 requires both careful planning and ongoing reflection;
5 requires comprehensive restructuring, not just tinkering at the edges;
6 requires the establishment of close links between home, school and the community;
7 requires district level support;
8 requires both external (advisers, cheerleaders, critical friends) and internal change agents; and
9 requires a multifaceted intervention strategy.

(Ames and Miller, 1994: xvii – xviii)

Again, the concept of holistic reform is reinforced. Restructuring requires changes in the roles and relationships of the participants, permeating beyond the way in which learning is organised, scheduled, delivered and supported. It does not need to be a gradual process, nor does it need to be planned in minute detail. Some changes can take place almost immediately. It is commitment and support that need to be long term.

A GUIDE TO STARTING MIDDLE SCHOOL REFORM

Understand the culture

Spend time, as a staff, accessing information regarding youth cultures. Understanding the nature and social context of young adolescents is likely to lead to more informed decision-making. Involve students and external agencies in these deliberations.

Establish a sound philosophical base

Theoretical considerations of differing constructs of alienation help teachers to examine their own stances on various teaching and learning issues. A sound philosophical base gives meaning and purpose to our actions.

Holistic change

Curriculum, pedagogy and school organisation are so interrelated that change in one area necessitates change in the others. Although the principal does not need to be the key change agent, overt and visionary support at both resource and morale levels is essential from the school leader.

Provide a teacher who is primarily responsible for each student's educational and social welfare

Young adolescents need the security of adult relationships. Schools that design their organisation around providing students with regular long-term contact time with a specific teacher who is primarily responsible for each student's educational, emotional and social well-being are more likely to attain success and respect from the student and parent cohort.

Team teachers together for both teaching and planning

Teaming overcomes professional isolation, allows combining of teacher strengths and fosters a positive view of students. Collaborative approaches engender collective wisdom and shared visions, assist in finding new ways to solve problems, and combine and complement teaching approaches. Team members should be given common, non-contact planning times within the timetable.

Believe strongly in democratic classrooms

Democracy begins in the classroom. It should be exemplified not just at a representative participation level, but also at more fundamental levels such as student choice. Students should be encouraged to participate in decisions about the way in which their learning is organised and monitored. This helps them to develop skills that are valued not just at the classroom level, but in wider areas of society. Students tend to react positively when they feel they are being listened to and when their views are being taken seriously.

Negotiated curriculum

Genuine consultation between students and their teachers enhances student learning as well as teacher effectiveness. Students learn in different ways, using different intelligences. Learning can be made more relevant and challenging if it involves students in practical activities that are related to real-life problems. Beane's integrated curriculum model is a good example. Teachers who afford students opportunities to decide how they learn, and with whom, are more likely to gain success.

Integrate the curriculum

Teachers who see children as whole learners, aim at making more sense of the disparate subject fields by using integrated approaches. They are more likely to assist students in making meaning of the world around them.

Vary the teaching and learning approaches

Flexible approaches reduce adolescent criticism of the routine, boring and uninteresting aspects of school. A repertoire of strategies is necessary to allow for different learning styles and needs. Teacher teaming and use of community and para-professional personnel are seen as effective means of achieving these ends.

Involve a wider audience

Education is a partnership. Agencies such as health, welfare and justice can make valuable contributions. Some recent successful initiatives have involved teachers in collaboration with university colleagues in identifying classroom problems, and trialing and evaluating new approaches. Involving parents in discussions of the nature of adolescence and constructs of alienation assists common understandings of the need for change.

Create new time and space models

Holistic reform requires major structural change. Greater flexibility in timetabling and student grouping increases the capacity of teachers to be more effective, and facilitates access to the wider community. Designating specific learning and leisure areas enhances students' sense of ownership and responsibility. The role of the principal in supporting greater organisational flexibility is a crucial factor.

PUTTING THE THEORY INTO PRACTICE

Structural and pedagogical reform at Oatlands

Oatlands School, Tasmania, is a K-10 rural school that has a middle years structure running from Years 5 to 8. Structural and curricular change has gone hand in hand with the development of a sound philosophical base for the reform, and a desire to cater better for the learning needs of young adolescents. The model has been adopted and adapted by a number of schools both in Tasmania and other states. The philosophy and genesis of this reform is documented in Scott (1994).

At Oatlands, teachers work in teams of two, each being the principal teacher of a group of 25–30 students. They teach these students for 60–75 per cent of their class time in mixed-year groups of 5/6, 6/7 and 7/8 classes. Principal teachers take their classes for English, maths, science, SOSE (studies of society and the environment), health education and all associated pastoral care roles. They work in pairs in double classroom units which have been created by making a sliding door between two adjoining classrooms. Each team of two is chosen on the basis of a male/female combination, and a requirement that at least one of the teachers has expertise in language and humanities and the other has expertise in maths and science. Each principal teacher and their students have one side of the double classroom as a home base where most of their core subjects are taught.

Within the unit, principal teachers are free to determine student group-ings, and when and how they will teach particular subjects. The two classes may be taught separately, as a composite group, or as multiple groups util-ising other teacher, student and adult help. In addition, one teacher can work with individuals or small groups while the other teacher supervises the remaining students. A particular feature of small group work in this model is the concept of tutorial time.

A flexible timetable designed to accommodate small group instruction

A typical weekly timetable for Years 5–8 at Oatlands might look like Table 6.1.

Principal teacher time

Sixty to seventy-five per cent of student time is dedicated to the core learning areas. Language and mathematics are central to the curriculum, and an integrated, cross-curriculum approach is encouraged.

Table 6.1   Oatlands School timetable

PERIOD	MONDAY	TUESDAY	WEDNESDAY	THURSDAY	FRIDAY
1	Principal teacher	Principal teacher	Principal teacher	Principal teacher	Principal teacher
2			TUTORIAL TIME		
			Recess		
3	Principal teacher	ARTS	Principal teacher	Principal teacher	DESIGN
			Lunch		
4	Principal teacher	DESIGN	Principal teacher	Principal teacher	ARTS

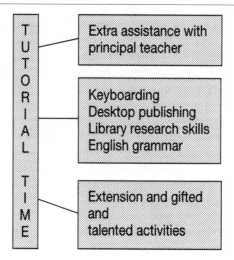

Figure 6.1 Tutorial time options

Arts and design time

Wherever possible, all Year 5–8 students are scheduled out to these learning areas at the same time. A discrete arts or design teaching team is responsible for student groupings, timetabling and pedagogy. This has enabled teachers to work separately on skill development, or to integrate the learning for activities such as the production of school performances and craft exhibitions. An important consequence of scheduling all students to one of these areas is the capacity to schedule all of the principal teachers off class at the same time. This has had a significant effect on planning and professional development capabilities.

Tutorial time

A basic principle of the Oatlands middle school philosophy is that there should be enough flexibility to enable the principal teacher to identify and aid those students who require extra assistance – both in terms of remediation and extension. The principal teacher is seen as the best person to assist in these circumstances, and so a tutorial session held in the second hour of each day has evolved to accommodate this need.

Normally, the tutorial groups run for about two weeks. The principal teacher might decide to work with a small group of students who are not performing well in a current mathematics area, or she may have identified a particular group who should be extended in poetry writing – the possibilities are numerous. For an hour each day these students will work with the principal teacher on these tasks. Students are encouraged to refer themselves to this group.

The remainder of the classes combine with a different group of teachers and adult tutors to study two-week courses which the parent community has deemed to be of importance. Some of these courses will be content-based, for example, Japanese, geography or English grammar. Others will be skill-based and include library research skills, music, keyboarding and desktop publishing. Research activities for events such as the Science Talent Quest can also be incorporated into this time (see Figure 6.1).

A more detailed study of time management at Oatlands was undertaken by Morgan (1993), and a comprehensive study of curricular and pedagogical practices was conducted by Kite (1996).

Dianne Andrewartha, a principal teacher at Oatlands, outlines some of the advantages of the reform for herself and her students:

> I am a primary trained teacher and have enjoyed being in my own classroom all my life. Initially I was worried about teaming in a dual unit with another teacher. I also had some concern about teaching science to grade 6 and 7 kids. My teaching partner, Scott, is maths and science trained, and pretty soon I was able to see that he would be of immense help to me in assisting with things I did not feel confident about.
>
> The beauty of the way that the timetable is arranged is that Scott and I are off class at the same time. This means that we can get around three to four hours' planning time together. While the children are out at specialist areas, we can discuss strategies, plan new units and assist each other with general daily routines. The shared time off has been great for incidental professional development, and once a week we have joint planning time with the other middle school teachers in which we all share strategies that we find are successful within our own programmes. You have professional development going on all of the time. It is not just concerned with cross-curricular teaching, but more with aspects of teaching within learning areas that enhance cross-curricular teaching practice.
>
> Tutorial time is one of the best aspects of our structure. It always bothered me that in the traditional primary classroom I had little opportunity to work over an extended period of time with a small group of students who I know would have really benefited from an intense burst on certain skill development activities. I know the practice is expensive in terms of needing extra teachers during this hour each day, but most of my colleagues now see the benefits in the longer term.
>
> I especially like the idea that I can be responsible for the remediation of students in my charge. Before our new system they got help from a special education teacher who did not know their strengths and

weaknesses as well as I did, and often I did not have the time to ensure that she used the topics and themes that were appropriate to what the child was doing when he or she came back to my class. Now I am responsible for giving the extra assistance, and this is always related to the rest of the classwork. Kids feel better about staying with me for remediation, and now their friends ask whether they can stay and catch up on skills as well.

Scott has used this time to run some really good extension programmes. Last year he had nearly forty of our kids doing Science Talent Quest projects. The school did really well in the Quest. He has done similar things with maths competitions and creative writing. Some students become absolutely engrossed in their research topics, and with block timetabling and us being in charge of so much of each student's day, it has been relatively easy to incorporate their projects into their study during principal teacher time. After all, isn't that what flexibility and relevance are all about?

Beane's thematic and integrated approaches to curriculum design

During 1994 the National Schools Network (NSN), in partnership with some state education systems, invited Professor James Beane from National-Louis University, Illinois, and Barbara Brodhagen, a primary and middle school teacher in Madison, Wisconsin, to conduct a series of workshops around Australia. These educators had devised a method of curriculum planning that took into account the nature of adolescent learners, and allowed them to participate in determining what they were to learn and how they would learn it. Their work was beginning to be applied in a number of Australian schools.

Beane (1991) advocates that the child should be at the centre of his or her learning. He proposes that children see little connection between the various separate subjects conventionally offered in upper primary and lower secondary school. Instead, he opts for a model that more purposefully integrates the curriculum and produces a community of learners who conduct research on questions that they consider to be important in their immediate lives. Central to his philosophy is a belief that if the curriculum is based upon the educational interests and concerns of young adolescents, then students themselves will be more open to learning.

Beane's research indicates that young people have two major areas of concern. The first is a personal concern about their role and contributions in a dramatically changing world. This is a concern for self, and adolescents often have questions about the physical changes that they are experiencing, their relationships with authority figures, their self-image, their identity and their ability to cooperate and communicate with others. Simultaneously, they share with all of us a set of concerns about the issues

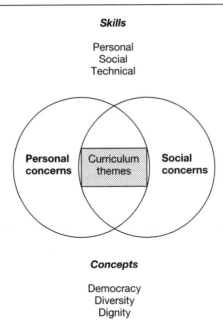

Skills

Personal
Social
Technical

Concepts

Democracy
Diversity
Dignity

Figure 6.2 Constructing a middle school
curriculum

Source: Beane (1991)

and problems posed by living in the larger world. Young people are
genuinely interested in the environment, cultural diversity and racism,
wealth and poverty, war and peace, freedom and interdependence, money,
and many other global issues.

In order to provide an appropriate and coherent curriculum, Beane
suggests that we should seek integrated themes that lie in the intersection of
the personal and global concerns of our young people (see Figure 6.2).

The Beane approach to middle school curriculum transcends traditional
disparate subject areas for those that are more content-centred. It emphasises
the development of generalist personal, social and technical skills taught
through unifying concepts of dignity, diversity and democracy. The process
itself is quite complex, because it involves intense negotiation with all of the
students in the class. To assist teachers in getting started, the NSN has
developed a multi-media package, *The Middle Years Kit* (1995), that facilitates teacher development.

FINAL COMMENT

Kathy Davis is a teacher at Lilydale District High School in Tasmania. The
school has set up reasonably homogeneous classes grouped in a two-year

range, i.e. Years 5/6, 6/7 and 7/8. Students spend about 60 per cent of the week with one teacher providing a core curriculum and pastoral care.

We have a strong team of teachers whose expertise ranges from K-10. We are able to communicate, share and support each other. With our personal background knowledge, experiences and ideas coming from other middle school programmes, professional development and relevant documentation, we were confident that we understood what the curriculum should contain. We knew that young adolescents need an environment and curriculum which helps them accomplish the developmental tasks that Andy Hargreaves identified.

Structural and timetable changes made in setting up the middle school programme effectively created the right environment; we had now to focus on curriculum. We decided upon an integrated and negotiated curriculum that provided greater coherence and relevance.

Our primary school colleagues were a great help. The timetable had been deconstructed to allow us blocks of time, and my partner was able to help me deliver learning in a more consistent and continuous pattern. Pretty soon we had moved away from a separate subject approach that presented fragmented organisation of loosely connected subjects with little or no coherent sense of unity in learning. Looking back, the analogy I make is like trying to fit together a difficult jigsaw without the benefit of the picture on the box – only the fanatic puzzle addicts will attempt such a task. Most of us will give up, as it is not worth struggling with the little bits if you can't see the big picture.

Through an integrated curriculum our students can experience and recognise the relevance of specific learning. For example, learning percentages took on real meaning because they had to make sense of the data they had collected in a humanities survey. They were able to discover why the process was necessary, and developed skills that added to their research and communication strategies.

Recently our team attended a two-day workshop conducted by James Beane, and he has been a great help in our coming to understand how to negotiate real learnings with our students. The real difference between his model and that of our previous experiences in primary schools was that the teacher no longer selected the topic or theme. For younger children, the teacher selecting how and what to learn seems to be an acceptable practice. Not so the young adolescent – they have concerns and interests which are specific to their age group that focus upon the cultures and times in which they live. Through a specific process outlined by James (and now available in kit form from the NSN) these concerns are identified and negotiated as a unifying theme.

Negotiating the curriculum with students means that adults do not have to think like adolescents. The curriculum gains relevance for students – they are empowered by seeing that the curriculum belongs to them. For teachers it is similarly stimulating for them. Jim Beane said it nicely at the seminar I went to: 'teachers are no longer dull disseminators of information, or glitzy instructional gymnasts; instead they are fully professional guides helping early adolescents explore their world'.

I feel good when I think about my teaching in this way. I am confident that the negotiated approach has improved my students' interests in school, and their parents are happy as well. We have had some parent evenings to explain what we are doing, and some parents now help at home and at school with the process. It is a powerful tool that has not only increased our satisfaction with our jobs, but it has also given me a new lease of life in watching kids who were turned off begin to take an interest and responsibility in their learning.

REFERENCES

ACSA (1996) *From Alienation to Engagement: Opportunities for Reform in the Middle Years of Schooling*, Vols 1–3, Canberra: Australian Curriculum Studies Association.

Ames, N. and Miller, E. (1994) *Changing Middle Schools: How to Make Schools Work for Young Adolescents*, San Francisco: Jossey-Bass.

Beane, J.A. (1991) 'The middle school: the natural home of integrated curriculum', *Educational Leadership* October.

Cormack, P. (1991) *The Nature of Adolescence*, Adelaide, SA: Education Department of South Australia.

—— (1996) 'Theoretical constructions', in ACSA, *From Alienation to Engagement: Opportunities for Reform in the Middle Years of Schooling*, Canberra: Australian Curriculum Studies Association, Vol. 2: 3–24.

Cumming, J. (1994) 'Catering for the needs of all young adolescents: towards an integrated approach', *Unicorn* 20, 2: 12–20.

Eyers, V., Cormack, P. and Barratt, R. (1992) *The Report of the Junior Secondary Review: The Education of Young Adolescents*, Adelaide: Education Department of South Australia.

Gardner, H. (1983) *Frames of Mind*, New York: Basic Books.

Hargreaves, A. and Earl, L. (1990) *Rights of Passage: A Review of Selected Research about Schooling in the Transition Years*, Ontario: Ontario Ministry of Education.

Hudson, M. and Carr, L. (1995) 'What causes alienation amongst male adolescents?', *Independent Education* July: 28–9.

Kite, L. (1996) *Implementing Cross-Curricular Practices in Schools*, Canberra: Australian Curriculum Studies Association.

Morgan, A. (1993) 'Oatlands School: A Middle School Programme for Years 5–8', in M. Bradley (ed.) *Proceedings and Papers Presented to the National Schooling Solutions Conference*, Darwin, July 1993, Canberra: Australian Curriculum Studies Association.

NBEET (1993) *In the Middle: Schooling for Young Adolescents*. Canberra: Schools Council.

NSN (1995) *The Middle Years Kit*, Ryde, NSW: National Schools Network.

Theme II

Curriculum and social justice

Chapter 7

National initiatives and primary schooling

Shirley Grundy and Stewart Bonser[1]

INTRODUCTION

Much of the rhetoric of 'restructuring' and 'reform' in relation to education and schooling over the last decade has been couched in the language of crisis, calling for school renewal and improvement. We assert that there is no crisis in Australian primary education in relation to the relative effectiveness of the teaching workforce. As borne out by evidence emanating from recent survey data (Schools Council, 1995b), Australia's primary teacher workforce is highly productive, competent and sufficiently professional to critique policy implementation in the light of the pragmatics of their work, that is, of primary schooling.

In this chapter we examine recent national initiatives designed both to monitor and to improve schooling. It is argued that these initiatives can be understood in terms of two interlocking themes: *accountability* and *quality*. However, we also notice that many of the key stakeholders within the primary schooling sector (students, parents, teachers and community) are marginalised within processes of educational policy development. Primary schooling and primary teachers have not been targeted for particular attention within the initiatives that we examine here. Thus, while the primary sector has responded to these initiatives, the specific needs, strengths and contributions of primary schools have been taken for granted. In particular, within the rhetoric of funding restraint, the resourcing of primary schooling has not only been falling quite severely,[2] it has been limited by a lack of initiatives on the part of educational administrators to identify the nature of the expenditure necessary to generate 'work patterns and arrangements . . . to meet the competitive requirements' (ACAC, 1988, cited in Ashenden, 1992) of a primary schooling industry.

In what follows we provide a broad overview of the national initiatives that have operated in Australian education and that have influenced the work of primary teachers and schools during the early part of this decade. It should be noted, however, that much of the debate about schooling, particularly about the importance of schooling to the economy, has centred upon the post-compulsory years. This has, to some extent, left primary schools as islands of continuity and consolidation within the sea of change.

THE BROAD POLICY CONTEXT

In keeping with trends in other Western countries (Beare, 1995: 134), the Australian federal Labor government vigorously pursued a broad platform of reform and restructuring policies throughout the period 1983–96, intended to increase the global competitiveness of the Australian economy. Education and schooling were not immune from these policy initiatives and in fact were very much part of the change agenda.

In this account the term 'agenda' is used to discuss a raft of national government initiatives in relation to school education. While these initiatives were not all pre-designed in detail, the direction was set early in the policy document *Strengthening Australia's Schools* (Dawkins, 1988). This was a watershed document in that it outlined the 'agenda' for the national initiatives that emerged in the years that followed. It articulated the Labour government's commitment to improving schooling. At the same time it provided rhetorical links between the structural changes taking place within the economy and the part that was to be played by schooling.

> Schools are the starting point of an integrated education and training structure in the economy. They provide the foundation on which a well-informed, compassionate and cohesive society is built. They also form the basis of a more highly skilled, adaptive and productive workforce.
>
> (Dawkins, 1988:1)

Although the document claimed that any demands for quality schooling ought not be taken to imply denigration of the schooling system or of its previous efforts, it nevertheless expected that schooling will and can make a difference without any increase in resourcing. The real issue underlying the policy statement is therefore one of *accountability*: that is, schooling systems accounting for, and providing evidence of, the effective use of resources.

> The issue here is not the level of our investment as a nation in our schools but rather the quality and appropriateness of their achievements. . . . The adjustment task before our schools does not require more money as much as it does more co-operation between those who work in the schools and those who have responsibility for making policy for them at all levels of the nation.
>
> (Dawkins, 1988: 1)

The agenda as it unfolded within the Dawkins (1988) document included developing

- a national effort for schools through a 'clear statement of fundamental purposes of our schools, their objectives and priorities'
- a common curriculum framework with common values to pursue
- a common approach to assessment
- priorities for improving the training of teachers
- education and equity

as well as

- increasing the number of young Australians completing school through retention targets[3]
- maximising our investment in education (implying increased efficiency).

THE NATIONAL AGENDA FOR THE 1990S

While 'national' should not be understood as meaning 'Commonwealth', there is no doubt that the Commonwealth government was shaping the agenda of restructuring and reform broadly within Australian society and specifically with respect to education. Historically, this interventionist role for the Commonwealth in relation to school education is both interesting and significant.

> While responsibility for schooling rests with the States ... the Commonwealth Government is playing an increasingly critical role in Australian education, both in terms of setting policy direction for the education sector and in financing education.
>
> (Schools Council, 1995a: 3)

Thus the national agenda was to be taken up through collaborative and consultative work with a broad range of educational stakeholders, including other state and territory government and non-government systems, unions and teacher professional associations.[4]

The agenda for this collaborative work was pursued through a two-strand approach.[5] We have called these the *accountability* and the *quality* strands. While we identify these as two strong themes in terms of national initiatives in schooling, they do not account for all of the work that was going on at this time. Another area in which work continued was around issues of 'equity' which is taken up in a later section of this text.

The strand that developed around the issue of *accountability* was pursued primarily through inter-governmental collaboration (i.e. by the states/territories and the Commonwealth jointly), but with broad consultation. The development of this strand was overseen by the Australian Education Council (AEC). The AEC was a council of government, Commonwealth and state/territory ministers for education and the Directors-General of the various government education systems.[6]

The initiatives forming this strand of the national agenda addressed and developed the concern for accountability articulated in *Strengthening Australia's Schools*:

> There is need for regular assessment of the effectiveness and standards of our schools. A common curriculum framework should be complemented by a common national approach to assessment . . . [including examining] how schools can report to parents . . . and we need to develop a method of reporting to the nation . . . [including establishing goals and benchmarks].
>
> (Dawkins, 1988:5)

Initiatives under this aspect of the agenda were financed jointly (on a proportional basis) by the Commonwealth and the states and territories. The first of these initiatives focused upon the development of 'agreed goals for Australia's schools'.

The most significant of these initiatives was the development of 'Statements and Profiles for Australian Schools'. Essentially this was an attempt to specify what should be the agreed learning outcomes for students in Australian schools. It was assumed that once statements of learning outcomes were agreed upon, teachers and education systems would be able to 'account' for the work of schools in terms of 'outcomes' rather than 'inputs'.

The second strand of the national agenda developed around the concept of *quality*. We have noted above how in *Strengthening Australia's Schools* it was asserted that the issue was not the level of investment in 'schools but rather the quality and appropriateness of their achievements' (Dawkins, 1988:1).

The quality strand of the agenda focused on work organisation and workplace reform as well as on teacher professional development. Initiatives arising from this aspect of the agenda were pursued through collaborative partnerships with other government and non-government systems, the teachers' unions, professional associations and other educational stakeholders. These initiatives took the form of a number of interrelated but separate projects funded by the Commonwealth. The National Project for the Quality of Teaching and Learning (NPQTL) and its sub-project, the National Schools Project (NSP), are examples of what transpired from this aspect of the agenda.

Parallel state agendas

It should be noted that all of these initiatives were occurring during a time of 'corporate' restructuring within state systems of education. This restructuring has been characterised by the devolution of budgetary responsibility to schools (Porter *et al.*, 1994: 225–6). Such devolutionary policies have been accompanied by an increase in demands for accountability in budgetary terms and also in terms of providing accounts of student learning outcomes and the quality of teaching through processes of teacher appraisal and school improvement (Cuttance, 1995).

PURSUING THE AGENDA: NATIONAL INITIATIVES

The accountability strand of the agenda

When considering the theme of accountability, which has underpinned a major strand of initiatives in Australia, it needs to be recognised that concerns with accountability remain part of a wider industrial ideology within Australia and elsewhere. Indeed, as capitalism has adjusted to changes in international markets (Watkins, 1994) the responsibility of management to account to the shareholders for company profitability has been further underscored. While profitability may be enhanced through increased production, in a competitive or contracting market it may well mean achieving efficiencies by producing the same, but improving the quality of what is produced without any increase in input cost.

In the period under discussion, accountability ideology began to permeate government thinking, resulting in demands to improve the quality of education (improved output) with no additional resources (McGaw, 1995). Indeed, government, along with the office of the Auditor General, saw need for more rigorous forms of accountability from the states regarding expenditure on education (Harrold, 1994: 210). Business management practices allied to 'performance measures' began to be applied to education. It is within this context that the development of the Statements and Profiles for Australian Schools should be considered.

Statements and Profiles for Australian Schools

We noted earlier in this chapter that the national agenda had been shaped and influenced strongly by the Commonwealth. Certainly the Commonwealth Minister for Education and the Commonwealth Department of Employment Education and Training (DEET) were influential in supporting the development of Statements and Profiles for eight learning areas. However, in 1993 the Commonwealth lost control of this aspect of the agenda. At the July meeting of the AEC the Liberal state ministers, who were by that time in the majority on the AEC, moved to make the further development and uptake of the Statements and Profiles a states' matter.

While the attempt to get some agreement about performance indicators in relation to school learning was not abandoned, it did signal the resistance of the state education systems to being accountable in terms of the outcomes of learning on a national level. Nevertheless, what started out as a national initiative to produce a coherent and agreed account of learning outcomes for Australian schools, continues to have implications for teachers' work and for education systems (Boston, 1995). We sketch below some of these implications for primary education.

Performance indicators of learning: a world-wide trend

Once again it needs to be recognised that these developments in Australia have their parallels elsewhere. Partly because of the strengths of the 'education is a state rights' issue and partly through strong professional resistance, Australia has avoided taking the path of a national curriculum and national testing, which has been a feature of the recent British experience. Closer parallels to the Australian experience may be found in some of the work being undertaken in the United States where national initiatives in 'standards-based reform' have been implemented since the 1989 adoption of a set of national education goals (McDonnell, 1995).

In 1994 the US Congress set three types of voluntary standards for schools and education authorities. McDonnell (1995: 234) describes these as follows:

- *content standards*: descriptions of the knowledge and skills that students should acquire
- *performance standards*: concrete examples of what students have to know and do to demonstrate proficiency
- *opportunity-to-learn standards*: the criteria for assessing the sufficiency or quality of the resources, practices and conditions necessary to provide all students with an opportunity to learn.

The 'content' and 'performance' standards in principle parallel the statements of learning outcomes and the work samples of the Australian Statements and Profiles. The 'opportunity-to-learn' standards are, however, not part of the 'standards' or the 'outcomes' discourse in Australia.[7] Here the link can be made back to the *Strengthening Australia's Schools* agenda which assumed that schools and teachers will demonstrate that learning outcomes are being achieved within existing resource provision, rather than that systems will be accountable in terms of whether the resource provision is sufficient for learning outcomes to be achieved.

Beyond accountability: implications for primary schools and teachers

Apart from the systemic accountability issue, the introduction of the Statements and Profiles has some particular implications for primary schools and teachers. The first is the challenge of being able to give an account of learning performance in terms of specific learning outcomes across a range of eight learning areas. For the primary teacher, who generally has responsibility for the whole curriculum, this could be seen as a daunting task. Yet the way in which primary teachers typically work also places them in a strong position in relation to this challenge. Planning for learning at the primary level is not necessarily bounded by strict subject divides and, in effect, learning experiences across the curriculum are often part of a pedagogical repertoire enabling learning to be contextualised. Australian primary teachers have a reputation as tending towards experimentation with cross-curricular possibilities through thematic and integrative approaches to curriculum planning.

With the advent of Statements and Profiles the potential to integrate syllabus content from across learning areas has been enhanced. Assuming that learning outcomes may be discernible from student performance on appropriate tasks, it is possible that students could demonstrate the integration of knowledge from across a range of subject areas. In primary classrooms, teaching practices grounded in theories of developmental learning and in understandings of literacy and social justice (Comber, 1993; Reid, 1993) have for some time utilised the integrative nature of syllabus content in the application and construction of knowledge. Language and learning philosophies developed throughout the period of the 1970s and 1980s, and which are couched in holistic developmental approaches to language and learning, lend themselves to an outcomes perspective. Teacher-based assessment models have a long association with this tradition. For example, a recent survey of primary school teachers conducted on behalf of the Schools Council (1995b) provides evidence that the identification of learning outcomes through the analysis of student work samples was an approach consistent with best practice in primary education. The authors of the report noted:

> Teachers recognised that teacher-based assessment models would always have problems of some degree of subjectivity. Some indicated that teacher assessment of progress against the National Profiles might resolve some of the subjectivity problems without creating the difficulties which standardised tests introduce. . . . The literature encourages the use of teacher observation and work sample analysis as these methods do not require students to perform under stress in the way that standardised testing does. The responses to the survey indicate that Australian teachers already practice assessment in the manner in which a large part of the developed world currently aspires to do.
>
> (Schools Council, 1995b: 51)

However, the pressure to provide standardised information about the outcomes of schooling is continuing (Masters, 1994). What is unclear is to what extent educational professionals will be able to determine the processes through which such information is identified. This includes both the form in which it is to be reported and the audiences to which such information needs to be addressed. Indeed, in Australia, an Industry Commission Review of Commonwealth and State Service Provision had 'benchmarking' school education in terms of performance measures as part of its brief. It is of concern if such non-education-based inquiries have more influence upon the form and function of outcomes information in relation to schooling than the teaching profession (Wilkins and Doyle, 1995). We identify this as an area for continued professional engagement, struggle and initiative on the part of the teaching profession.

The pursuit of the accountability strand of the national agenda is one that is fraught with tensions and contradictions. It appears to have been borne of suspicion that all is not well with our schools. Indeed, this sense of suspicion, the sense that non-educators, such as the Industry Commission and the Auditor-General, need to press education to get its act together, leads to a sense of crisis with respect to school education, particularly when the quality of teachers' work is neither understood nor acknowledged.

The quality strand of the agenda

While the Commonwealth, states and other stakeholders were positioning and repositioning around issues of accountability, another strand of the national agenda was affirming and strengthening the quality of schooling in Australia.

If *Strengthening Australia's Schools* was a watershed document in terms of the accountability strand of the agenda, then the paper prepared by the Schools Council of the National Board of Employment, Education and Training entitled *Australia's Teachers: An Agenda for the Next Decade* (1990) was similarly a direction-setting document in relation to the aspect of quality. It 'sets out a long term agenda for action' which is directed towards 'high quality teaching'. This agenda is constructed around the following issues:

Teachers' work

- more explicit teaching (a Charter was suggested as a start to this process)
- improved workplaces (schools should be decent places to work for both teachers and students).

Teachers' professional growth

- systematic and relevant professional development
- purposeful appraisal.

Teachers' careers

- an integrated career structure.

Public confidence

- more information (the authors expressed support for 'the AEC's move to introduce a scheme of national reporting')
- an orientation towards shared values (particularly at the local level)
- better leadership.

(Schools Council, 1990: i)

The vehicle created by the Commonwealth to pursue the 'quality' strand of the national agenda between 1992 and 1994 was the National Project for the Quality of Teaching and Learning (NPQTL).

National Project for the Quality of Teaching and Learning (NPQTL)

The NPQTL was a three-year project which commenced in February 1991. Its purpose was to provide research and development support for award restructuring in the teaching profession, leading to improvements in the quality of teaching and learning (NPQTL, 1992: 2). One part of the broad agenda for the project was to investigate the relationship between the organisation of teachers' work, teaching practices and student learning. The principal strategy for pursuing this agenda was through the National Schools Project (NSP). The *Annual Report* described the NSP as follows:

> The National Schools Project is an action research project . . . [which] involve[s] approximately [ninety] schools across all systems and sectors in an investigation of how changes to work organisation can lead to improved student learning outcomes. . . . The key principles [for the project] include:
>   commitment, on the part of the school, to improved student learning outcomes through greater student participation in the learning process; and
>   participative decision making and co-operative workplace procedures in identifying good practice in current work organisation and developing means of removing impediments to effective teaching and management of the teaching–learning process.

(NPQTL, 1992: 2–3)

In this project it was accepted that effective educational practices are not dependent solely upon the good practices of individual teachers. The situation in which the work of teachers takes place, the organisation of the school, was also recognised as having a crucial impact upon both the work of teachers and the learning of students. As argued elsewhere (Grundy, 1994), many of the earlier debates about the quality in teaching have focused upon the competence of the teacher within an ideology of individualism which in turn places the responsibility for educational improvement and the wellbeing of society upon teachers. Through their foregrounding of partnerships and collaborative action, the more recent initiatives have implicitly, if not explicitly, acknowledged that the ideology of individualism is problematic. There is need to consider further the influence of the professional community of the school upon 'quality' and 'accountability' mechanisms.

As the NPQTL was coming towards its end there was a reassertion by the Commonwealth Minister for Education of the Commonwealth's commitment to improving the quality of school education. This recommitment came in the form of the policy statement *Teaching Counts* (Beazley, 1993). This statement shows a continuing commitment on the part of the federal government to involvement in school education, as well as a degree of reassurance to the teaching profession that the dual strands of the bigger agenda were not to be seen as impacting negatively upon the education community :

> We are now in a stronger position than ever to work together with the States and Territories within the agreed national framework for schooling. This agenda for change has the potential to improve on the already sound quality of learning and teaching throughout our school system. The Federal Government is uniquely placed to ensure that a national perspective about schooling is promoted.
>
> (Beazley, 1993: 2)

To further these aims of ensuring the quality of teaching and learning, a number of programmes were identified and funding commitments made. It is interesting to note how these programmes continued to target areas identified in *Strengthening Australia's Schools* and in *Australia's Teachers* (Schools Council, 1990). The funding initiatives and the areas of focus were:

Quality Schooling Program
- school leadership
- school organisation in devolved education systems
- student welfare, particularly in the formative years of school

Key Competencies

Education Faculty Renewal

National Professional Development Program
- implementation of the AEC Curriculum Statements and Profiles
- implementation of the Key Competencies
- professional development strategies resulting from the NPQTL
- renewing discipline knowledge and teaching skills

Teacher Professional Development Fund – a redirection of funds designated for teaching practice supervision.

(Beazley, 1993: 10–15)

Two of these initiatives which had particular implications for primary schools and teachers are outlined below.

The Quality Schooling Program – A sub-project: the National Schools Network

As noted above, one of the sub-projects of the NPQTL had been the National Schools Project (NSP). At the conclusion of the life of the NSP, the external evaluators suggested that there were strong arguments for a larger and longer-term initiative. This longer-term initiative was to be the National Schools Network (NSN). The Network was funded under the Quality Schooling Program. Its purposes are identifiable in the following extract:

> The National Schools Network is a school reform network which links together schools, teacher unions, and government and non-government employers. The network consists of more than 300 Australian schools that are exploring ways to improve teaching and learning by changing the organisation of schools and the work of teachers.

(NSN, 1996)

The National Professional Development Project (NPDP)

The objectives of the NPDP were also directed ultimately towards the improvement of the educational outcomes for students. The vehicle for this improvement was to be the professional development of teachers through 'partnership' projects oriented to aspects of the national agenda. The specific areas to be supported by the NPDP projects were as follows:

- the facilitation of the use of Curriculum Statements and Profiles for Australian Schools
- the renewal of teachers' discipline knowledge and teaching competencies as well as the improvement of work organisation practices in schools
- the enhancement of the professional culture of teachers through the encouragement of a higher profile for professional organisations
- the promotion of partnerships between stakeholders in education, including employers, unions, professional associations and universities.

The link here with work organisation as a focus for professional development is interesting in the light of the later 1995 investigation into the elements of successful student outcomes undertaken by Price Waterhouse and commissioned by the Schools Council. In the section of that report dealing with professional development of primary teachers it is acknowledged that

> The working atmosphere of the school as a whole has a significant influence on student learning outcomes. . . . successful initiatives in staff development were enhanced by an atmosphere that was congenial to change and growth. The importance of the physical set-up and resources available within a school, especially the extent to which teachers control space, was recognised . . . as being an important factor.
>
> (Schools Council, 1995b: 39)

The importance of primary teachers controlling their own professional development at the school level through change-oriented, collegial endeavours was also emphasised:

> The social organisation of schools has also been found to be a critical factor to the success of any staff professional development initiatives as such programs are enhanced by an atmosphere that is congenial to change and growth. . . . Increased autonomy, discretion and control would allow teachers to use their professional knowledge and experience to the fullest, using only teaching methods which their best judgement says would work.
>
> (Schools Council, 1995b: 12)

It was these aspects of collegial development at the school level around issues of concern to the school community that formed the basis of one of the major sub-projects of the NPDP: the Innovative Links Project.[8] This project was grounded in the principle of 'partnership' enunciated in the NPDP objectives. In this case the partnership was between school teachers and university academics, the latter working in a facilitative role with teachers to support school-based projects. Employers and teacher union representatives also had important roles in the project's development and implementation. The Innovative Links project had a close collegial and networking relationship with the NSN, since the implications for work organisation practices of schools formed an important aspect of the school projects.[9]

A recent evaluation of the NPDP has reported positive outcomes in relation to the above aspects of the programme and in particular that

- Raising of awareness among teachers of the Curriculum Statements and Profiles for Australian Schools (or their local variants) has been one of the most significant outcomes . . .
- The NPDP is proving effective in meeting teacher demands for discipline renewal, especially when this is linked to activities to assist teachers in implementing the Curriculum Statements and Profiles for Australian Schools.

(National Curriculum Services, 1995: 96–102)

The Australian Teaching Council

A further initiative in the 'quality' strand of the national agenda had particular implications for 'teacher accountability' in the form of ensuring professional standards of competency. As a further development arising out of recommendations flowing from the NPQTL, the Commonwealth financed the establishment of the Australian Teaching Council which was charged with the task of attempting to develop a national process of teacher registration and accreditation.

Ensuring quality: implications for primary schools and teachers

Although primary teachers have embraced the initiatives outlined above, in general the primary teaching service has been building upon an already established base of quality practices. Teachers at the primary level over the past two decades have progressively maintained and developed a schooling system to a large extent by nurturing their own professional development and by experimenting with modern philosophies of learning. It has become more evident just recently that Australia's primary schooling system is highly regarded in the international literature on education. The strengths of Australian primary teachers are beginning to be recognised :

> Australian upper primary teachers use a variety of teaching methods including collaborative learning, peer tutoring and cross-age tutoring. Current international educational literature suggests that these methods enhance learning attainments as well as generate a greater spirit of congruence amongst educators and students. . . . It is interesting to note that the literature finds teachers overseas in most cases aspiring to achieve what Australian teachers have in fact already put into practice. The study findings thus indicate that Australian upper primary teachers already employ instructional models which educators overseas aspire to adopt.
> (Schools Council, 1995b: 29)

The high level of productivity generated within the primary schooling system relative to expenditure is a national achievement which is only now being evidenced and acknowledged. Primary teachers are beginning to gain opportunities to articulate the nature of their contribution. The following extract, which reports on the literature in this area, expresses teacher dissatisfaction with the lack of appreciation given to the quality of their work:

> The literature reflected current education decision models which have contributed to a sense of profound dissatisfaction amongst teachers. Teachers perceived that their role and their efforts were no longer valued

> or respected by the community, their professional judgements are often, if not usually, ignored, their input not valued at policy levels and they continue to work in the context of relative isolation.
>
> (Schools Council, 1995b: 34)

The NPDP has performed an important function in providing relevant and appropriate professional development opportunities as well as enhancing the sense of professionalism among teachers. The programme has also contributed to 'a greater valuing of the skills that teachers possess' (National Curriculum Services, 1995). However, the extent to which the positive aspects of the *quality* strand of the national agenda have been able to ameliorate the decline in teaching morale, is unclear. The NPDP has also foregrounded the role of professional associations in the professional development of teachers. However, the influence of professional organisations, such as the Primary English Teachers' Association (PETA), on the quality of literacy and learning in schools needs to be more clearly understood. Australian primary classrooms have been deeply influenced by the literacy debate of the past two decades and by the publications emanating from professional organisations. The literature on literacy and learning has predisposed primary teachers both to best practice and to recognising the resource implications of providing opportunity to learn.

CONCLUSION

In considering the initiatives discussed above, it is interesting to note the way in which the 'accountability' and the 'quality' strands of this agenda appear separate, but ultimately interweave through the NPDP. This interweaving has both political and conceptual underpinnings. On the one hand, when the Commonwealth lost control of the process designed to identify common student learning outcomes for Australian schools, it 'pulled the purse strings' of the NPDP to ensure that the states/territories did not abandon the endeavour to focus upon learning outcomes.

Conceptually, the linking of student outcomes with the quality of teaching and learning makes sense. It is not only budgetary concerns that have caused educators to focus upon learning outcomes. As the document *Australia's Teachers* (Schools Council, 1990) notes, public confidence in schooling is enhanced as information regarding student performance is made available, particularly to parents.

In considering these national initiatives in relation to the outcomes of primary schooling, however, the lack of emphasis upon resources is to be noted. We remarked earlier that there is no parallel in Australia to the United States' *opportunity-to-learn standards* which place the accountability responsibility for appropriate resourcing of learning upon education systems. The Schools Council (1995b) study noted that teachers were not simply demanding more financial and other resources but were very aware of how resourcing impacts upon learning and motivation: 'the physical setup and resources available within a school were perceived to have profound impact on children's educational outcomes as well as a direct influence on teacher motivation' (Schools Council, 1995b: 41).

The issue of adequately resourcing physical facilities of primary schools is becoming more urgent as the school buildings from the 1950s and 1960s are now showing both stress from a run-down in the maintenance budgets and a limiting effect on new-era learning couched in outcomes. Parent groups are becoming increasingly vocal regarding the lack of school maintenance and the inability of the system to provide infrastructure demands for education, particularly with respect to technology. While the capital and maintenance aspects of school education are not a Commonwealth responsibility, the quality of the physical plant which supports education is a national issue if education is to support national development.

The initiatives discussed here are being manifested in diverse ways within primary schooling across the Australian states. For the outcomes of such initiatives to impact positively upon Australian society it is timely to address seriously the importance of the 'issues arising' from the recent NBEET study (Schools Council, 1995b). Primary classroom teachers surveyed in that study were seen to have the expertise 'to generate a very comprehensive and accurate picture of upper primary learning attainments'. Of particular issue is the need for those outside the primary classroom to become more informed . 'Administrators, researchers, policy makers and the media should be encouraged to recognise the professionalism of Australia's [primary] classroom teachers' (Schools Council, 1995b: 62).

Finally, the potential for crisis is, of course, another issue. The challenge that must be met by educational administrators involves funding the development of *opportunity-to-learn-standards*, continuing appropriate professional development and creating initiatives for enhancing the status of primary classroom practitioners. It is not appropriate that the responsibility to maintain quality classroom learning should rest with primary teachers alone. Other, particularly higher status, stakeholders must make commitments to provide appropriate resources to support opportunities for learning.

We suggest that the challenge for policy-makers advocating standards-based reform is to translate political rhetoric into ways of funding resources to facilitate the engagement of teachers, parents and the community in guiding the continued advancement of Australia's primary schools. A critical starting point for future policy development must be the authentic identification of the strengths of Australian primary schooling as they relate not merely to economic imperatives but to social and environmental imperatives as well.

NOTES

1   The policy analysis that forms the basis for this chapter was undertaken as part of an Australian Research Council-funded project entitled Restructuring Australia's Schools.

2   Anne Morrow, Chair of the Schools Council, argues: 'Expenditure on school education . . . is now viewed more as a cost to the public purse rather than as an important area of public investment. There is no evidence that Australia is spending too much on schooling. On the contrary, by international standards we could almost be judged to be not spending enough. For example, according to OECD comparisons, Australia ranks 13th out of 16 countries in its level of expenditure on schooling as a percentage of GDP. It is therefore difficult to comprehend why our education systems are under such constant pressure to reduce their expenditure. This is particularly puzzling when the long-term effect of reducing education infrastructure is unknown' (Morrow, 1995:3).

3   These have been achieved.

4   These other stakeholders were not simply supporters of the agenda. In the case of the teachers' unions (the Australian Education Union and the Independent Education Union) they were also 'shapers' of the agenda through the Teaching Accord.

5   The portrayal of the 'agenda' in terms of 'strands' is merely a conceptual device to facilitate analysis of this broad range of initiatives. In practice, the initiatives undertaken nationally during this period were much more interrelated than our separation of them into 'strands' suggests.

6   In December 1993 the AEC was replaced by a new Council: MCEETYA (Ministerial Council on Education, Employment, Training and Youth Affairs).

7   McDonnell (1995: 251) notes that opportunity-to-learn standards have remained fairly much symbolic in the United States. 'OTL standards became the most controversial part of the Goals 2000 legislative debate. Opponents argued that they . . . might serve as the basis on which students could sue states to spend more on schooling inputs.'

8   The full title of the project is Innovative Links Between Universities and Schools for Teacher Professional Development.

9   A more detailed analysis of the Innovative Links Project is available in *Making the Links* (Yeatman and Sachs, 1995), a formative evaluation of the first phase of the project.

REFERENCES

Ashenden, D. (1992) 'Award restructuring and productivity in the future of schooling', in D. Riley (ed.) *Industrial Relations in Australian Education*, Social Science Press Australia, pp. 55–74.

Beare, H. (1995) 'New patterns for managing schools and school systems', in C. Evers and J. Chapman (eds) *Educational Administration: An Australian Perspective*, Sydney: Allen & Unwin, pp. 132–52.

Beazley, K. (1993) *Teaching Counts: A Ministerial Statement by the Hon. Kim Beazley, MP, Minister for Employment, Education and Training*, Canberra: Australian Government Publishing Service.

Boston, K. (1995) 'Benchmarking education systems: professional and political possibilities', *Unicorn* 21, 2: 33–42.

Comber, B. (1993) 'Literacy and social justice', in A. Reid and B. Johnson (eds)

Critical Issues in Australian Education in the 1990's, Adelaide: Painters Prints, pp.112–24.

Cuttance, P. (1995) 'Quality assurance and quality management in education systems', in C. Evers and J. Chapman (eds) *Educational Administration: An Australian Perspective*, Sydney: Allen & Unwin, pp. 296–316.

Dawkins, J.S. (1988) *Strengthening Australia's Schools: A Consideration of the Focus and Content of Schooling*, Canberra: AGPS.

Grundy, S. (1994) 'Action research at the school level: possibilities and problems', *Educational Action Research* 2, 1: 23 – 37.

Harrold, R. (1994) 'From process to product: changing directions in public education policy', in F. Crowther, B. Caldwell, J. Chapman, G. Lakomski and D. Ogilvie (eds) *The Workplace in Education: Australian Perspectives*, ACEA 1994 Yearbook, Sydney: Edward Arnold Australia, pp. 208–17.

Masters, G. (1994) 'Setting and measuring performance standards for student achievement', in *Public Investment in Schools Education: Costs and Outcomes*, papers presented at a conference sponsored by the Schools Council and the Centre for Economic Policy Research at the Australian National University, Canberra, 17 March, pp. 35–60.

McDonnell, L.M. (1995) 'Defining curriculum standards: the promise and the limitations of performance assessment in schooling', paper presented at a conference in Canberra jointly convened by NBEET and the Centre for Economic Policy Research of the ANU, September, in *Efficiency and Equity in Education Policy*, Canberra: Australian Government Publishing Service, pp. 231–76.

McGaw, B. (1995) 'Benchmarking for accountability or improvement' *Unicorn* 21, 2: 7–12.

Morrow, A. (1995) 'Policy implications of the Industry Commission's review of Commonwealth and state services provision and the Schools Council's review of primary schools' resources', in *Public Investment in Schools Education: Costs and Outcomes*, papers presented at a conference sponsored by the Schools Council and the Centre for Economic Policy Research at the Australian National University, Canberra, 17 March 1994, pp. 1–12.

National Curriculum Services (1995) *Evaluation of the National Professional Development Program*, report of the NPDP for the Commonwealth Department of Employment, Education and Training, December.

NPQTL (1992) *National Project on the Quality of Teaching and Learning Annual Report*, Canberra: Department of Employment, Education, and Training.

NSN (1996) World Wide Web Home Page http://www.schnet.edu.au/nsn/Welcome.html

Porter, P., Lingard, B. and Knight, J. (1994) 'Changing Administration and Administering Change: An Analysis of the State of Australian Education'. in F. Crowther, B. Caldwell, J. Chapman, G. Lakomski and D. Ogilvie (eds) *The Workplace in Education: Australian Perspectives*, ACEA 1994 Yearbook, Sydney: Edward Arnold Australia, pp. 218–28.

Reid, A. (1993) 'Accountability in education: the case of attainment levels', in A. Reid and B. Johnson (eds) *Critical Issues in Australian Education in the 1990's*, Adelaide: Painters Prints, pp. 31–41.

Schools Council (1990) *Australia's Teachers: An Agenda for the Next Decade*, paper prepared by the Schools Council of the National Board of Employment Education and Training, Canberra.

—— (1995a) *Resources and Accountability: Commonwealth Funding Scenarios for Government Primary Schools 1996–2000*, paper prepared by the Schools Council of the National Board of Employment Education and Training, Canberra, August.

—— (1995b) *The Elements of Successful Student Outcomes: Views from Upper Primary Classroom Teachers*, Commissioned Report No. 41, paper prepared for the Schools Council of the National Board of Employment Education and Training, Canberra, December.

Watkins, P. (1994) 'The Fordist/post-Fordist debate: the educational implications', in J. Kenway (ed.) *Economising Education: The Post-Fordist Directions*, Geelong: Deakin University Press.

Wilkins, R. and Doyle, K. (1995) 'Benchmarking school education', *Unicorn*, 21, 2: 24–32.

Yeatman, A. and Sachs, J. (1995) *Making the Links: An Evaluation of the First Phase of the Innovative Links Project*, Murdoch University: Innovative Links Project.

Chapter 8

Extending options for gifted and talented pupils

Miraca U.M. Gross and Jacinta H. Howard

If priorities for resources must be determined among educationally disadvantaged groups, it could be argued that gifted children are currently among the most disadvantaged of these groups.

(Commonwealth of Australia, 1988: 5)

This quote is taken from the report of a cross-party Standing Committee of the Australian Senate which spent two years investigating school provisions for gifted and talented pupils. The Committee was critical of the low level and poor quality of the provisions that it observed and noted that 'many academically talented children not only fail to achieve their potential but actually drop out of school in large numbers' (*ibid.*, 1988: 4). Their report concluded that 'most Australian schools do not appear to make any provision for the education of gifted children' (*ibid.*, 1988: 82).

During the 1970s and 1980s many schools that might otherwise have developed provisions for their most able students were deterred by the concern that such provisions might be perceived as 'elitist'. The extreme egalitarian ethos of this period led to a misunderstanding, among many teachers and teacher unionists, of the concept of equality of opportunity. Equal opportunity requires that all students, regardless of their level of ability, should be encouraged and facilitated to develop their potential to the fullest. Unfortunately, however, this was often misinterpreted as implying that no child should be *given* an educational 'opportunity' that was not appropriate for, or available to, his or her classmates.

In several states this misunderstanding acted, for many years, as a powerful barrier to the development of special programmes for the gifted and talented. More frequently than is sometimes acknowledged, it led to serious abuses of the educational rights of students.

'Ian', a Year 4 student in a state primary school, was identified as having truly exceptional mathematical ability; he scored considerably above the mean on a university maths test which he was given, as part of a research study, to assess his level of achievement. His teacher, however, insisted that he undertake Grade 4 maths with the other 9-year-olds, and the school principal was adamant that he should not receive any provision that was not offered to the other children in his grade. She told Ian's parents, candidly, that it would be 'political suicide' for her to develop any special provisions for gifted students within her school (Gross, 1993).

'Margaret' entered school, aged 5, with the reading accuracy and comprehension of a 7-year-old, but her teacher insisted that she take reading readiness exercises with the other children, in case their self-esteem might be damaged if they realised that she could already read.

Braggett (1986) outlined the major difficulties facing gifted education in Australia. These include the egalitarian belief that special provisions should not be made for able students because of the more pressing needs of other, more visibly disadvantaged, groups; a lack of educational commitment to the concept of providing effectively for individual differences; the lack of awareness among Australian teachers of the special needs of gifted and talented children; and 'an educational philosophy in which social factors are sometimes considered to be more important than educational factors' (Braggett, 1986: 15).

Ten years after Braggett's analysis, Australian teachers are more aware of the need to make differentiated responses to different learning needs. There still remains, however, a widespread lack of understanding of the characteristics and needs of gifted and talented children. Many teachers still believe that gifted students are easily identified; that they come predominantly from professional families and from the dominant culture; and that they are automatically high achievers. As a result, the majority of highly able students work significantly below their true ability level, and gifted children in minority and disadvantaged groups go largely unidentified (Gross, 1993).

It is often said that a nation's gifted children are its most valuable resource. It is these young people who, if their talents are allowed to develop, will enhance their country's cultural, scientific, economic or industrial development in future years. As the Senate Report noted, without the contribution of its gifted citizens, Australian society would be poorer both materially and culturally. We would be less able to sustain a level of prosperity that allows our education systems to provide for physically and intellectually disadvantaged students. We would fall behind in social and medical care, and in medical and scientific research. The timely investment in the talented youth of a community for the benefit of all has been called 'enlightened self interest' (Gallagher, 1991: 177).

THE POLICY

In New South Wales, between 1988 and 1990, the *Carrick Review*, the Government White Paper *Excellence and Equity* and the 1990 *Education Reform Act* provided the framework for an evaluation of the equity and effectiveness of education within the state, and set the tone for a major re-examination and restructure of educational provisions for gifted and talented students.

In early 1991 the Government of New South Wales published its *Strategy for the Education of Gifted and Talented Students*. This was supplemented by two support documents: *Implementation Strategies for the Education of Gifted and Talented Students*, published by the NSW Department of School Education, and *Guidelines for Accelerated Progression*, published by the NSW Board of Studies.

These three documents detailed a comprehensive policy structure and management plan designed 'to maximise the educational outcomes of schooling for gifted and talented students' (NSW Government, 1991: 1). Their publication, and the resultant educational initiatives in NSW schools, have influenced several other states to undertake major revisions of their own gifted education policies and provisions.

The current policy reflects international thinking and research on the nature and needs of gifted students:

- The focus on giftedness as high ability or potential, rather than on achievement or performance, recognises that many gifted students currently underachieve in school.
- The identification of gifted students is not left to teacher nomination alone. A combination of objective and subjective procedures is recommended, including behavioural checklists, standardised testing of ability and achievement, products and performance, class grades, and nomination by teachers, parents or peers.
- Teachers are alerted to the need to identify gifted students from disadvantaged and minority groups and to 'allow for the highly talented to emerge from the larger talented group' (*ibid.*, 1991: 5).
- It is acknowledged that an intellectually gifted student with specific learning difficulties may require remedial assistance concurrent with placement in a special programme for gifted and talented students.
- Whereas provisions for gifted students prior to 1991 were largely limited to 'in-class enrichment', the current policy, while noting that 'the implementation of appropriate and specific strategies in the regular classroom will form a solid basis for the education of gifted and talented students', goes on to outline a range of grouping and accelerative strategies which schools are also encouraged to employ.
- The current policy includes a strong focus on teacher in-service and training, requiring that 'all schools should facilitate the participation of all staff members in at least one introductory in-service course addressing the education of gifted and talented students in 1992–1993' and that 'after 1995 all schools, where feasible, should seek to employ at least one teacher who has training in the education of gifted and talented students' (*ibid.*, 1991: 11).

The Department of School Education (DSE) responded by making in-service on gifted and talented children a priority for schools' use of professional development funding in 1992–3.

A significant weakness in the policy, however, is its adoption of an arbitrary and impractical definition of giftedness which proposes that 'Gifted students are those with the potential to exhibit superior performance across a range of areas of endeavour', while 'Talented students are those with the potential to exhibit superior performance in one area of endeavour' (*ibid.*, 1991: 3).

This definition reveals nothing about the nature of giftedness, fails to acknowledge the influence of personality and environment, as well as ability, on student achievement, and provides no indication of how gifted students may be identified or assisted to develop their potential. Many NSW schools have found it unsatisfactory and have sought alternative definitions which are more solidly grounded in the educational and psychological research on giftedness and talent, and which are more readily operational. One such school is St Ives North Primary.

THE SCHOOL

St Ives North Primary School (SINPS) is a government school in New South Wales, which serves a population of 600 students in grades K-6. It is sited in a relatively affluent area of Sydney where it has to compete, in an increasingly crowded educational environment, with a decreasing number of children to service.

The community of St Ives and its neighbouring suburbs tends to be highly educated and aware of educational and social issues. They hold high expectations of the local schools in terms of educational standards and the provision of opportunities to meet the individual needs of children. A range of economic, social and cultural factors, including the gradual 'aging' of the region's population, has led to steadily declining enrolments of children into the state school system, and two nearby primary schools were closed in 1988 and 1990. A demographic profile undertaken by the local Council of the Municipality of Ku-ring-gai in 1991 predicted continuing attrition from the district's government schools over the next ten years.

Through the mid- and late 1980s SINPS was active in promoting the needs of students who were recognised as being especially at risk for under-achievement, including students with learning difficulties, students from non-English-speaking backgrounds, and Aboriginal and Torres Strait Islanders. It became increasingly obvious, however, that the school was not offering enough in the way of academic challenge to its many gifted and highly able students, and these students tended to leave SINPS at the end of Year 4 to attend local state primary schools which had 'opportunity classes' – full-time self-contained classes of gifted students in Years 5 and 6 – or private schools which claimed to offer a differentiated curriculum for academically able pupils. Parents of these children admitted, to the SINPS staff, that while they would prefer to keep their children at SINPS, they felt constrained to move them to schools that would offer programmes specifically oriented towards high ability students.

SINPS did, indeed, offer a pull-out programme for gifted and talented students, which had been in place for several years, but many staff members had doubts about its efficacy. The pull-out structure, where gifted students are withdrawn from the regular classroom for a few hours, or less, each week, to work on extension material with a resource teacher, has been criticised as one of the less effective interventions for gifted students (Borland, 1989), while VanTassel-Baska (1989), alluding to the fact that the typical time frame allotted to enrichment through pull-out is no more than 150 minutes per week, called it an 8 per cent solution to a 100 per cent problem. SINPS began to question the efficacy of basing its interventions for gifted students solely on the pull-out model.

The publication, in 1991, of the NSW Government *Strategy*, focused the school's attention even more sharply on the need to evaluate its current provisions for gifted students, and a Steering Committee was established to develop a strategic plan for the development of defensible and effective programme structures. The Steering Committee, chaired by the deputy principal, Ian Foulcher, included the principal, Jan Fredericks, staff members, parents of a representative cross-section of the SINPS student population, members of the local community and local council, and faculty members from the Ku-ring-gai campus of the University of Technology Sydney who had a special interest in the education of highly able students.

The strategic plan, developed by the Steering Committee for submission to the school community, was strongly influenced by the Government *Strategy*. As noted earlier, the *Strategy* had recommended that schools consider a number of approaches to programme development for gifted students, including accelerated progression, in-class enrichment, mentor programmes, pull-out programmes and full-time classes, and had also advised that 'these approaches, in many cases, may be implemented concurrently' (NSW Government, 1991: 6). The strategic plan proposed that, as a first step towards an integrated structure of programme offerings, a full-time class of academically gifted students should be established at SINPS for the following year.

This was a bold and ambitious project. Thirty-two full-time classes for gifted students had already existed, for several years, in NSW Department of Education Schools, but these 'opportunity classes' (OCs) had been established by the central bureaucracies of two of the DSE's administrative regions, which also retained responsibility for student identification and placement. Some members of the SINPS community were unsure as to whether the DSE would permit individual schools to establish full-time classes for gifted students which might be seen as competing with the centrally established OCs in neighbouring schools.

None the less, the strategic plan was enthusiastically adopted by the school community and in 1991 SINPS presented a formal proposal to the DSE, for the establishment of the special class. The DSE expressed its delight at the school's initiative and, to show its support, arranged for the project to be launched, during Education Week, by the then Minister of Education and Youth Affairs, the Hon. Virginia Chadwick.

The school community decided to establish the first full-time class at Year 5 level. Advertisements placed in local and Sydney-based newspapers attracted an overwhelming response. Parents with children of all ages – pre-school to Grade 6 – expressed great interest and enthusiasm for the concept, and parent evenings held by the school to explain the proposals were extremely well attended.

The principal had consulted regularly and openly with the parent body of SINPS regarding the proposals, and the general reaction was extremely positive. Some parents were concerned that the influx of 'strangers' would change the image, and focus, of the school, but this concern was balanced by the assurance that a focus on the talents and strengths of students would benefit many of the school community, rather than a small minority. With the strong support of the community, planning went forward for the establishment of the new class in February 1992.

THEORETICAL UNDERPINNINGS OF THE PROGRAMME

The decision to establish a full-time class was undertaken after a thoughtful consideration, by the Steering Committee, of the educational research on the academic and social outcomes of grouping gifted students. Research has shown that ability grouping

- allows gifted students to advance at their own pace with other students of similar ability
- permits teachers to offer gifted students methods and materials geared to their ability and achievement level
- gives gifted students regular access to other students of like ability and like interests
- raises gifted students' levels of social and general self-esteem
- leads to a significant drop in underachievement among gifted students, particularly deliberate underachievement for peer acceptance
- makes teaching easier and more effective by reducing the range of ability and achievement within the classroom.

(Gross, 1993; Kulik, 1992; Rogers, 1991; VanTassel-Baska, 1989)

In 1991 and 1992 the American National Research Center on the Gifted and Talented (NRCGT) published two major syntheses of the research on ability grouping. The conclusions of the studies, and the resulting recommendations by the NRCGT, strongly endorsed the validity of full-time grouping of gifted students.

> Students who are academically or intellectually gifted and talented should spend the majority of their school day with others of similar abilities and interests. Both general intellectual ability grouping programmes and full-time grouping for special academic ability have produced marked academic achievement gains as well as moderate increases in attitude towards the subjects in which these students are grouped.
>
> (Rogers, 1991: xii)

Kulik (1992), however, cautioned that little benefit arose from programmes that simply grouped gifted students together but required them to work on the same material, at the same level and pace, as they would have if they had remained in the mixed-ability classroom. The SINPS staff were keenly aware that the gifted education class must have a programme that was strongly differentiated in pace and content. Equally, the choice of teacher would be critical to the success of the programme.

Tina Howard, the assistant principal of SINPS and a member of the Strategic Planning Committee, was asked to teach the special class in 1992. As Tina had no special training in gifted education, she asked that the school support her enrolment in a training programme so that she could decide whether she was suited to such a role.

In September 1991 Tina enrolled in the Certificate of Gifted Education (COGE) programme at the University of New South Wales (UNSW). COGE comprises three weeks of on-campus lectures and seminars held during consecutive school vacations. UNSW's own lecturers in gifted education are supplemented by experts in this field from overseas. The September week of COGE had two significant outcomes for SINPS; it resulted in Tina Howard agreeing to teach the special class, and it introduced the school to the model of giftedness and talent developed by Françoys Gagné of the University of Quebec in Montreal, who taught as a visiting professor in the COGE programme.

As discussed earlier, SINPS was one of many NSW schools that found the government definition of giftedness and talent impractical. By contrast, the Gagné definition contributed to teachers' knowledge of gifted students, and could be operationalised in schools.

Gagné (1993) defines giftedness as the ability to perform at a level significantly beyond what might be expected from one's age-peers, in any domain of human ability. A child can be gifted in any one of the cognitive, creative, socio-affective or sensori-motor domains; or in several, or in all. Importantly, giftedness is viewed as outstanding potential, rather than outstanding performance; this model, therefore, recognises the existence, and the dilemma, of the underachieving gifted child.

By contrast, Gagné defines talent as *achievement* significantly beyond what could normally be expected from age-peers. Numerous fields of performance are associated with any ability domain, and a child may be talented in one or many fields of performance.

Within this model a child can be gifted (having unusually high potential) without being talented (demonstrating unusually high performance). To explain the relationship between the two, Gagné points to a cluster of catalystic variables which can either facilitate or impede the translation of giftedness into talent.

Crucial to the process of talent development is the quality of the child's learning, training or practising. Impacting on this process, however, are personality factors within the child herself, including motivation, self-esteem, self-confidence, and the degree to which she accepts her own abilities. Equally important are environmental factors such as the quality of teaching and parenting that the child receives, the provisions that the school makes, or fails to make, to develop her gifts into talents, and even the social ethos of the community which can dictate which gifts are valued and, there-fore, which programmes of talent development will be established or funded.

Within the Gagné model, the community's responsibility is to identify children who are gifted but not yet talented, and assist them to bring their gifts to fruition, as well as further assisting those talented students who are already performing at high levels.

Gagné emphasises that, although his model is rather more inclusive than former definitions which limited giftedness to the cognitive domain and to the top 2–5 per cent of the population, he does not suggest that every child possesses a gift or talent. He suggests that up to 15 or 16 per cent of chil-dren may be viewed as gifted or talented, and he cautions that within this population there is still an enormous range of ability and achievement.

In adopting the Gagné model, SINPS was committing itself to the devel-opment, over time, of a range of programmes which would respond to the types and levels of giftedness and talent among its students.

DEVELOPMENT AND EXPANSION OF THE PROGRAMME

Since the establishment of the Ku-ring-gai Unit for Gifted and Talented Students, as the full-time classes came to be called, in 1992, the SINPS programmes for gifted and talented students have grown considerably. The school population has increased from under 400 in 1991 to over 600, and the considerable majority of incoming students have been gifted and highly able children, and their brothers and sisters. Visibly, the school community of SINPS had identified an area of need, and its effective response to that need has led to an enlargement of its community. No geographical limits are imposed, by the school or the DSE, on student intake, and students are drawn from a broad geographical area, some travelling significant distances to attend the SINPS programmes.

In 1996, five years into the establishment of the programme, SINPS offers the following programmes for gifted and highly able students. The NSW Government *Strategy* has provided the framework for school policy and programme development, and the staff have modelled each new programme on similar, successful, interventions reported in the international research literature in gifted education. Conscious of the research which shows that teachers trained in gifted education develop more effective teaching strategies and a more positive classroom climate for gifted students (Hansen and Feldhusen, 1994), SINPS has funded the training of six staff members through the UNSW Certificate of Gifted Education, while staff regularly attend gifted education in-services run by UNSW, Macquarie and Charles Sturt universities.

Ability and achievement grouping

SINPS offers a range of programmes which allow students access to a challenging curriculum with students of like ability and interest.

- *Self-contained classes.* The school now (in 1996) houses four full-time classes of gifted students in Years 3, 4, 5 and 6. These classes comprise the Ku-ring-gai Unit.
- *Pull-out programmes.* Children with specific abilities in a range of subject areas are withdrawn from the mixed-ability classroom each week for extension and enrichment in maths (Years 3–6), creative writing (Years 3–6), research skills (Year 2) and creative and performing arts (across the school).

Acceleration

Australian teachers are often reluctant to accelerate academically gifted students, in the belief that it may lead to social or emotional difficulties; yet research shows that carefully planned and monitored acceleration can have extremely positive academic and social benefits (Kulik, 1992; Rogers, 1991; Shore *et al.*, 1991). SINPS offers several of the acceleration options recommended in the NSW Board of Studies *Guidelines for Accelerated Progression* (1991).

- *Grade advancement.* Gifted students who excel in several subject areas may grade-advance, i.e. a student may 'skip' Year 3, or may enter high school at the end of Year 5 rather than Year 6. These students are required to show that they have already mastered the work of the grade that they will 'skip'.
- *Subject acceleration.* Gifted students who excel in single, specific subjects

may take that subject with an older grade while remaining with age-peers for the remainder of their work.

- *Half-year skips.* Gifted students may 'telescope' two years into one by spending the first half of the year with age-peers, and advancing to the next grade after the July vacation.
- *Early entrance.* Young gifted children who are already performing at kindergarten or Year 1 level, and who are clearly ready for school both academically and socially, may start school before the usual age of enrolment.

For some highly gifted students, the school uses a combination of two or more methods of acceleration. Since 1992, approximately twenty academically gifted students have undertaken some form of acceleration at SINPS, and some students enter the Ku-ring-gai Unit classes having already been accelerated in their former schools.

ENRICHMENT

It is an axiom of education at SINPS that every student, regardless of ability or achievement, receives academic enrichment. It is accepted, however, that enrichment for gifted students must provide a differentiated level of pace, challenge and complexity.

Academically gifted students in Years K-2 and in the mainstream classes at other grade levels receive fast-paced, academically challenging in-class enrichment. Students in mainstream classes who are talented in specific subject areas join the Unit classes each day for work in their particular talent area. Children with high levels of ability and interest in specific subject areas may also work on short-term projects or investigations with adult mentors – members of the wider community who have expertise in the child's area of interest – and mentorships have been established in such differing areas as mathematics, aeronautical engineering, German, mythology, computer studies and chemistry.

The school participates in state and regional enrichment programmes such as Tournament of the Minds, Future Problem Solving, debating, public speaking and chess, which provide excellent enrichment opportunities for many students, not only those of high ability, while the school's two orchestras, choir and sports teams extend students with a wide range of strengths or talents. A Saturday enrichment programme, 'Step Ahead', is held at the school once each semester, and is open to gifted and talented children within the wider community.

IDENTIFICATION PROCEDURES

As already discussed, the NSW Government *Strategy* requires NSW schools to use a range of objective and subjective procedures to identify gifted and talented students, and this recommendation is strongly supported by research (Shore *et al.*, 1991). SINPS believes that its systematically planned and evaluated selection procedures have been an essential factor in the success of its programmes.

- When making application for their child to be considered for entry to the Ku-ring-gai Unit, parents complete a research-based checklist of cognitive and affective characteristics of gifted and talented students, and list their reasons for wanting their child to be considered for enrolment.
- Parents are invited to include, with their application, any supporting documentation such as school reports, test results, comments from school counsellors or teachers, etc.
- The research literature in gifted education strongly supports the use of IQ testing to assist in the identification of intellectually gifted children (Shore *et al.*, 1991). All children applying for admission to the Unit attend a testing day at the school. Tests of both verbal and non-verbal reasoning (the latter is essential to ensure that children from non-English-speaking backgrounds are not disadvantaged) are administered by qualified psychologists. All tests employed have a high ceiling to ensure that the full extent of the children's abilities can be assessed (Gross, 1994).
- Children complete a test of reading comprehension, and a writing task which requires them to retell a narrative that has been presented to them orally.

The full range of information gathered on each applicant, both objective and subjective, is reviewed by the selection committee, which consists of the principal and four or five teachers trained in gifted education, and placement in the Unit is offered to gifted and talented students who would benefit, academically and socially, from the fast-paced, academically rigorous work of the full-time classes. Gifted and highly able students who already attend SINPS, and who participate in the many other enrichment and extension programmes, are selected through ongoing assessment using a combination of standardised achievement testing, classroom performance and teacher nomination.

EVALUATION AND PROGRAMME OUTCOMES

Formative and summative evaluation are essential components of any educational programme. Evaluation assesses the worth and effectiveness of educational policies and the programmes and teaching strategies that arise from them.

Carefully collected evaluation data assist SINPS teachers to assess student needs, plan appropriate learning experiences, and ensure that instructional objectives are being met. Measurement of student progress through a range of formal and informal assessment strategies is an essential element of programme evaluation, and provides needed evidence that the differentiated curriculum and programme structures do indeed have a positive impact on the students' learning. Student assessment occurs through norm-referenced and criterion-referenced testing, work portfolios, class grades, products and class performance, student interviews and anecdotal records.

While teachers make many individual decisions about gifted students in their classes, SINPS has established a support group of staff members which has three principal roles:

- to provide suggestions and advice when required
- to review periodically the placement of gifted students to ensure that the programme in which they are enrolled is still appropriate for them
- to suggest alternative placement or courses of action where a placement no longer meets the needs of individual students.

Teachers, parents, students and mentors complete evaluative questionnaires, commenting on the effectiveness of SINPS programmes. The responses are overwhelmingly positive. Indeed, the community has demonstrated direct and practical support for the programmes through the rise in enrolments from under 400 to over 600 since 1991.

The Unit and its associated school-wide enrichment, acceleration and grouping programmes have impacted strongly and positively on programme development and classroom practice throughout the school. Teachers are much more aware of the individual strengths and interests possessed by all students at SINPS, as well as the gifts and talents of the highly able. While the curriculum developed for academically gifted students differs significantly in content, process and product from that offered to age-peers of more moderate ability, the enhanced teaching and programming skills that have been developed in the SINPS teachers through specialist training and in-service have benefited students across the school.

Staff and parents have noticed striking improvements in SINPS students' attitudes towards school and learning. They are engaged in instruction at an appropriate level and pace; they are actively involved in their own learning; they set personal goals and value excellence. Students demonstrate positive and responsible attitudes towards their own and others' talents and abilities, and both teachers and parents comment that the 'tall poppy' syndrome, which results in deliberate underachievement for peer acceptance among gifted students in many Australian schools, is virtually unknown at SINPS.

The gifted education policy at SINPS took a full year to draft. It is grounded in sound educational research, and responsive to government policy. It is the collaborative effort of a committee of teachers, parents and community members and, as a result, the school community 'owns' the policy and the programmes that have developed from it, and takes justifiable pride in them. Indeed, in acknowledgement of the quality of identification, curriculum development and programming for gifted and talented students at SINPS, the Department of School Education has designated the school a 'Centre of Excellence' in gifted education.

REFERENCES

Borland, J. (1989) *Planning and Implementing Programmes for the Gifted*, New York: Teachers College Press.

Braggett, E.J. (1986) 'The education of gifted and talented children in Australia: a national overview', in K. Imison, L. Endean and D. Smith (eds) *Gifted and Talented Children: A National Concern* (pp. 13–27), Toowoomba: Darling Downs Institute Press.

Commonwealth of Australia (1988) *The Report of the Senate Select Committee on the Education of Gifted and Talented Children*, Canberra: Australian Government Publishing Service.

Gagné, F. (1993) 'Constructs and models pertaining to exceptional human abilities', in K. Heller, F.J. Monks and A.H. Passow (eds) *International Handbook of Research and Development of Giftedness and Talent* (pp. 69–87), Oxford: Pergamon.

Gallagher, J.J. (1991) 'Programmes for gifted students: enlightened self-interest', *Gifted Child Quarterly* 35, 4: 177–8.

Gross, M.U.M. (1993) *Exceptionally Gifted Children*, London: Routledge.

—— (1994) 'The highly gifted: their nature and needs', in J.B. Hansen and S.M. Hoover (eds) *Talent Development: Theories and Practice* (pp. 257–80), Dubuque, IA: Kendall Hunt.

Hansen, J.B. and Feldhusen, J.F. (1994) 'Comparison of trained and untrained teachers of gifted students', *Gifted Child Quarterly* 38, 3: 115–23.

Kulik, J.A. (1992) *An Analysis of the Research on Ability Grouping: Historical and Contemporary Perspectives*, Storrs, CT: National Research Center on the Gifted and Talented.

NSW Board of Studies (1991) *Guidelines for Accelerated Progression*, Sydney: NSW Board of Studies.

NSW Department of School Education (1991) *Implementation Strategies for the Education of Gifted and Talented Students*, Sydney: NSW Department of School Education.

NSW Government (1991) *NSW Government Strategy for the Education of Gifted and Talented Students*, Sydney: NSW Government.

Rogers, K.B (1991) *The Relationship of Grouping Practices to the Education of the Gifted and Talented Learner*, Storrs, CT: National Research Center on the Gifted and Talented.

Shore, B.M., Cornell, D.G., Robinson, A. and Ward, V.S. (1991) *Recommended Practices in Gifted Education*, New York: Teachers College Press.

VanTassel-Baska, J. (1989) 'A comprehensive model of gifted programme development', in J.F. Feldhusen, J. VanTassel-Baska and K. Seeley (eds) *Excellence in Educating the Gifted* (pp. 123–42), Denver: Love.

Chapter 9

Responding to the pupils' culture and language

Georgina Tsolidis

WHERE LANGUAGE AND CULTURE EQUAL ENGLISH AND MAINSTREAM IN SCHOOLS OF THE FUTURE

Introduction

Imagine the primary school. An inner-city school, small but getting bigger. A reputation for excellence, particularly in regard to the teaching of English literacy. A new principal, a school moving into the 'Schools of the Future' programme and, as a result, a new school charter. There exists an abundance of committees and a reasonable number of committed 'education-literate' parents to participate on these committees. The staff provide an enormous amount of their own time to the children, the parents, the committees and the social and political life of the school in general.

The school community is solid, involved and seems to have more than its fair share of 'schoolies' as parents. Parents send their children to the school because they like the atmosphere, the commitment of the staff and the many progressive policies and ways of doing things. It is a school that is difficult to fault – except when it comes to understanding broader issues related to language and culture. Language equals English and culture equals mainstream.

How common it is for schools such as these inner-suburban schools, which over time have developed progressive curriculum strategies, as a response to diversity among other reasons, to forget this diversity once the majority of students are understood to have English as their major language?

A closer examination of the school will reveal that, like many of its kind in inner-city suburbs becoming gentrified, it still has a culturally diverse underbelly. There are a dozen or so languages other than English which its students speak in their homes. While most of the students (and parents) would be understood by the school to favour English as their language of communication, there is a sizeable number of students who are likely to be ambivalent bilinguals.

There are the children who are part of that generation whose non-English-speaking grandparents have remained in the gentrified inner-suburbs but whose parents have shifted to the new homes in the outer suburbs. However, these children remain with their grandparents before and after school and, by virtue of this relationship, their parents often choose to send their children to schools far away from home but close to grandma and grandpa – often the very same school that they themselves attended when they were inner-city, newly arrived 'migrant' children.

There are the children of bilingual parents who live in the immediate community – these are the children of the 'assimilated', upwardly mobile 'migrants' – and there are the children of mixed marriages, where one parent is attempting to hang on to the last vestiges of another world, another culture.

There are the children of the newly arrived immigrants from the neighbouring language centres and commission flats. The colourful clothing from places such as the Horn of Africa adds the much-sought-after dimension of difference that allows the community to boast that it is not homogeneous. Yet for many of these children, the far-away look in their eyes betrays the lack of English as a Second Language (ESL) provision, which is increasingly the reality at these inner-city schools.

There are also the children of monolingual English families who share a community within which cultural diversity is commonplace: the children who know that many of their school friends, neighbours and shop-keepers have insights into other places and other ways of doing things; who know that their friends go to another school on Saturday morning or Tuesday night at which they learn other languages, dances and traditions. These children are somehow cut off from these opportunities. All in all, there is a cultural and linguistic diversity of which the school programme does not take advantage.

While the school described above is not a real school, it is typical of a range of schools within the inner-city suburbs of Melbourne. Demographic shifts and upheavals in government policies over the years have created immense changes in these schools, not all of which have been welcomed by teachers, parents and children. Of particular concern here are how these shifts relate to cultural and linguistic diversity.

Policy context

The Labor government elected in Victoria in 1982 ushered in a period of policy-led reform. The Ministerial Papers appeared in the early to mid-1980s and offered new ways of administering schools (*Ministerial Paper No. 1*, Minister of Education, 1985) and new platforms on which to build curriculum (*Ministerial Paper No. 6*, Minister of Education, 1985). In broad terms, the orientation was to provide local school councils, constituted to include teacher, parent and principal viewpoints, with local decision-making authority within the parameters of a centrally determined policy framework. Of particular concern within this policy framework were notions of inclusivity. These were applied both to the school-based decision-making processes themselves as well as to the curriculum that was offered to students as their outcome.

Ministerial committees and the State Board of Education undertook a range of projects intended to inform and include groups prone to marginalisation within school governance. Emphasis was given to women and ethnic minority parents as two such groups. As examples of this, *Ministerial Papers* were translated into a range of languages other than English and those involved in the local selection of school principals were provided with briefings on equal opportunity.

Similarly, in relation to curriculum, concern with inclusivity was often enacted in relation to gender and ethnic diversity. A range of school-based practice concerned with these issues was consolidated by support for materials development and professional development, often through Commonwealth-funded programmes such as the Participation and Equity Program and the Multicultural Education Program.

A range of criticisms have been made of this policy period and its emphasis on inclusivity. In terms of seemingly generic understandings of inclusion, where it became almost passé to list gender, ethnicity, class, disability, etc., in reference to schooling, the question has been asked whether such an approach served to submerge rather than address the specific needs of groups of students such as girls (Yates, 1987). Attention has been drawn to the role that a political process that relies on categories such as 'women and girls' and 'non-English speaking' plays in denying the subjectivity of groups that fall between such categories, such as ethnic minority women and girls, and to the implications of this lack of articulation between such categories for curriculum approaches (Tsolidis, 1993a). Comment has also been made on the success of such processes in actually including marginal groups in school governance (Terry, 1989).

As part of this policy process, the government issued two documents centred on multi-culturalism and the teaching of languages other than English, respectively. These are most relevant to the issues under consideration here.

The 1986 document, *Education in, and for, a Multicultural Society* (Ministry of Education), proposed a rationale for teaching to cultural difference in all schools and to all students. It reiterated arguments about the historic nature of Australian cultural diversity, the benefits of this and the benefits for all students of a curriculum that stressed the positive aspects of this diversity. It proposed few strategies and the task of translating the policy into practice, in Victoria, was taken up through Commonwealth-funded programmes. As was common during this period, an emphasis of such programmes was school-based curriculum development and professional development with the assistance of 'outside' funding and consultancy staff. (Much of the teaching material that eventuated from such programmes, unfortunately, did not receive the necessary funding for adequate publication and distribution.)

The Place of Languages Other Than English in Victorian Schools (State Board of Education/MACMME) was issued in 1985. It set in place a policy, which was followed by a strategy plan, *Victoria Languages Action Plan* (Ministry of Education) in 1989, for the teaching of LOTE (languages other than English). In the interim, the *National Policy on Languages* was published (Lo Bianco, 1987). The emphasis in this policy was to separate the issue of LOTE teaching and learning from multi-culturalism (Ozolins, 1993). There has been a common tendency within multi-cultural policy to link LOTE with ethnic minority status and to argue that, along with ESL, in particular bilingual approaches to this, it is a necessary adjunct to maintaining bicultural Australian identifications (NACCME, 1987). The *National Policy*, however, challenged dichotomies that had been drawn between foreign and community languages in the past. Instead it opted for an approach that stressed the benefits of LOTE learning for a range of reasons including those concerned with economics and trade. In doing so, however, it may have helped to consolidate a dichotomy between community and trade languages and helped to sever the political link between culture and language which had functioned as a mainstay for a politics of difference within Australia (Tsolidis, 1993b).

Clearly, this period was policy-rich and, some would retrospectively argue, also relatively well resourced. What is the legacy of this period where reformist Labor governments tackled curriculum issues through a political process, whereby school communities were encouraged to consider issues such as which LOTE to teach?

Subsequent to the election of the Liberal government in 1992 further shifts have taken place in Victoria. The ways in which school councils are constituted have changed and school councils now have responsibility for budget management at the local level. While policy processes related to cultural diversity seem to have lost their momentum, in relation to LOTE teaching and learning there has been a new impetus. In 1993 the Victorian Department of School Education issued a directive, making the teaching of LOTE compulsory in every school. While the previous government had shied away from such an explicit directive, opting instead for incentives, the new government matched the directive with a resourcing strategy which included satellite provision as a means of operationalising it in times of economic restraint.

The Conservative government in Victoria has introduced many changes. These are difficult to consider in isolation from each other and in isolation from the mood of defensiveness and apprehension that many school communities continue to feel as a result of over ten years of rapid policy shift.

Changes to the ways in which school councils are constituted and the range of their responsibilities, changes to staffing and special needs allocation, changes brought about by Schools of the Future, and changes to assessment procedures and the Learning Assessment Project are some of these shifts.

Where schools were already feeling under siege, the directive that all schools provide a LOTE has been met with cynicism, if not hostility. In this context, a range of issues related to linguistic and cultural diversity arise. These relate to both pedagogy and school governance.

Governance

If we return to our fictitious inner-city school, how is a directive to teach a LOTE interpreted by a school council, constituted relatively narrowly, with more authority and with more responsibility to make financial ends meet? Within the new arrangements, where management is undertaken at the school level under the Schools of the Future programme, there exists increasing need and incentives for school councils to make decisions about school offerings in relation to 'market forces'. What will make the school attractive to parents? Which parents are attractive to the school? What is affordable? In such a context, it is easy to understand why curriculum-led decision-making may fall by the wayside. For example, if an inner-city school is surrounded by schools that adopted Italian as a LOTE in the times when this was considered a community language, a so-called trade language such as Japanese can appear attractive. This may not be because Japanese is easy to teach, nor because it will be reinforced in the students' community. Japanese may in fact appear attractive because it is not offered in other neighbourhood primary schools or because people assume, in an unexamined way, that it is useful for future careers. Japanese may appear attractive because it is offered at surrounding private secondary schools and in this way the primary school can cater for the parents who plan for this type of secondary schooling but do not insist on it at the primary level.

How are decisions reached as to school offerings? Most of us who have experience of school governance realise that school council membership is unrepresentative of the whole parent body. It is the parents with the time and the commitment who find themselves on school council. The parents without English, the shift workers, those who are not 'education-literate' – these parents are less likely to be involved in school-based, decision-making processes.

More to the point, regardless of time and experience, most parents realise that there exist real disincentives for them to 'rock the boat' within the school community. Few parents consider LOTE teaching and learning at all, let alone enough to make themselves unpopular over it. Many bilingual parents despaired of having their home language reinforced within schools a long time ago and instead opted for after-hours schools-based programmes within ethnic communities. For many of these parents, school-based LOTE teaching is neither here nor there.

There are also the politics of the staff room and how these interact with decision-making processes. If LOTE is introduced, who teaches it? Is this person adequately trained? Who is displaced by a new appointment? Where is LOTE in the school priorities over and above a music or PE teacher, for example? Whose expertise is being challenged when there are pronouncements that a LOTE can be taught and taught well in ways compatible with existing programmes? Whether the considerations are related to industrial issues, added stress and lack of time, or less professional development opportunities, many teachers are reluctant to reassess a way of doing things which has consolidated over time. This can be the case particularly when the trigger for such a reassessment is LOTE teaching (a notoriously low priority) and especially if it is in response to what is seen as a policy directive from on high.

Pedagogies

How is a directive to teach LOTE understood in relation to the hows and whys of marrying the teaching of LOTE with an English-language programme which centres on language immersion, a whole-school approach and integrated curriculum?

Literacy, albeit simply English literacy, is the stuff of primary schools. While the debate about phonics may still be alive and well, many schools have committed themselves to an English literacy curriculum that is underpinned by cross-curricular, experientially based approaches. How does a school like this marry LOTE provision by satellite with the existing programme? How can a staff that has a successful whole-school approach to English literacy come to terms with a LOTE programme which, almost by definition, can be nothing more than an add-on? This is particularly the case when a school has not developed a LOTE programme in the past and merely sees itself as responding to a policy initiative that it was not a party to making.

Then there are real issues of resourcing. Of course, it is possible to teach LOTE in a way that is compatible with an English literacy programme such as the one described above, particularly if the LOTE chosen is one spoken within the immediate school community. This, however, requires time for the professional development of the school staff. It requires adequate staffing, materials and time for curriculum development. In many ways this list of requirements reads more like an explanation of why it might be tempting for a school to opt instead for a token LOTE programme. This fulfils the Department of School Education requirements. It adds a dimension to a school's curriculum which many parents find attractive, particularly, those parents tempted by private schools where so-called trade languages are offered. It also allows everything else to continue as it always has.

Within many schools, issues related to cultural and linguistic diversity are not placed uppermost on teachers' agendas. In some schools, where students obviously bring with them competency in a LOTE and perhaps not English, this is understood in deficit terms framed by the lack of English rather than the competency in Vietnamese, for example. In such instances, the home background can be problematised and a compensatory rather than affirming curriculum developed. In instances where English competency is sufficient enough to mask the diversity, schools can be content to add a further layer of camouflage to such diversity by pretending that it does not exist; by teaching to the English and the mainstream, rather than teaching to the difference.

Teaching to difference

Australian society incorporates an almost unique level of ethnic and linguistic diversity within its population. Its long history of immigration and the rapid demographic shifts that resulted from post-war immigration in particular, have provided real opportunities to challenge monolingualism and monoculturalism. The role of schooling in such a process has been acknowledged. Since the late 1970s, national governments have issued policy statements about the role that education can play in maintaining this diversity and fostering a tolerance towards it (Commonwealth Education Portfolio Group, 1979). While the limitations of such policies, most commonly positioned under the rubric of multi-culturalism, have been pointed out (Jakubowicz et al., 1984; Kalantzis and Cope 1984), there is nevertheless scope to consider the advantages of the imperatives to teach to difference.

Over the years, there has been a shift away from frameworks that have constructed linguistic and ethnic diversity as disadvantage. Rather than adopt a deficit framework which sought to compensate ethnic minority students for the fact that what they brought with them to the classroom was not of the mainstream, alternative frameworks have been developed. In Victoria, these frameworks have often been encapsulated by notions of inclusive curriculum. Such attempts have been premised on the understanding that existing curriculum should value difference, not only for those students who are themselves from ethnic minorities, but for all students (Ministry of Education, 1986). All students should access images of themselves and their communities within the curriculum. This is an important way of creating a positive self-image. Moreover, students who may not share a minority location, through such a curriculum, are provided with understandings of what the world is like and of understandings that there exist multiple ways of doings things, expressing things and valuing things. Importantly, such a curriculum is an important means of combating racism (Troyna, 1993).

In broad terms, what is required is a shift of understanding which challenges the privileging of monolingualism and monoculturalism within the culture of the school – within the staff room, the council meeting room and the classroom. There exist other ways of doing things, seeing things, describing things and understanding things which are linked to perspectives and languages that are not mainstream. All students benefit from exposure to these and this can be done in ways integrated within the whole-school curriculum. All students can be exposed to more than one (or two) languages and cultures. In everyday ways, mainstream Australian institutional practice still favours the misunderstanding that cultural difference is a problem. Schooling is an important form of this institutional practice and can challenge the privileging of monolingualism and monoculturalism within Australian society.

TEACHING TO DIFFERENCE: AN EXEMPLAR

Background

Exemplar Primary School is a suburban school in Melbourne. The population of the school could be described as a slice of society with various cultural and socioeconomic locations represented. Demographically it is similar to the school discussed earlier.

Recent school principals have believed passionately in the developmental learning model. Children come to school with enormously varied experience, backgrounds and expectations and school programmes should match these needs and expectations. At the school, this view is applied to academic, physical, social and emotional learning. As teachers, the question we need to consider is 'Why do we organise schools in the way we do, when we know so much about difference?' We know that children learn much from interacting with each other, particularly in families, and that younger children model and learn from older children and older children help and teach younger children while learning much themselves from the experience.

In order to address these issues Exemplar Primary School has been organised with students grouped according to needs within multi-age structures. Over the years, these structures have been modified and changed to respond to student, teacher and community needs and ideas.

Curriculum

In terms of curriculum, there are benefits in this multi-age structure. The staff is committed to the provision of an integrated curriculum, based on the principles of developmental learning, social integration, cross-age tutoring, mixed ability and flexible student groupings. The teachers strive to provide a balanced curriculum across the Eight Key Learning Areas, always planning for the development of critical thinking and problem-solving, communication and negotiation skills. The approach is student-centred, with hands-on activity-based learning a common characteristic. Teachers plan units and themes together and negotiate the learning with the children. Literacy and numeracy acquisition and development are the building blocks and tools for their learning.

The curriculum is organised around themes that are negotiated with students. So while teachers may start with what students already know, this is extended to what they wish to know in ways that incorporate the Key Learning Areas. Priority is given to open-ended themes that are capable of accommodating understandings of diversity. For example, approached in this way, a theme such as 'Neighbours' can extend beyond the people who live next door to include Australia's Asian neighbours.

Through the school structure and pedagogic approaches, difference does not become a way of categorising students but rather something that is celebrated through a range of curriculum contexts. An exemplar of this approach is the school's LOTE programme. Here the LOTE that is taught is integral to the school community – it is one of, if not the main, community language. LOTE has a long history at the school and is taught in a way that dovetails neatly with the existing integrated curriculum approach. The school operates a programme that combines the enjoyment of art, craft and design with LOTE learning. It is premised on the understanding that language is best taught and learnt in a meaningful context. As a result, teacher instructions and student responses and requests, whenever possible, are made in the LOTE. In this way, subjects that students enjoy are being used to motivate and stimulate the language-learning process.

Clearly, there is much being done at Exemplar Primary School that is premised on the value of difference, including ethnic and linguistic difference. However, key staff will readily admit that, increasingly, issues related to this linguistic and ethnic difference are being crowded off their agendas. Two reasons are identified for this state of affairs. One relates to the changing nature of the school population. Like the other primary school described above, Exemplar Primary School is in an area rapidly becoming gentrified. As a result, the cultural difference made obvious by newly arrived, non-English-speaking immigrants is being replaced by less obvious forms. Second, there are the policy imperatives faced by such schools to become self-managing and, some would argue, entrepreneurial. In this climate, there is less time and probably less incentive to value diversity.

Schools of the Future and teaching to difference

The concept of the self-managing school, which is at the heart of the Schools of the Future programme, brings with it a range of new responsibilities for school principals. It has been argued that, rather than devolving authority to school communities, Schools of the Future has reinforced a hierarchical relationship between schools and the centre and placed the school principal in the invidious position of being a line manager with dual accountability – to the centre, with all the responsibility that this entails, and to a school council constituted with parents in the majority. Increasingly, there is a separation between curriculum and administration, with more pressure being placed on principals and teachers who aspire to promotion to be expert in management rather than curriculum (Brown and Angus, 1995).

This move has been consolidated by a shift away from school-based curriculum development to a model that is centralised. This is exemplified by the Curriculum and Standards Framework, and in Victoria through accountability measures associated with this, such as the Learning Assessment Project.

Whether in relation to administration, curriculum or assessment, Victorian school principals and teachers are being asked to account for their practice in ways that many of them find overly time-consuming and sometimes intrusive and an assault on their professionalism. All this is in the context of increased class sizes, a reduction to many of the regional support structures and a reorientation to professional development programmes which have left many teachers bemoaning the loss of many of their previous supports.

What are the implications of such changes for teaching to ethnic and linguistic difference? Beyond LOTE and ESL, there is no direct reference to cultural difference within the Eight Key Learning Areas. While it is important for understandings related to cultural difference to be integrated into the Key Learning Areas, in most cases this requires an understanding that this is possible and desirable and support in order to do so. Previously, centralised and regional support and consultancy staff existed to provide school staff with professional development and curriculum support in this area. Much of this support is no longer available in the same ways. Consequently, teachers with an interest in these issues have to actively seek such support. In a situation where teachers are faced with an increasingly centralised curriculum structure, where they are under pressure to account to the centre and to school councils which may be constituted quite narrowly, will they have the opportunity to consider the merits and implementation requirements of a curriculum programme that works against the grain of so much that is now taken to be the stuff of schooling?

Conclusion

In a school like Exemplar Primary School, the diversity of the school community is valued in explicit and implicit ways. However, teaching to cultural difference is being crowded off the agenda because of the imperatives that are part of the new policy context. Additionally, ethnic and linguistic differences are now less obvious within the immediate school community. There are issues worth exploring in relation to the visibility of ethnic and linguistic difference. First, there are the limitations of a commonly made association between the need to teach to cultural difference and an obviously ethnically and linguistically diverse school population. Such an association can translate into a compensatory curriculum premised on the notion of disadvantage, that is, a curriculum that concentrates on what students do not have rather than on the skills that students do have and how these can be expanded. While it is important for all students to speak English, it is also important for teachers to acknowledge that students who lack English also have an alternative set of linguistic skills which can be built on. Similarly, in relation to cultural difference, it is important for a curriculum to be developed that is inclusive of a set of alternative understandings. Instead of seeking to compensate 'different' students for their cultural and linguistic diversity, a curriculum should introduce, incorporate and value cultural and linguistic diversity in ways that are meaningful to the entire school population.

Second, there needs to be some consideration of why, in a country like Australia, where cultural and linguistic diversity are such a historic fact of life, teaching to this reality is so readily crowded off school agendas, even in the current policy context. Australia stands as an example of a successful immigration programme. In relation to the scope of this programme, the demographic shifts that are its result and the relative ease with which this has translated itself into cohesive citizenship, Australian multi-culturalism stands almost as a unique example of success. In part, this has been due to the emphasis that has been placed on education and its potential to foster tolerance, to combat racism and to provide affirmation of minority languages and cultures. The step of targeting the entire population in spreading these understandings needs to be confirmed. The challenge that faces us now is in relation to the children and grandchildren of immigrant parents. These students have the potential to form the backbone of a cultural shift which allows bicultural identifications to come to the fore. Through them Australia may reap the benefits of previous education policies which stressed the benefits of diversity and challenged notions of assimilation.

In the current policy context, the issue becomes one of whether teaching to difference is better served by a policy climate that emphasises school-based curriculum development relative to one that stresses centralised curriculum frameworks and accompanying accountability measures. If we are to judge this question in relation to the Victorian experience and compare the 1980s where the centre issued policy guidelines to be interpreted by school communities with access to regional professional development and curriculum support, or the 1990s where schools are required to implement curriculum imperatives with relatively little practical support, it would seem that there is less opportunity and less incentive to consider the educational advantages of teaching to difference.

The professional terrain that teachers are allowed to traverse is becoming increasingly narrow. Their sense of curriculum expertise is threatened by demands placed on them to account for their practice in relation to externally determined demands, be they those imposed by the centre, the principal or the council. A range of issues exist that threaten their goodwill, their inclination and their capacity to be creative and expert in directions that move outside an increasingly restricted curriculum domain. Even if one were to imagine a set of centrally determined imperatives to account for linguistic and ethnic diversity, what chance is there of these being implemented successfully? If the LOTE example is anything to go by, there is an almost natural resistance within schools accustomed to making curriculum decisions in-house which works against the creation of the goodwill required for this type of change. Top-down policy imperatives are unlikely to create attitudinal shifts. The merits of teaching to difference are less obvious than the merits of English-language literacy or numeracy. There is a lot of cultural baggage embedded within Australian society which provides little support for notions such as multi-lingualism and multi-culturalism. Asking teachers, most of whom are themselves reared in such traditions, to make the attitudinal shifts required, needs to be negotiated carefully and with adequate support and resourcing.

NOTE

The teachers and principals who were interviewed for this chapter and with whom discussions took place wished to remain anonymous. In order to respect this request, schools described are amalgams and have fictitious names.

REFERENCES

Brown, L. and Angus, L. (1995) 'Reconstructing teacher professionalism: curriculum in Victoria's Schools of the Future', paper presented at ACSA conference, University of Melbourne.

Commonwealth Education Portfolio Group (1979) *Commonwealth Education Portfolio Discussion Paper on Education in a Multicultural Australia*, Canberra: AGPS.

Jakubowicz, A., Morrissey, M. and Palser, J. (1984) *Ethnicity, Class and Social Policy in Australia*, University of New South Wales: Social Welfare Research Centre.

Kalantzis, M. and Cope, B. (1984) 'Multiculturalism and education policy', in

G. Bottomley and M. de Lepervanche (eds) *Ethnicity, Class and Gender in Australia*, Sydney: Allen & Unwin.

Lo Bianco, J. (1987) *National Policy on Languages*, Canberra: Commonwealth Department of Education, AGPS.

Minister of Education (1985) *Ministerial Papers 1–6*, Victoria: Ministry of Education.

—— (1986) *Education in, and for, a Multicultural Society: Policy Guidelines for School Communities*, Victoria: Ministry of Education.

—— (1989) *Victoria Languages Action Plan*, Victoria: Ministry of Education.

NACCME (1987) *Education in and for a Multicultural Society: Issues and Strategies for Policy Making*, Canberra: AGPS.

Ozolins, U. (1993) *The Politics of Language in Australia*, Melbourne: Cambridge University Press.

State Board of Education/MACMME (1985) *The Place of Languages Other Than English in Victorian Schools*, Victoria: Ministry of Education.

Terry, L. (1989) *'We Are Ready to Give Our Views': A Ministerial Discussion Paper on Non-English Speaking Background Parent Participation in Victorian Government Schools*, Melbourne: Victorian Ethnic Affairs Commission.

Troyna, B. (1993) *Racism and Education: Research Perspectives*, Buckingham: Open University Press.

Tsolidis, G. (1993a) 'Difference and identity: a feminist debate indicating directions for the development of a transformative curriculum', in L. Yates (ed.) *Feminism and Education: Melbourne Studies in Education*, Bundoora: La Trobe University Press.

—— (1993b) 'Re-envisioning multiculturalism within a feminist framework', *Journal of Intercultural Studies* 14, 2: 1–12.

Yates, L. (1987) 'Does "all students" include girls? A discussion of recent policy, practice and theory', *Australian Education Researcher* 15, 1: 41–57.

Chapter 10

The gender-responsive classroom

Judith Gill and Jill Heylen

INTRODUCTION

In 1987 the National Policy for the Education of Girls was launched, the culmination of nearly two decades of attention to gender-based inequity in schooling outcomes. Much of the initial work was based on the identification of girls as educationally disadvantaged, a position that is in itself problematic (Yates, 1993). By the 1990s the orientation has changed to an examination of the ways in which gender operates in schools to the detriment of both boys and girls in educational experience and post-school options. Many of the arguments that were used to present the case for girls needing special treatment in education have been recycled by the 'boys and education' lobby. Consequently the popular press has carried many articles focusing on gender as a fundamental educational divide, either operating for the boys or for the girls but inevitably biased towards one or the other. This chapter investigates these tensions within the context of one Australian primary school.

From the considerable literature that addresses the issue of gender and educational practice there can be at least one safe generalisation, namely that discussions of gender always need to be located within particular social and historical contexts and that pedagogical practice needs to take account of such contexts if it is to be successful. In this chapter we will attempt to describe one primary school setting and one teacher's efforts to develop teaching approaches which both take account of the gendered awarenesses that the students bring to the task of learning and, in cases where such awarenesses are counterproductive to successful learning and/or to the maintenance of a safe and happy school environment, to transcend them. While the setting of this particular school may be different in some important aspects from that of other Australian primary schools in terms of its socio-economic background, its ethnic mix, its non-urban location, its size and its level of staff expertise, we hope that in setting out our account, readers will find some points of comparison and some possibilities for rethinking educational practice.

SETTING THE SCENE

In many ways Mylor Primary School can be seen as both an idyllic and archetypal Australian primary school. Located in a small town in the gently rolling Adelaide hills, the old stone schoolhouse in its delightful bushland setting would be replicated in countless rural schools around the country and yet Mylor is only some 25 minutes away from the city centre. The original stone building, which dates from 1892, still stands by itself with its high ceilings and long sash windows which proclaim its Victorian school-days origins – the ghosts of past principals and their 80-odd pupils sitting in ranks can be felt around the now brightly coloured library which, along with the Reception/Year 1 classroom, is located in the old building. The adjacent schoolyard contains several large portable buildings (particularly familiar to South Australian schools) which house the three other classes, i.e. Years 2/3, 4/5 and 6/7. There is a separate science room, a language room (dedicated to the learning of Indonesian and decorated accordingly) and a music room.

Altogether the school caters for around 100 students; its numbers have been stable at around this figure for many years. The buildings are set within a sloping site which contains several grassy stretches, many splendid gum trees, a creek bed, a sand area and two 'adventure play-ground' facilities, some paved areas and a roofed area for sheltered play, assemblies and wet lunchtimes. The orientation is perhaps less than clearly planned; like so many schools of its era there was evidently a time at which it grew like topsy, spawning outbuildings and portables to cope with the division into smaller classes. The general effect is pleasant and more homey than that encountered in some of the purpose-planned school layouts of more recent times.

In terms of its social setting Mylor Primary School draws students from the local hills community which encompasses parents who are reasonably well off and others who are struggling. Around 30 per cent of the students are recipients of the means-tested school card whereby their books are provided by the school. This is slightly lower than the average for South Australian (SA) schools (currently 46 per cent). The students are predominantly Anglo-Celtic in origin, so much so that the observer can feel as though in a time warp – surely this school is more typical of schooling in an earlier era than of Australian public education in the late 1990s? And yet, as we shall see, there are other features of this school that locate it clearly in its late twentieth-century setting, not the least of which are the attitudes, both official and unofficial, of parents, teachers and students with respect to gender.

As befits the school size, staff numbers are small – four full-time teachers, several of whom have multiple roles, e.g. the language teacher is also the Year 4/5 teacher, and the principal, Jill Heylen, teaches classes (five half days per week). Jill relishes the opportunity to interact with the children as their teacher as well as their principal and it is immediately evident that she is known to the children on this level too – she is theirs just as much as they are hers. There are several fractional appointments, e.g. the librarian is at Mylor three half days per week, the Year 2/3 class is shared between two part-time teachers, the choral and musical instrument teachers see a large number of students each week and there are also some private tutors who teach music and dance.

There is an active parents group which helps in the school in a range of ways – it appears that in this hills community there are many mothers who do not have paid work outside the house and are prepared to give considerable time and energy to assist in their children's schooling. Again this feature may be different from that of other schools and again there are interesting gender implications for the running of a school in which persons in authority, i.e. teachers, principal, library staff, support officers and parent helpers are very largely female. A particular feature of the mothers' involvement in the running of the school has been that they are often in positions that would once have been reserved for males, e.g. one mother is the chair of the school council, and another very active and visible group of women take responsibility for the landscaping and grounds. Fathers' involvement is more likely to be in evening meetings although there have been some instances in recent years of individual fathers having a good deal to do with the daily life of the school, as in the computer installation, to be discussed in a later section.

Jill Heylen is in her sixth year as principal at Mylor Primary School. She had worked as deputy principal at a neighbouring hills school for some years and is committed to the concept of small schools integrally related to their communities. A recurring point at issue in discussions with parents at Mylor has been a concern, raised by a small group of mothers, at the lack of male involvement in the official school positions (Jill won the position, replacing a male principal who retired after seventeen years at Mylor). In dealing with this concern Jill takes time to describe to these parents the breadth of the school's range of curriculum offerings and in particular her own involvement in the promotion of physical education and sporting activities with all the students. There is no way that any students at Mylor miss out on science or computers or are less involved with football or other sports as a consequence of the all-female staff. However, the idea that boys need 'a male role model' appears to have gained some currency, albeit ill defined, in some sections of the parent community. This situation appears to render the principal's position as somewhat defensive – one cannot help but wonder whether, if the situation were reversed and there was an all-male teaching staff, there would be similar charges concerning the lack of female appropriate models. Mylor is an Australian school of the 1990s and gender operates here as an issue, a site of potential controversy, just as it continues to do in the wider society.

TALKING GENDER: POLICY AND PRACTICE

South Australian public education has long been committed to the development of strategies to promote gender equity in schools. There are sexual,
gender and racial harassment policies which all schools are expected to
follow. Through the 1980s most SA schools included a position (or a fractional part of a position) dedicated to promoting equal opportunity (EO) in
the school – often this person was understood as centrally concerned with
the education of girls. There have been numerous debates about whether or
not the setting up of specialist positions was productive of widespread
change. Suffice it to note here that by the 1990s SA schools have been beset
with industrial and economic concerns and while the previous emphasis on
gender equity has not faded, it has been incorporated into a more general
commitment to equity and social justice. Currently the urgent issues facing
schools have more to do with survival in times of economic stringency and
management of the implementation of National Curriculum; in this environment the gender issue appears to be less of a focus than previously.

Mylor Primary School does not have its own policy on gender. In Jill's
view, the provision of equal opportunity is the responsibility of all staff and
gender equity forms one of the totally accepted and taken-for-granted philosophical commitments of the school and of all the teachers. Equity is
identified as a core value of the school in its promotional literature. There is
written school policy on issues such as sexual harassment and student
behaviour management and these matters are interwoven with gender
justice. During our initial discussions about this chapter, Jill commented
thoughtfully:

> I guess we don't necessarily talk about gender issues much lately . . . we
> sort of assume a commitment to gender justice and almost take for
> granted that girls and boys should have equal access to what the school
> offers. . . . I think all the teachers would agree with that.

What we established was that while Mylor held copies of the official policy
relating to girls and education and the National Action Plan, the dimensions of this work were considered to be widely understood and accepted.
However, on closer questioning, Jill felt that most teachers would take the
position that being fair with respect to gender meant affording similar experiences to both sexes, giving the girls the same teaching, encouragement,
access to resources as the boys, rather than seeing the gender groups with
different sets of needs and differently prepared to enter into the world of
school.

Sexual harassment appears to be rare at Mylor – Jill recalled an incident
some time ago in which a boy was calling the girls 'rude names' and the
girls had come to her to complain. The boy was brought in too and it transpired that he did not know the meaning of the word that he had been

using. When this was explained, he appeared embarrassed and crestfallen and was told that such behaviour would not be tolerated. There have not been other incidents. In this recollection Jill was pleased that the girls had known and been comfortable with following a course of action technically known as a grievance procedure and that the matter had been resolved clearly and quickly. 'It is ironic that you almost need something like this to happen so that you know you're doing all right,' she commented.

In the classroom Jill maintains her commitment to the principles of gender justice and related an incident in which she was challenged by one of the Year 5 girls for implying that a particular characteristic applied to boys only. The incident provoked an interesting discussion with the girl after class. Jill was at pains to defend herself in that all of the students of whom she had been speaking were in fact boys, but she was also keen to congratulate the girl on her alertness to the possibility of sexist assumptions and her readiness to challenge the teacher on this basis.

In the classroom research on the topic of gender one finds repeatedly that children – and many teachers – take the position that to name any group in terms of the sex of its members is being sexist. Teachers, including those at Mylor, have frequently stressed their commitment to treating the children as individuals rather than seeing them as girls or boys. However, this assertion has been seen to mask an interaction style in which gender is highly significant – the individuals in the classroom are also girls and boys and the range of suitable individualities is circumscribed by their gendered locations within it (Clark, 1990).

What is needed is an awareness that classroom practice which routinely uses sex as an organising structure supports the idea that the sexes differ in basic human potential – a position that is sexist. However, to fail to recognise someone as girl or boy would appear to be erring on the other side. Young children recognise gender as an organising feature of their experience of the world – to pretend otherwise would mean risking the loss of credibility and respect (Davies, 1989). The sensitive and complex task for the classroom teacher becomes one of balancing a recognition of the child's importance and sense of self as a girl or a boy and an awareness of the danger of allowing such recognition to limit what the child may learn and hence the people they will become.

THE CLASSROOM BEYOND THE WALLS

A good proportion of Jill's teaching is done beyond the classroom. A fine sportswoman herself, she is committed to promoting physical coordination and the enjoyment of a range of sporting activities in all her students. Hence she organises a whole-school swimming experience for the first week of the year – all students spend this week at a neighbourhood swimming pool where they learn a range of water safety techniques and swimming strokes.

This environment offered the possibility for Jill to carry out some whole-school observations with respect to gender.

In the first week of 1996, she noticed a Year 7 girl who was put in the group of non-swimmers in which she stood out by virtue of her size and physical maturity. Last year she had succeeded in being excused from swimming and had somehow got through previous years without ever having learnt. Jill was uncomfortably aware that, had the non-swimmer been a Year 7 boy, he would likely have come in for a good deal of ridicule from his peers – and probably been given special help by the swimming teachers to overcome the problem. In the girl's case, not only was this not happening, but she was also able to adopt the role of 'helping with the little ones' and remain relatively unnoticed, until Jill devoted herself to this one student and succeeded in teaching her to float. In reviewing the incident Jill registered an acute awareness of the gender factor which had led to this student's being able to hide within gender-appropriate behaviour which meant that she had missed out on important learning. It is this dimension, the interaction between traditional gender roles and areas of knowledge, that must be the continuing focus of educational work.

The playground also forms an important arena for primary students to act out gendered roles. Mylor is a little different from the average primary school in this respect. There is no large stretch of open ground known as the oval, but rather the playground consists of a range of possible play spaces from a wild scrubby area along the creek, an adventure sandbox area, grassy slopes under shady trees, a covered area and a fair-sized rectangular stretch that the students call 'the oval'. The children seem to spread themselves around all these spaces in play groups that are usually, but not always, same sex. While the groups of girls are generally smaller than groups of boys, there is not the roving pack of boys dominating the largest playing area, a feature so typical of primary school study. There is a homeliness about the school grounds that allows for a less determined approach to activities. This year a group of Year 2 boys are preoccupied with teddies and they bring these to school and engage in mutual teddy-oriented activity during playtimes.

In a more structured way Jill takes all the classes for sports lessons at least once a week and makes sure that girls and boys are encouraged in all activities. Sometimes activities are organised in single-sex groups. Jill uses these learning sessions to concentrate on skills that each gender group may lack – large muscle activity for the girls and coordination tasks for the boys. After some experience in learning the skills of, say, basketball or soccer, the children participate in mixed games – wherein Jill notes that they tend to put themselves against same-sex opponents.

Parental involvement in community sporting activity is one area in which Jill has noted gender differences in levels of support. Mothers and fathers of boys are more likely to be involved with their son's sporting activities than with their daughter's and consequently, at Mylor, boys' sporting teams have a stronger following than those of the girls. Also more of the boys play sport than do the girls, again reflecting the gender differences within the parent community.

Wandering around the playground at Mylor the visitor will likely note that although there is some mixed play among the senior Year 6/7 students, by and large the playground groupings are same sex. The boys seem to play in larger groups than do the girls, the older ones around a ball game, the younger ones maybe in the sandpit. Previous studies of primary schooling have registered the boys as more likely to be known throughout the school than the girls, and boys' bigger public presence has been connected to their larger playgroups (Gill, 1991).

At Mylor, the children's self-chosen patterns of play – with the boys oriented around a ball game and the girls generally in smaller groups less clearly game-based – coupled with the combined classes, means that there is a good deal of cross-age interaction; in this environment some boys readily become known throughout the school. Jill commented on some hero worship existing, with some of the small boys idealising the older ones – with the same feature happening with some girls, especially the netballers, albeit to a lesser degree than with the boys. 'By the same token', Jill added, 'the girls don't take themselves nearly so seriously as do the boys – the boys actually seem to believe that they are heroes!' At school assembly girls and boys routinely take turns at speaking; while Jill says that in her view the girls are superior in their public speaking, it is important to give equal time to the boys. Once again it is a question of balance, being seen to be fair is as important as the recognition of gender difference.

INSIDE THE CLASSROOM

As a competent and experienced teacher Jill is aware of the need to ensure that public roles within the classroom are seen to be distributed fairly and not on the basis of gender. There is a good deal of rotation of tasks and each class has two student representatives, a girl and a boy. Similarly the bank monitors, who are involved in keyboarding at a level of public performance and responsibility, also comprise a girl and a boy. Talking about how this was organised, Jill commented, 'well, I think it's been that way for so long and it's seen to be fair . . . they never comment on it'.

One new area of gender sensitivity in the school involves the setting up and use of computers, and Jill is alert to the ways in which the computers can quickly become the province of boys. The story of the computer set-up at Mylor offers one example of the way in which schools are powerfully locked into the resources, attitudes and values of their communities. Initially expertise with computers and the installation of computer systems was provided by three of the fathers associated with the school. These men put in many hours assisting with the installation and developing teachers' familiarity with and confidence in the new medium. Subsequently the role of 'computer expert' fell to one of the sons who, as a consequence of his father's knowledge and interest, knew a good deal about computers too. In his final year at Mylor this lad was an invaluable help to the teachers and to the other children in using the new computers. Jill was aware of the danger of setting up the male guru and has watched closely what is now happening. Another boy who is also very familiar with the technology, but not as confident or outgoing as the first boy, also appears to be taking on the power role. Jill plans to ensure that some of the other children, including some of the girls, will increasingly share in this knowledge. Advances in educational technology will continue to provoke issues for school administrators as well as classroom teachers – there is a need for ongoing professional development in the area if schools are to be able to counter, rather than replicate, the association between technological interest and male power and control.

In terms of general classroom treatments Jill sees gender operating differently with different year levels. For example, in discussing the use of competition, she said:

> I do use competition as a motivator on occasions – after all, there's some degree of competing that goes on in whatever you find yourself doing so I don't automatically shy away from it. But yes, I agree that competition is usually a more effective motivator for most boys than for girls. But then again, when I'm teaching the Year 2/3 I'll introduce some sort of competition and they are all very keen, girls as well as boys. But then I'm always careful to arrange them in mixed groups for this sort of an activity – I'd never set up the girls against the boys routine. As they get older, in 4/5, say, or in 6/7 they respond a little less keenly to competition – certainly the girls in Year 5 aren't very keen to compete and any of the Years 6/7 are less motivated by competition than they were in 2/3 – I think they understand more about the value and benefits of cooperation. So it's a matter of balancing the way you use competition along with everything else.

When asked about the use of routines such as 'Hands up who got ten out of ten', Jill said that she did use these sorts of whole-class strategies some of the time, but always her policy was to 'start from the other end'. Thus if the exercise were out of 20 she would call for a show of hands from those with 10 or more, 11 or more, followed by 'who has improved?' In this way most of the children get to own an achievement and it is not a case of increasing embarrassment with decreasing success levels, as has traditionally been the case. This strategy also provides a public recognition of achievement for most of the children, a recognition particularly important for girls' learning.

Seating arrangements in the classrooms at Mylor vary from freely chosen tables to paired desks in rows. As Jill works across all classrooms she has developed an awareness of gendered seating patterns. In the free choice on the mat, she has noticed a tendency for the boys to place themselves to the back and sides, with the girls in the centre front position. In this arrangement the boys not only take up considerably more room than do the girls, but their distance from the teacher means that they are required to speak more loudly and forcefully to make themselves heard – and have greater opportunity to misbehave. Jill believes that seating arrangements need to vary according to the task, but she does favour a circular seating arrangement for group discussion such that the teacher position can vary within the circle and that all students are equally visible within the circle – both to the teacher and to one another. Such an arrangement precludes gender-based seating patterns in which boys are positioned more powerfully and more publicly than girls.

Discussions of gender-based oppression in schooling often include issues to do with sex and sexuality education (Szirom, 1988). In the R/1 classroom recently Jill had been confronted with a complete Ken and Barbie set, proudly brought in by its owner as part of the ubiquitous show-and-tell. Some of the children commented on the fact that Ken's pants are moulded on but Barbie may be totally undressed at will. In discussing this difference with the children and asking how they would explain it, Jill anticipated that there would be some mention of the need to hide the obvious male genitalia as compared to the more hidden female parts. However the children's explanation bore no relation to this theory – rather they opted for an explanation about the difficulty of fitting and fastening male trousers whereas Barbie's more flexible gear is amenable to Velcro fasteners! Jill offered this anecdote as an example of the way in which teachers can become preoccupied with getting the gender thing right and, in so doing, complicate things for themselves unnecessarily.

By contrast, when talking with the Year 4/5 Jill noticed some giggling at the mention of menstruation and decided to clear away any embarrassment or half knowledge by giving full information on female reproduction and the necessary role of menstruation. In part, her rationale was that the prevalence of TV commercials for feminine hygiene products made it unlikely that the area would be totally unknown to any of the children and she believes that it is important for boys as well as girls to know the facts. In the ensuing discussion Jill felt that she had all the class interested and attentive and willing participants – no longer a giggling matter! And she commented later:

> And you know this sort of thing [reference to sex or sexuality] can come up any time within the context of the primary school. I think it is enormously important for women and men teachers to deal with such matters as honestly and openly as possible, because somehow it's behind a lot of the confusion about gender for children.

Relatedly, when asked if she thought that girls and boys should learn about gender oppression in the wider society including facts about women's exploitation in the paid workforce and the higher suicide rate of young males, as has been suggested (Gilbert cited in MCEETYA, 1995), Jill felt that such things were inappropriate for the primary school – 'they haven't really got the concept of how their neighbourhood fits into the wider world, they're certainly not ready for those larger social understandings'. It seems that the blanket term 'inclusive curriculum' – a familiar feature of gender policy – is too glib a commitment and one that disregards the real issues of teachers' and students' daily lives. It needs to be refined by teacher awareness of children's readiness to absorb information in meaningful ways. Curriculum content that is shaped by gender consciousness must be sensitive to cultural differences and embedded in a process that acknowledges and addresses counterperceptions.

GENDER EQUITY IN SCHOOLING: THE ONGOING CHALLENGE

The gender-responsive classroom is nurtured within the climate of a gender-responsive school. Teachers need the support of an administration that takes account of its responsibility for gender equity in structural ways and in interactions with teachers, students and parents. The work at Mylor has demonstrated the need to maintain a constant vigilance over accepted schooling practices, to see who is missing out at the swimming pool, who is taking too much time in the school assembly or the classroom. Because as primary school teachers we wish to encourage young people to settle in to the world of school, to accept the institutional structures and processes, it is particularly difficult to maintain a critical stance which disturbs this newly acquired comfort zone, which asks difficult questions about 'normal' schooling practice.

The very tenets of progressive education which so many practising teachers took on as their own, tenets that involve a belief in the self and individual expression, have been shown to facilitate and reward behaviours that are more typical of and tolerated in boys than girls (Walkerdine, 1984). To some degree a gender consciousness troubles what we have learned as good teaching practice. If we open our classrooms to self-expression and free choice, we are unwittingly encouraging behaviours that are profoundly gendered. Surely the answer is not to be found in a reversal to the more strict norms of classroom management of an earlier era. Rather, solutions must be generated in terms of the particularities of each classroom encounter. Changes in gender relations both at home and in the workplace are to be a significant feature of life in Australia in the twenty-first century, and schooling must take responsibility for preparing students to enter that differently ordered world.

A final word from Jill and her teachers:

At Mylor we are fortunate to be a small school in which all of our children are known and valued. We are committed to developing in our children a mutual respect that celebrates community and recognises difference. Responding to gender issues is an essential part of this recognition and working for gender equity is a central feature of this respect.

REFERENCES

Clark, M. (1990) *The Great Divide: The Construction of Gender in the Primary School*, Carlton: CDC.

Davies, B. (1989) *Frogs and Snails and Feminist Tales*, Sydney: Allen & Unwin.

Gill, J. (1991) 'Differences in the making: the construction of gender in Australian schooling', unpublished PhD thesis, Adelaide University.

MCEETYA (1995) *Gender Equity: A Framework for Australian Schools*, Canberra: Ministerial Committee for Education, Employment and Youth Affairs.

Szirom, T. (1988) *Teaching Gender : Sex Education and Sexual Stereotypes*, Sydney: Allen & Unwin.

Walkerdine, V. (1984) 'Developmental psychology and the child-centred pedagogy: the insertion of Piaget into early education', in J. Henriques, W. Hollway, C. Urwin, C. Venn and V. Walkerdine (eds) *Changing the Subject*, London: Methuen.

Yates, L. (1993) *The Education of Girls: Policy, Research and the Question of Gender*, Hawthorn: ACER.

Theme III

Classroom practice

Chapter 11

What is being learned here?

Trends in assessment and reporting

Susan Groundwater-Smith and Vivienne White

INTRODUCTION

We are starting this chapter with a question for ourselves: *What would we want to say to primary school teachers and administrators about assessment and reporting in the context of social justice?* In other words, what are the key ideas that we are working with and how do we make them explicit for our readers? This chapter is the result of the conversations that we have had over several years regarding the ways in which teachers might best work to support student learning; Vivienne is coordinator of the National Schools Network and Susan is a tertiary teacher educator. Both of us have had extensive experience in working in primary classrooms and know how complex and challenging that work can be. We are also well aware, nationally, of policy trends in assessment and reporting from both systems' and parents' perspectives.

Our first premise is that any assessment work that teachers do is fair, ethical and transparent. That is, we work in honourable ways and make the reasons for our judgements available to learners. It is not enough to award a mark, or determine a level, or tick a box; our students need to know on what grounds decisions are made about the quality and progress of their learning. We need to interact with them in such a way that they know what is going on and why it is going on. This holds equally true for their parents and guardians.[1]

We are also concerned that assessment and reporting should be connected to the 'real work' of the classroom, not developed as a series of discrete tasks. We have to build into the daily work of the classroom ways in which we can find evidence for student learning, ways that are also available to the students themselves. To be effective we need to begin by asking assessment questions. What is it that we want our students to have learned and why? And how will we, teachers and students alike, know what kind of learning has occurred? For undoubtedly, learning is happening all the time, not all of which is intended.

Consider this interview with Nancy Mohr, principal of University

Heights High School in the Bronx, by Jane Figgis, reporter for the Radio National Education Report (29 November 1995).[2]

> And a lot of that [school reform] did come out of our work in assessment, which started by looking at what we wanted our students to be able to know and do. And bit by bit, that changed the curriculum, that changed the instruction, that changed the whole structure of the school. They work on projects, all day. Those projects incorporate the various subject areas but are not really labelled as such.
>
> And they have a construction which always consists of the three simple questions: the first one is 'what' – 'what did I do'; the next one is 'so what' – 'what does it mean, what does it mean to me, what does it mean to the rest of the world'; and the third question is 'now what' – 'what are the implications for further study for me, what are the implications for society', or whatever it is that they're looking at.
>
> And these questions apply, whatever it is that they've learned. And the question is, 'Is this work good enough for the next step, or the next benchmark'.

Here is an instance of assessment being built into curriculum design. The project work of the students is substantial, integrated and open to public defence. Assessment is of both process and product.

Another concern underlying our discussion is the matter of 'high stakes assessment'. Unquestionably there is a trend for school systems to be gathering information about student learning for purposes that go beyond the classroom. State-wide testing is now common throughout Australia; also in some states there is selection for specific classes, such as those for gifted and talented students and nominated secondary schools. Students and their parents equally need to be informed of the purpose of such assessment and the stakes that are involved. Even during the primary years of schooling the stakes may be high.

In summary, any assessment and reporting must be to improve and inform. The two actions are interactive and cyclical and they assume that teachers and children are both engaged in the learning going on in the classroom.[3] Assessing learning means being analytic. Children, when asked to, are well able to talk and write about their learning in insightful and constructive ways; this is a matter to which we shall return later. Improvement is not only related to student learning; it is also a fundamental goal for us as teachers as we go about improving our provisions for learning in the classroom. Sound assessment and reporting practices give us feedback on our own professional work.

Good teaching is hard work. Teachers are making decisions about student learning, on a daily basis, at furious pace. Is Max able to hear, sitting over there? Can Adnan understand enough spoken English to know what he needs to do next? Judy has finished early; will she go over to the quiet reading corner or is it better that she helps her friend who is having quite a struggle with the work? Mona's team have done a great job investigating the tadpole life cycle; would this be a good moment to stop everyone and celebrate their achievement with some words of praise? Have I time to sit down with Lin Lin and discuss her writing progress?

Even after the children have left there is more to be done. Organisation of learning for future days and months means that teachers have to consider what students already can do, make and know and what will be appropriate for further development. Evening meetings are undertaken with parents to map progress and to provide them with evidence of achievements. Discussions need to be conducted to find ways for providing appropriate assistance for those who need it as well as possibilities for extension and enrichment. These are challenging responsibilities for both classroom teachers and school administrators.

In this chapter it is our intention to recognise the complexity and challenge of good teaching and management and recommend that we take the adage 'do less, better' as a focus for making decisions about which strategies to adopt and to what purpose.

Each of the key ideas outlined here will be discussed more fully in the chapter. But first we think it essential that we consider the current context for assessment and reporting in Australian primary schools; what are the prevailing policies and how are they affecting work in this area? Our first consideration is in relation to the perspectives of parents.

NATIONAL PARENT CONSENSUS ON ASSESSMENT AND REPORTING PRACTICES

The education of young people is not the exclusive domain of the schooling system. At its best it is the result of a constructive partnership between home and school. Parents are the first educators of their children. It is under their tutelage that children learn their first words, take their first steps, play and interact with others. Parents have a different relationship with their children than teachers do with their students. Parents are deeply concerned about what and how their children are learning. Not all parents feel confident about showing this regard to the school for all sorts of reasons (see, for example, Groundwater-Smith and Forster, 1994), but care they do.

As an indication of this care a project has recently been undertaken Australia-wide in which parent organisations, using a national consultative process, investigated and debated views about assessment and reporting student achievement in schools (Australian Council of State School Organisations Inc. (ACSSO) and Australian Parents Council Inc. (APC), 1996). The process was one that enabled a range of views to be collected and then discussed over several cycles. We were both able to be participants in this process and would wish to emphasise how keenly the parents, from

every state and territory, expressed their wish to see the home/school partnership enhanced in the interests of improving and celebrating student
learning.

The result was the documentation of twelve key principles for assessment
and reporting. These are outlined below:[4]

- Parents are entitled to continuing, quality information regarding their
  children's education through a variety of reporting mechanisms.
- Any form of assessment should be integral to the curriculum and
  designed to inform, support and improve learning outcomes.
- Assessment and reporting processes should make provision for parent and
  student input about teaching and learning.
- Parents and their organisations must have an active role in developing
  and implementing assessment and reporting policies and processes at the
  school, the system, the state and the nation.
- Schools, systems and governments, state and federal, must make explicit
  and public the purposes for which they wish to collect assessment data.
- Assessment data must not be used for the purpose of establishing and
  publishing competitive judgements about schools/systems/states or territories.
- Parents must be informed by all those who seek such data about student
  performance, of the uses to which such information will be put.
- Data collected from students in schools should be used in accordance with
  its stated purposes. Any other subsequent uses should be specifically
  negotiated.
- Individual student assessments are confidential to the student, his/her
  parents and appropriate school staff.
- Parents have the right to withdraw their children from specific system,
  state-wide and national testing.
- Assessment data for state-wide or national purposes should be collected
  by statistically valid, light sampling procedures only.
- Appropriate appeal mechanisms should be established and made public to
  protect the rights of students and parents in matters of student assessment and reporting at the school, state and national level.

(ACSSO and APC, 1996: 6)

These principles reflect a number of parent concerns. The first of these is that
of the goal of improvement, an issue that we have already discussed above.
The second is in relation to developing an authentic partnership for learning.
It is believed that there is insufficient recognition of the range and variety of
information that parents themselves have of their children's experiences: life
histories; health; relationships; likes and dislikes; accomplishments and
worries. Too often they are told of their children's progress in school with no
reference to the wealth of knowledge that they may also offer about their out-
of-school experiences. Schools are now attempting to redress this by

including opportunities in school reports for parents to provide written comments and feedback which go well beyond a mere acknowledgement that they have read the report. As well, people are providing time during parent–teacher interviews to listen and probe what it is that parents may have to say about their children's experiences and the ways in which they may discuss their school work at home.

The third concern is to do with the provision of transparent, quality information. Parents are not looking for summative judgements, nor for evasions. They want to know how their children are performing at school, across the Key Learning Areas, and ways in which the school intends to support and develop learning outcomes. Information needs to be grounded in sound evidence which is available to the parents. Portfolios of learning are seen as documents which may include work samples, photographs, descriptions of class programmes and so on. They need to be vital and focused. After all, as Wylie (1994) indicates, parents will find other sources of information for themselves, if they are not adequately advised. What children bring home in the way of homework, notes and finished projects, becomes the evidence: 'Parents' most regular source of knowledge about their child's progress is what comes home in the school bag' (p. 1) .

At the same time parents do want some basis for interpreting information. They believe that by jointly analysing and discussing learning with their children and their children's teachers they will come to a better understanding of what is being achieved and the ways in which difficulties might be addressed. They also do want some benchmarks: not so much in relation to place in class, but at least as an indication of whether learning is progressing at the rate that one might expect of that particular age cohort.

Paramount to parents' concerns is the wellbeing of their children. They do not want to see their children's confidence and sense of self-worth eroded and they do want to genuinely understand what is going on. Sometimes it is believed in schools that parents' non-appearance at various events signals a lack of interest in their children. Very few parents are not interested and caring about their children, but many are alienated because of their own school histories, lack of English, or the educational language used, which seems clear to us, as education professionals, but which is perceived as bureaucratic jargon by others. Sadly, it is still the case that some teachers' judgements may be affected by their perceptions of their students' social class, the ways in which they dress and speak (Filer, 1993).

These all tend to be individual family concerns. At the same time ACSSO and APC are peak organisations for parent bodies in every Australian state and territory. Parent bodies are also concerned with policy. They argue that government policies in education, particularly in relation to assessment, are made without sufficient reference to parents themselves. Employer and media representations of schooling are more likely to drive an agenda that leads to particular forms of state-wide testing and the possibility of placing schools in competition with each other based upon results of such testing, than parents' needs themselves. Hence a number of the principles make reference to the purposes of government assessment policies and practices and the role that parents should play in determining such purposes.

Clearly, then, parent policies are essential in the consideration of assessment and reporting. We have foregrounded them, because too often they are seen to come well behind the policies determined by state and federal governments. Nevertheless government policy is critical to any discussion regarding assessment and reporting and should be addressed.

GOVERNMENT POLICY IN ASSESSMENT AND REPORTING: NATIONAL TRENDS

The last decade in Australia has seen unprecedented cooperation between states and territories in the development of curriculum and assessment frameworks. Ministers of education from across Australia have agreed to the development of a series of curriculum statements in the areas of the arts, health and physical education, mathematics, studies of society and environment, English, languages other than English, and science and technology. Statements are designed to define the area and outline its essential components. They convey what is distinctive about the area and nominate a sequence for developing skills and knowledge. Accompanying the statements are profiles which are designated as descriptions of the progression of learning outcomes typically achieved by students in each area of learning. National statements and profiles have been taken up variously by the states. Some, such as Western Australia and the Australian Capital Territory, have, in practical terms, adopted them intact. Others, such as New South Wales, have sought to make them commensurable with existing and developing syllabus frameworks. In any case it is unarguable that the orientation is towards an outcomes-based education model.

Outcomes-based education is seen, nationally, to have significant merit in that the goals are explicit and clear. It is linked to processes of continuous improvement and quality assurance (Rowe, 1994). Also, the strategy is seen to take account of student diversity, but to hold high expectations that ultimately almost all students are capable of high levels of performance, given time and resources.

A prime advocate of outcomes-based education has been William Spady. He argues:

An outcome is a culminating demonstration of the entire range of learning experiences and capabilities that underlie it. It occurs in a performance context that directly influences what it is and how it is carried out. The word 'based' means to direct, define, derive, determine, focus and organise what we do according to the substance and nature of the learning result that we want to have happen at the end.

(Spady, 1993:5)

He sees that by naming the learning outcomes the destination is clear; however, the route towards them may vary, depending upon the students' abilities and aptitudes. It is the culminating achievement that counts rather than the time taken to reach it. This strips out some of the normative expectations that all students will move lock-step at the same rate. Spady sees that there are three different responses to outcomes-based education: traditional, where existing curriculum statements are restated in outcomes terms; transitional, where some attention is paid to curriculum rethinking; and transformational, where focus is given to life-long learning in a changing world with an emphasis upon generic higher order competencies.

Eltis (1995) claims that the ways in which New South Wales has taken national frameworks and melded them with the state's syllabuses is an example of a traditional response. There is little evidence in other states or territories that any initiatives have gone beyond the transitional. It is interesting to speculate that the key competencies drive, while deriving from an investigation of the post-compulsory years of schooling, does have the potential to be of a transformational kind. Dellit (1993) suggests that the key competencies, which would overlay the learning areas to form a learning matrix, are skills and knowledge in operation:

These are useful skills and knowledge. . . . They are highlighted as student attributes and should be developed. There are rare teachers who embark on teaching self-organisation and management, team working skills, communication skills and so on within the curriculum content of their teaching. Yet before the release of the Mayer discussion papers, there was little if any systematic recognition of the importance of *teaching* these skills.

(Dellit, 1993:59)

There can be no doubt that the trend to outcomes-based education as a government policy initiative has a second effect also; that is, that teachers and schools can be held more accountable for student learning. Hence the related trend to state-wide testing. The British experience, which closely linked the national curriculum to national assessment, is a clear demonstration of this. (For a case study of this link see Groundwater-Smith and White, 1995, ch. 11). Linking teacher accountability to student learning outcomes has an appeal for governments who have a liking for displacing their own accountability in terms of educational resources and professional development and placing the responsibility on the shoulders of teachers and school administrators, who are often working under the most difficult of conditions.

ETHICS AND ASSESSMENT

We would argue that teacher accountability is of an ethical kind. Teachers have an ethical responsibility to work in ways that enhance their students' wellbeing and advance their opportunities to learn to become well-integrated, functional members of a caring and compassionate society. Similarly, they have an ethical responsibility to parents to keep them informed of their children's successes and difficulties so that a sound learning partnership may be maintained. It is for these reasons that teachers and school administrators need to think carefully about ways in which they might improve their assessment practices.

While it is not within the scope of this chapter to outline the many ways in which schools might go about developing more authentic assessment procedures, we do believe it appropriate to pay attention to a range of innovations that are exercising the educational imagination and to derive from them some significant understandings which might be used in policy-making at the local level.

MEETING THE CHALLENGE

An important development for schools has been the recent emphasis upon notions of constructivism. Children make meaning of their world irrespective of the intervention of schooling. In other words they are active, rational learners. 'Accumulating evidence suggests that children's natural learning during the pre-school years is impressive and that youngsters should be recognised as remarkably competent active learners with an ability to learn rationally in natural settings' (McNamara, 1994: 35).

This insight, while apparently simple, has important consequences. If we accept that children *are* learning all of the time, then the objective for the teacher is to find out *what* and *how* they are learning. Assessment practices need to investigate the actual learning itself. In the past too much emphasis has been placed upon what has been in the teacher's mind rather than what is in the learner's mind. Taking a constructivist approach means that there must be space for teacher's to co-investigate learning with the learner. We might call this 'having a learning conversation'. What makes for a good learning conversation? We would argue that principally there must be a condition of mutual regard between teacher and learner, a capacity to hear each other out and to support each other in trying to develop interpersonal understanding.

This mutuality lies behind the design of the Australian Council for Educational Research's *Assessment Resource Kit* (*ARK*) (Forster and Masters, 1996) which has as its focus developmental assessment.[5] The principal motif used by the Australian Council for Educational Research is the progress map; this is consistent with the statements and profiles now currently in use in Australian curriculum design. Using the descriptors provided by the statements and profiles, a developmental map can be constructed and the learners' progress documented. In order to place learner's achievements on the map it is essential that teachers and learners engage in sustained interactions. Among the resources provided, the *Kit* will contain handbooks on portfolios, performance assessment and project assessment. We shall briefly consider each of these, bearing in mind ways in which both teacher and learner may contribute.

Portfolios are carefully collected selections of evidence. They may be working portfolios, whose principal audience is the student, and are formative and diagnostic in nature; or they may be documentary in nature, in which case they are a selection and showcasing of the student's best work in a summative sense. Even so, documentary portfolios will still contain evidence of process as well as the actual product. For example, a student might include a well-crafted piece of writing and the working drafts that led to the final published account. In a primary school a working portfolio could follow a student's progress throughout the years of attendance. He or she might also have accumulated several documentary portfolios, the culminating one being that which goes on to the secondary school. The important matter to consider is how the maintenance of the portfolio should be managed so that it is part of the classroom's practices. It should not be an add-on; neither should it merely be a collection of work. The more a class teacher engages in teacher-led instruction, the less time there will be for selecting and discussing examples of work in progress. Teachers who use learning logs and journals and regularly conference with their students about the nature of their learning will find themselves quite comfortable with these ideas (cf. Stenmark, 1991; McLean and Campagna-Wildash, 1994).

PERFORMANCE AND PROJECT ASSESSMENT

Performance assessment is based upon the actual doing of the work, whether independently or as a member of a group. It focuses upon processes. These may be learning processes related to the apposite subject matter or learning processes related to being a member of a team. The conduct of performance assessment may be informal or planned. For example, a teacher may be observing athletics or gymnastics skills as the lesson progresses; or may require students to engage in a routine that is the culmination of several weeks of teaching and learning. Either way it is possible for the students themselves to be active in the observation and analysis of their learning.

Project assessment is seen by Forster and Masters (1996) to hold great promise, not only for the assessment of subject-specific knowledge, but also for assessing generic competencies such as problem-solving, information-handling and communicating. Students are encouraged to reflect upon not only what they learned, but also how they learned (Henry, 1994). It is possible to build into the project specifications a brief for students to consider how they set about the task. Again, it is a matter of connectedness, connecting the assessment to the learning in powerful ways.

Teachers and learners cannot afford to drown in assessment. It must be focused and doable. We have suggested elsewhere (Groundwater-Smith and White, 1995) that schools plan their assessment over the year. It would be possible to take literacy and numeracy as the core running throughout the year and intersect them, term by term, with specific Key Learning Areas such as human society and its environment. We encourage practitioners to build time into the day when talking about learning is a part of the learning itself. We cannot say it enough – assessment must be thoroughly embedded in the curriculum. Equally it must be embedded in the corporate thinking of the school. Staff and faculty meetings should themselves be learning conversations about curriculum and assessment processes. Sometimes it may be more appropriate to report to parents *en masse*, about assessment and reporting procedures, not in the formal school council or parent/citizen/friend meeting, but in an open forum where there is an exchange of views and ideas.

Below is a case study of a school that took as its principal focus, over a two-year period, 'How might we more authentically work with our community to assist in the learning of our students through assessment and reporting?' Claims are modest, but there is no question that the school is finding itself more and more interested in refining its principles and procedures so that school is a good workplace for students and teachers alike.

A CASE STUDY OF CHANGE: THE MALECK PEAK STUDY

Maleck Peak School is nine years old and is situated in Darwin.[6] It is adjacent to urban housing, sections of bush and a developing new housing estate. The community is a sprawling one with few facilities within walking distance. Over 30 per cent of the students are from urban Aboriginal families, with some being recent arrivals from remote and traditional communities for whom English is a second, and sometimes third, language.

A large number of families are ones under the care of a single parent, many of whom are not able to be in paid employment. The school is characterised by high mobility, with students leaving and re-enrolling in the school a number of times. Disadvantage caused by poverty is recognised by Commonwealth programmes.

For many children and their parent(s) the school is a haven. It is the site where advice is sought about parenting and social support. Clearly it is a place where teachers are working under great pressure but with commensurably great rewards.

The school has a council, but with the rapid turnover of the population there is little continuity. A great deal of help and support is needed in order to build up the skills and confidence of parents. It is in this context that the school, over the past two years, has been rethinking its reporting procedures. It has sought to address four fundamental questions:

- Why do we report?
- To whom are we reporting and for what purpose?
- What exactly are we reporting about?
- How can we make reporting reflect the value that our school community places on communication?

Using an open-door policy, the school encouraged parents to voice their concerns regarding current reporting procedures – what did they like or dislike, and why? It was clear that parents felt that school reports gave little indication of their children's learning in the fullest sense of the word.

It was resolved to develop reporting strategies that included what teachers planned as well as what students achieved; so that, for example, in science and technology it was indicated that the teachers planned that students will

- discuss what they see and suggest reasons that things will or will not work
- use what they have discovered in other situations
- conduct simple tests and describe what happens
- work with others on group tasks and cooperate to improve the solutions to problems
- design and construct
- record and present information.

The report indicated whether the student had achieved these outcomes beyond expectations, at the expected level, or working towards the expected level. Evidence was provided through a learning folder which accompanied the report. Also, extensive verbal communication supported the written report.

Teachers recorded the many forms of informal communication also undertaken. They compiled a list of the kinds of things that they discussed with parents, in school, over the fence and in the local shopping centre:

- academic achievement/progress
- sporting ability/attitude
- social interaction/development
- emotional development
- strategies for implementation of school programmes
- contribution to class goals, e.g. fund-raising, ways to make the class more productive
- possible strategies for improving behaviour/performance

- something positive that the child has achieved
- family issues/gossip . . . things that can affect behaviour
- physical/mental problems
- special interests
- review teachers' roles with parents
- review reporting processes and procedures with parents
- ways in which parents can support learning at home, e.g. reading, playing word games
- support services available to parents, e.g. Disabled Children's Allowance
- parent programmes (STEP)
- personal habits/likes/dislikes/routines/interests
- responsibilities of parents in their child's education
- options, so that teacher and parent are seen by students as working as a team
- strategies that parents could attempt in order to enhance their role, e.g.class-based/school-based parent support group.

The school is a vital, busy place with much evidence of parental presence. Parents feel valued rather than patronised. They understand that they are part of a partnership rather than apart from their children's learning.

CONCLUSION:

Madeleine Grumet, in her challenging text *Bitter Milk* (1988), argues that in order for curriculum to be truly transformative, all of the stakeholders must participate in the processes of its making. Part of that making is related to the ways in which students and their parents experience the work of the school. Throughout this chapter we have argued that curriculum and assessment are inextricably linked. Assessment and reporting of student learning is the junction where all the participants meet. Current policies and trends in Australia, from both the systems' and the parents' perspectives, hold great promise for the emergence of a more transformative practice. Classroom teachers and school administrators can use these trends to great purpose, but only to the extent that they are seen as educational rather than bureaucratic; as liberating rather than constraining; and as improving rather than changing for change's sake.

NOTES

1 From this point on we shall take parents to also mean guardians. We are sensitive to the fact that many children in our schools are now in the care of adults who may not be their biological or adoptive parents.
2 This extract was derived from the transcript that is published by the ABC on the World Wide Web.
3 By the 'classroom' we mean those places where the school's programme for

student learning is being conducted. It could mean the soccer field, the creek down the back paddock, the local museum, the jetty or the municipal library.

4 A copy of the report, with an accompanying broadsheet poster, can be obtained by writing to the Australian Council of State School Organisations, Hughes Primary School, Kent Street, Hughes, ACT 2607, Australia.

5 At the time of submitting this chapter the *Assessment Resource Kit* (*ARK*) was still under trial. The *ARK* will contain videos, guides and a workshop manual. The issues covered are: developmental assessment; progress maps; assessment methods; judging and recording; estimating attainment; and reporting. The methods used are: portfolios; performances; projects; products, and paper-and-pencil processes.

6 We have changed the name of the school in the interests of confidentiality. However, the account that we present here derives from the documentation that the school prepared about itself. We thank the principal and her staff for giving us access to their reports and allowing us to use them as a basis for the professional learning of others.

REFERENCES

Australian Council of State School Organisations Inc. and Australian Parents Council Inc. (1996) *Assessing and Reporting Student Achievement: A Report of the National Parent Consensus*, Canberra: ACSSO and APC.

Dellit, J. (1993) 'Key competencies and schooling in South Australia', in C. Collins (ed.) *Competencies: The Competencies Debate in Australian Education and Training*, Canberra: Australian College of Education, pp. 57–67.

Eltis, K. (1995) *Focus on Learning: Report of the Review of Outcomes and Profiles in NSW Schooling*, Sydney: NSW Department of Training and Education Coordination.

Filer, A. (1993) 'Contexts of assessment in a primary classroom', *British Educational Research Journal* 19, 1: 95–107.

Forster, M. and Masters, G. (1996). *The Assessment Resource Kit*, Hawthorn: Australian Council for Educational Research.

Groundwater-Smith, S. and Forster, K. (1994) 'Don't patronise us', *Set Research Information for Teachers* No. 1, Item 3, New Zealand Council for Educational Research.

Groundwater-Smith, S. and White, V. (1995) *Improving Our Primary Schools: Evaluation and Assessment through Participation* Sydney: Harcourt Brace.

Grumet, M. (1988) *Bitter Milk*, Amherst: University of Massachusetts Press.

Henry, J. (1994) *Teaching through Projects*, London: Kogan Page in association with the Institute of Educational Technology, Open University.

McLean, K. and Campagna-Wildash, G. (1994) *Using the English Profile*, Carlton: Curriculum Corporation.

McNamara, D. (1994) *Classroom Pedagogy and Primary Practice*, London: Routledge.

Rowe, A. (1994) *Quality and Outcomes Based Education*, ACSA Workshop Report No. 8, Belconnen, ACT: Australian Curriculum Studies Association.

Spady, W. (1993) *Outcomes Based Education*, Belconnen, ACT: Australian Curriculum Studies Association.

Stenmark, J. (ed.) (1991) *Mathematics Assessment: Myths, Models, Good Questions and Practical Suggestions*, Virginia: National Council of Teachers of Mathematics Inc.

Wylie, C. (1994) 'The too hard basket', *Set Research Information for Teachers* No.1, Item 4, New Zealand Council for Educational Research.

Chapter 12

Introducing lap-top computers in the junior school
Changing cultures and structures

Richard Smith, David Adams-Jones and Stephen Lewis

This chapter deals with the introduction of a technology-based teaching and learning programme into a private P-12 co-educational school in Australia. The chapter deals with the introduction of lap-top computers into the school and the policy issues invoked in what was a relatively radical innovation. The chapter is centrally concerned with the predisposition and capacity of a school to move beyond continuous improvement of existing programmes to the development of new categories of clientele and new uses of curriculum. The discussion indicates that a school that wants to move to new and emerging markets and technologies requires a different set of organisational capabilities and a high level of innovativeness and competitiveness.

THE POLICY INITIATIVE

In 1991, the Head of the Junior School visited a prestigious ladies' college junior school in another Australian state to review a nationally acclaimed technology programme. The intention was to review the programme and to judge the feasibility of introducing a similar programme into the head's school. The head was particularly interested in the lap-top computer programme in which elementary school children used computers across the curriculum. After viewing children using lap-tops in Year 5 and conducting lengthy discussions with the principal and teachers, the head concluded that such a programme would place his own school at the cutting edge of technologies in education. A detailed report was prepared, outlining the benefits of such a programme and presented to the headmaster. Subsequent discussions of the technology concept led to the resolve to introduce a lap-top programme.

The decision to move in this technological direction was far from self-evident, despite the success of the exemplar school. It was necessary for the head and some members of the staff to develop the logic of the literature dealing with computer use in schools which suggested that computer technology would have a far-reaching potential for educators.

In 1991, it was apparent that the increase in computer processing speed meant that computers would have increasing capability for doing more things more quickly. It was recognised that the combination of increased speed and extensive memory made it feasible to think about using computers for video, telecommunications, audio, text and graphics processing in colour.

In addition, the miniaturisation of computers, exemplified by the lap-top, suggested that computers had become flexible enough for use at school and at home. A critical factor with such devices is that they are relatively easy to use and their use is intuitive enough for young children. Such devices, while not inexpensive, were within reach of the school's clientele.

Further, convergence was already evident in the computers of the early 1990s. It was recognised that the possibility to link the television, telephone and computer, so that video and audio signals are converted to computerised data, would expand the educational possibilities of computers. Staff looked to the imminent capacity to construct, retrieve, read, process and store curriculum materials and student work, and to the computer as a gateway to navigation tools for non-linear access to information. The Internet, especially, offered intriguing potential as another text and graphics package to be cut and pasted.

Finally, in 1991, it was increasingly apparent that CD-ROM-based materials added to the resources available for teachers and students. If these were to be used educationally, then it was clear that the school required the means to build them into its teaching programmes.

Nevertheless, a move into computer-based education was a risk. The school was young, having been recently established in the sun-belt of South East Queensland. It had already developed a reputation in the community for academic achievements, enjoyed encouraging feedback from the school community and had waiting lists for enrolment. The obvious demand for places in the school depended on a model of schooling that has been unchanged for decades and the physical appearance of the classrooms reinforced the model. Whatever else it was doing, the school was a financial and educational success in a very competitive environment for private education.

There was no doubt that a radical decision to enforce or implement a technology programme requiring all students in Year 5 to purchase their own lap-top computer was a risky strategy. The risk was exacerbated by the general lack of awareness in the school community about technological matters. They knew that they could not draw on definitive educational research in primary schooling that demonstrated the educational worth and cost-effectiveness of lap-top computer programmes. There was much to lose in the proposed technological innovation.

In spite of the risks and unlike many other schools of a similar kind in the area, the school made the decision to accept the technological age and to adopt lap-top computers as an appropriate classroom tool. It embarked on a compulsory lap-top computer programme. Other schools showed great interest in such a programme but decided to take a 'wait and see' approach.

Once the decision was reached, considerable research and lengthy discussions took place in the year prior to the start of the programme. Apart from curriculum and teaching considerations, there were key concerns about hardware, software and classroom requirements to be formulated. In retrospect, dealing with the computer industry and the sales people who represent it, stand out as particularly difficult.

CHALLENGES

The implementation of innovations such as this generate a multitude of problems and issues that need to be solved. These challenges include inappropriate classroom design in buildings that were virtually new, the need for adequate printing stations, the need for ongoing technical support, the need for software training, the need for staff training, the need for parental awareness seminars, the need for administrative support and awareness workshops, and the need for policy statements to be communicated to the staff and general school community. Some of these challenges were unanticipated and have been dealt with over the time that the programme has been in operation. Because of the special context of the school mentioned earlier, matters concerned with the school community are discussed in more detail in what follows.

The challenge for parents

Because the decision had been made that the lap-top programme was compulsory and parents were being asked to double their financial commitment to the school, it was necessary to engender parental support. It was crucial to the success of the programme to ensure that the parent body was aware of the rationale underpinning the decision to head in this direction and the need for what appeared to many of them as radical change. Parent information nights were held in which key staff enunciated and supported the rationale behind the programme and parents were able to debate the issues. This was particularly the case in the first year when there was only six months between the final decision and implementation.

At the time, economic conditions in Australia were such that interest rates were high and the Australian dollar had declined in value. Therefore it was necessary for the school's commitment to be absolute before the parent body was included in the discussion of the decision to proceed with the project. The school was determined not to alienate parents who, for financial and other reasons, precluded their children's involvement in the programme.

This was not an inconsequential matter. One of the key aspects of the programme was that computers should be used in all areas of the curriculum and, in turn, be built into all classroom operations. For this plan to be realised, it was essential that all students had access to a computer throughout the day. Given the then child–computer ratio in the school, it was necessary to purchase computers so that the computer ratio was increased. Parents were therefore asked to make a financial commitment to buy computers without the school making a substantial financial outlay.

From a parental viewpoint there was very little true consultation and collaboration regarding this initiative. As might be predicted with this less than consultative model, the initial meetings with parents were volatile. Parental questions centred on the cost involved and the educational value of the initiative. Parents queried the choice of brands of machine available and their cost and the long-term value of the machine itself. They were especially insistent that the machines should not be 'optioned up' to a level where the cost exceeded the potential use by school children. Indeed, during these early negotiations and meetings it was clear that parents, who are representative of the region's middle class, were suspicious of the presentations made by multi-national computer company sales people. On their part, the staff of the school were careful to recommend computers at the 'low end' of the market. This concern motivated some parents to form a lobby group which sought a more favourable purchase price from retailers across Australia than that obtained by the school. Other factions debated whether the use of lap-tops was superior to a network configuration and the future direction of the lap-top programme. To some extent, subsequent hardware decisions confirmed the fears of a segment of the school parent body.

In the initial discussions, some parents challenged the assumption that appropriate software in the elementary school curriculum areas was available. They also queried the mechanisms of timetabling subjects for the more integrated approach that was fundamental to the lap-top programme. Their concerns were the possible diminution of the academic curriculum for which the school was renowned. Others opposed the programme proposal, arguing that the computers-in-the-classroom model was educationally out of date in the Northern Hemisphere. The school countered with assurances that, on educational grounds, the objectives of the programme were indeed sound and forward-looking. However, the issues of cost of the machine and the maturity of the children who would eventually own the lap-top were less easily resolved.

The outcomes of these meetings had little or no effect because the school management was committed to a belief in the educational advantages of the programme regardless of opposition from parents and teachers. In this sense, the school predetermined the direction and implementation of the lap-top programme. Eventually, the junior school head was able to negotiate a settlement with parents so that tacit support was provided for the programme and the school quickly purchased low-end twin floppy drive lap-tops in the first year. By the end of the first year, the computer company was no longer able to supply a model that suited the school's needs and in the following year, the school purchased another brand of 386 computers. These computers were quicker and able to run Windows, thus opening up a greater range of relevant software.

The challenge for teachers

During the time of the parent meetings, considerable pressure was placed on the school's administrative staff, in particular the junior school head. Not only did he have to justify his position to the parental body but he had to appease the staff as well. His management style is best described as robust as he prosecuted the case for establishing the project. Consequently many staff, who at this stage were peripheral to the planning, were disenchanted by the lack of negotiation with teachers to that point. Some felt excluded from the programme while others believed that their career aspirations were under threat. Staff meetings witnessed frank discussions, and staff letters and deputations against the programme were dealt with autocratically. The subsequent refusal of one staff member to teach in Years 5–7 where the laptops were required was symptomatic of the unsettling effects of this innovation. At the conclusion of the initial round of staff meetings and negotiations, the philosophy underpinning the programme was accepted by teachers as educationally grounded and sufficiently innovative to be worth pursuing.

Even so, unresolved issues remained. A major concern was the supply of lap-top computers to staff. Each year, staff teaching year levels where lap-tops are required receive the latest computers. Remaining staff who want lap-tops are required to purchase their own. Because the technology is superseded literally year to year, some teachers are left with obsolete equipment. This iniquity disadvantages some teachers and remains a serious point of friction among staff.

Another concern was the teacher selection criteria set by management. The failure to think through the unanticipated consequences of selection for the lap-top programme created a series of ongoing problems for some teachers. It is not difficult to understand why this situation eventuated in the rush to establish the programme. The teachers who wanted to teach the lap-top years, 5–7, were selected by management mainly for their computer skills and supportive demeanour. The camaraderie and bonding between these teachers was cemented by attendance at a residential computer workshop in Melbourne at the site of the school first identified by the headmaster and the head of the junior school. Other teaching staff quickly developed the perception that the lap-top programme received undue emphasis which in turn detracted from the excellent teaching practices in other areas of the junior school. This perception was reinforced by the exclusion of lap-top teachers from the mainstream activities of the school. For example, when there is a need for lap-top specific activities to occur, the Years 5–7 teachers are unavailable for normal school tasks. Again, there is extreme reluctance by the lap-top teachers to teach classes below Year 5 and some opposition to the lap-top programme has developed by those teaching below Year 5. The programme thus has the potential to establish relatively impermeable boundaries between the seemingly privileged lap-top teachers and the others. These unintended characteristics of the lap-top programme cause some disharmony among junior school teachers and hinder the flexibility of the junior school.

A differential valuing of teachers' work has emerged. The lap-top programme offers unique opportunities to develop new skills and knowledge that were not previously available and are presently restricted to a subset of teachers in the school. Teaching at the lap-top years has ignited a flame of enthusiasm and a renewed awareness of professionalism within those teachers involved. In effect, the lap-top programme constructs an additional career line for those teachers who do not aspire to administrative roles, if they can gain entry into the cohort. The baulkanization of the curriculum because of technological specialisation and the evolution of different status due to the inadvertent exclusion of teachers from the technological know-how of lap-top computers are not usual in a primary setting. The cultural effects of teacher discontent and the structural implications of the baulka-nization of teachers and the school remain.

Response to the challenges of introducing the programme

The progression from year to year has brought new challenges and dilemmas. Each year it has become progressively easier to convince the parent body of the value of the programme and considerable effort and time are dedicated to the continuing education of the school community. Perhaps the most effective counter to criticism and opposition has been the momentum and success of the programme each year since its inception.

The year in which the school introduced the low-end twin floppy drive machines to staff and children was the most exciting and challenging time and provided opportunities for publicising the innovation. The major soft-ware component at that stage was LogoWriter and the school hired a North American consultant who had advised the school on which the project was modelled. He spoke to numerous local schools that were monitoring the progress of the project, thus enhancing the original decision to proceed with the lap-top programme. Local and national media groups visited the school and their reports gained wide media coverage. Such activity proved to be a significant marketing strategy not only for technological approaches to education of interest to other schools in Queensland, but also for justifying the programme to the school community.

A critical element of the consultant's work was the provision of in-service to teachers on ways of best utilising the Logo software. These sessions not only provided the technical skills required to develop pedagogical strategies but also provided the opportunity for teachers to relate their professional experience to a technological environment. In this way, the knowledge of practising teachers is extended while providing avenues for them to devise ways of using the computers to develop their own curriculum and teaching approaches. The in-service sessions did much to quell the fears and uncertainties of teachers who were on the margins of the original decision to implement the project and who felt threatened by a teaching medium that was at best a mystery. Nevertheless, there is still much to be achieved in preparing the existing teachers to use the technology to its full potential.

A significant change in the project's direction took place in 1994 when Macintosh Powerbook 145b computers were introduced. These machines are capable of audio input and output and multi-media development. Even though the financial considerations discussed elsewhere in this chapter remained key issues, the new machines injected fresh life into the programme as the full potential of the machines was realised by teachers and students. Applications such as HyperCard fitted the primary education environment perfectly, as well as being an excellent vehicle for publicising the programme. Classrooms came alive with new challenges as teachers and students explored the novel technology and operating system. At this time, links were established with the Griffith University School of Education and the school's classrooms became sites for teaching, research and professional development.

These developments, especially the outside recognition and increasing stream of visitors to the school, had a major impact on a number of the teaching staff. Some of those who were reticent to be involved with computers as such, felt confident enough to attend briefing and training sessions. One senior teacher with extensive teaching experience and peer acknowledgement embraced the technology with gusto. The need for in-house professional development received a fillip from the staff-generated enthusiasm for knowing more. Food and childcare facilities were provided to support staff during professional development sessions and many of the barriers that previously existed between teachers in the junior school broke down.

By 1996, the programme has evolved sufficiently for the junior school to integrate computer technology into classrooms in a seamless way. The Internet is fully utilised along with a vast range of easily used peripheral devices, including scanners, digital cameras, video cameras and AV computers. A technology centre has been established within the junior school to support the lap-top programme.

Work with parents has been a continuing theme of the programme. Parental observations are encouraged and monitored and a regular series of open days has paralleled curriculum and teaching developments. These factors reinforce the obvious enthusiasm shown by the children so that the project has quickly gained an aura of excitement and value that permeates the school and its community. The key management people involved in the project noticed changes in student–teacher dynamics, as students produced work of high quality regardless of their different grade levels. As one teacher put it, 'a student can now produce a page of punishment lines in seconds!'

Parental feedback indicates that there is strong and continuing support for the lap-top project, but concerns remain about the development of hand-writing skills and the relative allocation of time to all curriculum areas. As indicated earlier, the rationale of the school curriculum remains that of the academic curriculum and parents expect to see the 'traditional' subjects being taught and examined.

One of the unanticipated problems that had to be solved was that of technical support. With the introduction of the 386 series lap-tops and the extension of the programme into a second year of the school, the servicing level of the computers rose significantly and the turnaround time between dispatching computers for service and return became an issue. This was a serious problem that threatened both the academic goals of the programme and parental support. Children were increasingly left without a machine, to their detriment, and school–parent relations were strained as delays generated frustration. The problem was exacerbated by the mismatch between the lofty promises of computer companies at the point of purchase and what they deliver day to day. The appointment by the school of a technician and successful negotiations with the current computer supplier have created a more appropriate collegial network for solving computer servicing difficulties. In addition, the school administration has realised that innovative programmes require a strategic plan with evaluation mechanisms if the full potential of the philosophy is to be fulfilled. The experiences of the school in this respect indicate that the rigours associated with using a lap-top computer in a primary school setting should never be underestimated.

In viewing the lap-top project from the perspective of several years of operation, there are lessons to be learned about the introduction of technology-based programmes into a primary school. First, the personal qualities of the head and the senior staff are quite critical. As we indicated earlier, the vision and the commitment to undertake the lap-top programme were decided by senior management and supported by key change agents in the teaching staff. The commitment of the head and the senior staff to developing the philosophy, aims and logistics of the programme provided the authority and emotional energy to undertake discussions with parents and staff. In the case of the head of the junior school, his carriage of the programme in a strong sense proved decisive; a lesser commitment and a more faint-hearted approach may well have been fatal.

Second, projects such as the lap-top programme confront teaching and administrative staff with the unknown and, for some, with the unthinkable. In retrospect, it may have been a more productive course to expend greater energy on informing the staff about the 'big picture' that senior administrators had in mind. In this way, staff might well have understood the philosophy underpinning the programme at its inception. It is also possible, of course, that teaching staff in particular might have formed a more formidable opposition to it.

Third, the teaching staff acceptance of the lap-top programme relies on substantial and systematic professional development at the early stages and throughout the development of the programme. The fears and uncertainties that many teachers have about computers are real for those who are not comfortable with them. Again, it is one thing for a teacher to prepare word-processed documents and overhead transparencies using computers, and another for the same teacher to develop resource-based curriculum materials using partially understood software. A concomitant of this point is that teachers need the time and the resources to develop their understanding of both the technology and the new materials. There are clear implications here for the calculation of teacher workloads.

Moreover, as programmes like the one described in this chapter develop, there is a key strategic need to extend teachers' knowledge and skills by introducing a greater range of more powerful software such as authoring languages that are appropriate for curriculum development. Not all teachers will accept such opportunities but some will and these are the growth points in the system. Finally, it is probably the case that the recruitment policies of the school need to include some elements of computing proficiency and predisposition to develop computer-based learning programmes.

THE CHANGE PROCESS

The model of educational change described in this case study is problematic in several respects. It is certainly an example of what Hargreaves (1994) refers to as the tension between vision and voice. As the discussion indicates, the vision of the headmaster and the head of the junior school extinguished the voice of the teaching staff, except for a small band of committed followers. It also ran counter to the voice of the parent group, at least initially. In both instances, staff and parents had the choice of remaining within the contrived and cooptative collaborative framework around the lap-top project, refusing to work in the programme or abandoning the school.

The intervention of the headmaster and the head of the junior school in curriculum development exemplified by the lap-top project was decisive. As the previous discussion emphasises, these people provided leadership by setting the vision and providing the direction for the innovation while simultaneously managing the project by being involved in planning and working with staff and parents (Fullan and Stiegelbauer, 1991). Of special importance to the success of the project was the capacity of the headmaster and the head of the junior school to solve the particular problems of a small but growing private institution with an already established reputation for academic excellence in the academic curriculum.

As Connell (1985) points out, such schools are linked to their clientele by the market mechanisms of competition for fee-paying students and consequential demands by parents for particular models of schooling that are perceived to prepare students for university entrance and well-paid jobs. Teachers, presumably, are attracted to employment in such schools because they share the goals of private education and have some affinity with the models of education that private schools espouse. These characteristics set the school in which the lap-top programme was introduced, apart from most Australian government schools. Prima facie, the perceived need to innovate in technological approaches to teaching and learning was far from self-evident for the school community. The cultural circumstances of the school in its historical development formed a high-risk context for introducing the lap-top project.

The risk factor lies in the apparent restructuring of the dominant models of education propounded by the school. The school's prospectus apparently promises excellence in educational outcomes by appeal to the academic curriculum, therapeutically based concern for 'individuals' and criteria for conduct that are drawn from the private school traditions of the past, while accounting for contemporary trends such as gender equity. The lap-top project can be viewed as an attempt to widen the market appeal of the school, to position the school for a technologically minded, future-oriented middle-class constituency, as well as an educationist curriculum development. The headmaster and the head of the junior school read and interpreted technological and sociological trends and related these to the strategic needs and capabilities of the school. They correctly read the 'market pull' before it was overtly a demand, thus anticipating changes in the competitive balance between schools. In particular, these people and the team they constructed to implement the vision had the wherewithal to relate the lap-top programme plans, their implementation and support to parental and student needs. The 'vision', given the cultural context of the school, is clearly based on the notion that 'the past is no necessary guide to the present, let alone the future' (Bernstein, 1996: 77). It is this element that provided parents and teachers with the initial 'shock of the new' and the reasons to resist the proposed lap-top programme. In this sense, the lap-top programme was always a kind of wager against *future* customer requirements (Myers and Rosenbloom, 1996).

There are several explanations for why the school was able to overcome the fear of the unknown and nostalgia for the past. First, the commitment to the lap-top programme by the headmaster and the head of the junior school and the school council leadership was never in doubt. They and the implementation team reinforced the commitment at every opportunity. They also had the organisational authority, resources and experience to make things happen (Hutton, 1994). Second, the senior staff of the school worked with enthusiastic teachers who took ownership of the project so that priorities were set and milestones reached, despite opposition. These people were empowered to proceed by their own desire to develop new skills and knowledge and a shared vision about the compelling logic of the arguments for a technological direction in teaching and learning. Third, as the project progressed, the practical implementation implications were identified so that an understanding of the route to be followed was clarified. These were progressively communicated to the school community so that the vision became achievable, despite setbacks and unanticipated difficulties. Of crucial importance here was the engagement of the Logo consultant and other professional development opportunities so that teachers were able to contribute to the school effort and deal with their own computer use and computer-related curriculum problems.

The successful resolution of parental objections to the lap-top programme was largely a function of information-giving and celebration of successes as they accumulated. In addition, it was always predictable that for younger parents who are themselves involved in information technology at home and at work, the programme would have both a market appeal and an inevitability (Bernstein, 1996). To this extent, the vision of the headmaster and the head of the junior school may well be judged as defensible as a school policy initiative in spite of parental opposition. In a broader frame-work, the history of the relationships between the school and the parent community underlines the dilemmas of collaborative processes identified by Hargreaves (1994: 260), namely that 'attention to the change process should never be allowed to detract from or displace the paramount importance of change purpose and change substance – of what the change is for!'

REFERENCES

Bernstein, B. (1996) *Pedagogy, Symbolic Control and Identity: Theory, Research, Critique* London: Taylor & Francis.

Connell, R. W. (1985) *Teachers' Work* Sydney: Allen & Unwin.

Fullan, M. G. and Stiegelbauer, S. (1991) *The New Meaning of Educational Change* London: Cassell.

Hargreaves, A. (1994) *Changing Teachers, Changing Times: Teachers' Work and Culture in the Postmodern Age* London: Cassell.

Hutton, D. W. (1994) *The Change Agents' Handbook* Milwaukee, WI: ASQC Quality Press.

Myers, M. B. and Rosenbloom, R. S. (1996) 'Rethinking the role of research: leadership in marketplace innovation requires mastering radical incrementalism', *Research, Technology Management* 39, 3: 14–18.

Chapter 13

Discipline in the classroom
Policy and practice

Phillip Slee, Laurence Owens, Janice Flaherty and Andrew Laybourne

The issue of school discipline is one of the single biggest concerns of the classroom teacher and can occupy an inordinate amount of a teacher's time and energy. In this chapter the term 'discipline' is considered to be mutually agreed-upon teacher and student behaviour that is a response to any action that detracts from an optimal learning environment and which threatens the order and safety of the classroom. The focus in the present chapter is on understanding the relationship between policy and classroom practice in relation to discipline.

THE SERIOUSNESS AND NATURE OF DISCIPLINE PROBLEMS IN AUSTRALIAN SCHOOLS

A frequently asked question in terms of managing student behaviour concerns the seriousness of discipline problems in Australian schools. In a study of teacher's views of discipline, Adey *et al.* (1991) found in their metropolitan school survey of 1,335 primary and secondary teachers that over one in five teachers reported 'serious' or 'very serious' discipline problems in schools. Fitzclarence (1995) has mounted a convincing argument that violence is on the increase in Australian schools. The recent House of Representatives inquiry, *Sticks and Stones* (Australian Government, 1994), concluded that, while violence was not out of control in Australian schools, bullying violence among students was in fact a major problem that needed addressing. Slee (1992) has strongly argued that the increasing alienation of students in our school system inevitably results in resistance and violence. In response to such evidence, consideration is increasingly being given to the development of programmes that address the issue of violence.

As reported by Adey *et al.* (1991), the most common discipline problems faced by primary teachers which occur on a daily basis include: hindering other students, work avoidance, talking out of turn, infringing class rules, not being punctual, unneccessary noise, rowdiness, out-of-seat behaviour, and verbal and physical abuse of other students. A disturbing feature of their findings was that in primary schools, pupil verbal and physical aggression occurred in about one in six classes almost daily.

Burke *et al.* (1994: 2) have noted in their recent paper dealing with behaviour management in Australian primary schools: 'The research indicates that disruptive and anti-social student behaviour is a product of intrapersonal, interpersonal and contextual factors.' In this regard Slee and Knight (1992) have convincingly argued that school organisational structure, policy development and administrative procedures are related to the nature and incidence of disruptive and anti-social behaviour within schools. It is with these points in mind that the discussion now turns to a consideration of the manner in which policy informs classroom discipline practice. To achieve this, the underpinning theoretical principles of the most recent South Australian Department of Education and Children's Services (DECS) discipline policy are described. This policy has much in common with other Australian states' discipline policies, particularly in relation to emphasising, in systemic terms, the active participation of students, teachers and parents in developing a school discipline policy.

A DESCRIPTION OF THE DECS DISCIPLINE POLICY

The DECS policy provides a broad school discipline framework for the development of a safe, orderly, productive and successful school learning community. The policy is intended to be considered in relation to other legislation, departmental policies and action plans, and is based on a number of shared principles. The policy presents various strategies to achieve the main objective of creating positive learning communities which encourage the development of student learning and responsibility. Drawing on this information, individual schools are expected to develop specific discipline policies that are responsive to the needs of their local communities. Consideration is now given to describing the shared principles and their practical implications.

The shared principles

The principles may be considered as underlying values which provide the foundation stone for the overall policy. In turn, the values may be associated with various psychological theories, which seek to explain human behaviour. A recent Australian book (Porter, 1996), provides a very comprehensive overview of theory relating to student behaviour.

'DECS operates within the context of the wider society'

One of the first principles espoused is that DECS operates within the context of the wider society and has a responsibility to prepare young people for successful participation in society. This principle is an overarching one which acknowledges that school is a significant part of the preparation for adult life. This means that schools play a crucial role in providing a safe, inclusive and encouraging environment in which students can learn. To fulfil this charter, schools need to develop discipline policies that build on the following other principles.

'All individuals should be treated with respect at all times'

This Rogerian humanistic principle (Rogers, 1983) so easily remains an empty cliché not translated into practice. As Egan (1995) argued, respect is not just an attitude, but it must be demonstrated behaviourally. The DECS policy explains that schools need to maintain respect for students by taking account of individual differences in learning and social knowledge and skills. There is an important role for schools in trying to understand irresponsible behaviour and supporting students in learning more appropriate ways of behaving.

'Individuals choose their own behaviour to meet their needs, although some circumstances may limit the ability to exercise choice'

Here the influence of the neo-Adlerians (e.g. Dreikurs and Cassell, 1990; Dinkmeyer et al., 1980) and Glasser (1986) is obvious. This principle is a clear rejection of deterministic behaviourism which suggests that a student's behaviour is shaped by the environment, i.e. the teacher's role is to arrange the environment (antecedents and consequences) to achieve desired student behaviour. Instead, the neo-Adlerians and Glasser suggest that students choose to behave in certain ways to achieve desired goals or to satisfy important needs (e.g. attention, power, belonging). The implications of this position for schools is that they need to equip students with opportunities to practise choice and decision-making. The bottom line is that students are responsible for their own behaviour so that discipline is not so much imposed from without by teachers but students choose to behave in certain ways and thereby choose the consequences of their behaviour. The caveat at the end of the principle is an important one because it acknowledges the individual differences that may make choice difficult for some students.

'Families, society, peers, staff and other significant adults influence the choices of young people'

This principle stresses the importance of the various interacting social systems which are part of a child's life. The child is not alone but, in a systemic sense, teachers, parents and peers play important roles in guiding and encouraging the child. This principle advocates a partnership between staff, students and families which aims at the creation of safe, caring, orderly and productive whole-school communities.

'Behaviour has consequences which increase or reduce choices in life'

Again the influence of the neo-Adlerian link between choices and consequences is evident. Responsible choices improve a student's future life chances, while irresponsible choices reduce future opportunities. Consequently, it is important for schools to focus on responsible behaviour by spending time encouraging it. On the other hand, responses to irresponsible behaviour must provide opportunities for students to learn how to behave more appropriately in the future. The consequences need to be non-violent and logical, and specifically related to the student's behaviour. Clearly, the notion of punishment (physical, verbal or emotional) as a consequence that terminates an incident is discouraged. Instead, discipline becomes part of a structured learning process for each child.

'Individuals must accept responsibility for their own behaviour according to developmental ability'

This principle overlaps with the idea of choice and is a re-emphasis of the concept of individual responsibility for behaviour. Older notions of teachers taking responsibility and making students behave are gone. Development of self-responsibility is the aim. Again, individual differences are acknowledged and discipline is placed within an educative context. Schools need to provide opportunities for students to discuss and practice appropriate behaviour and they must accept that children need to learn to behave appropriately.

In summary, the various principles that underlie the DECS behaviour management policy emphasise that individuals are active agents who have an impact on the system of which they are a part. In turn, the system needs to be responsive to the needs of the individual. The principles provide a foundation from which to implement strategies.

KEY STRATEGIES FOR IMPLEMENTING SCHOOL DISCIPLINE

Success orientation

Success orientation is a strategy whereby schools can respect the individuality of students. In practice, this means that a curriculum ought not be designed to fail students but should be inclusive so that all students have opportunities to succeed. Attention to a safe and happy environment is a crucial aspect of this strategy. The development of a learning programme that highlights student competencies and achievements is also a significant element that will enhance student learning and in turn prevent discipline problems. The humanistic orientation popularised by Gordon (1974; 1991) seems to inspire this strategy.

Student responsibility

This strategy involves encouraging responsible student behaviour so that all members of the school community will benefit. Respect for self, others and the school environment is encouraged. Teachers play an important role in directly teaching students to take responsibility for their behaviour (Rogers, 1995).

Consistent practices

Too often schools have been guilty of violating their own policies through inconsistent practices by staff. Consistency involves developing and maintaining positive relationships with all those in the school system. Consistency is reinforced in terms of the language used and the responses made to students, parents and teachers.

Partnerships

School staff are expected to take a leading role in the involvement of the whole school community in the development of behaviour codes. Such participation in decision-making is more likely to lead to ownership of the school behaviour code and support for its implementation. As presented in the DECS discipline policy, behaviour codes and student development plans are part of partnerships.

1 Behaviour codes expand the school discipline policy into specific expectations and consequences which take into account local circumstances.
2 Student development plans provide for negotiated agreements between the school and the student/caregivers to support individually developed behaviour change programmes. Such plans would take into account the individual needs and circumstances of the students.

SCHOOL DISCIPLINE: LINKING POLICY AND PRACTICE

An overall departmental policy provides a framework for schools to develop practices and discipline procedures at the local level. A school-wide policy prescribes how members of the school community behave toward each other. The interpretation and implementation of the policy at school level requires a clear understanding of the principles of effective discipline and its translation into school, yard and classroom practice particular to the individual school. As already noted in the South Australian discipline policy, the 'behaviour codes' represent a school's individual adoption of the principles to the needs of its community.

The discussion now turns to the practical application of policy and theory to classroom discipline practice, with a particular focus on the various strategies described in the preceding section. To highlight the links, an actual primary school teacher's experience is called upon. In this instance the teacher ('Tom') had called in an education consultant to assist him in managing his classroom better. Broad details of this case study are as follows.

Tom had taught for several years in a small school where class sizes were low and few discipline problems presented. When he transferred to a bigger school, he found himself with what seemed like a large group of boisterous students. As the year progressed it seemed that the amount of teaching that Tom could do was limited by the constant movement around the room and the non-compliance of his students. His class seemed noisier than the classes nearby and he seemed to be constantly reprimanding students without any improvement in their behaviour.

By the third term Tom felt overwhelmed by what was happening in the class. He did not want to go to school, he was tired and he was on the verge of tears several times. Through the principal, he requested support from a behaviour management consultant.

A SUCCESS ORIENTATION

The physical environment

As Tom noted, 'From the details provided here, you can see that I was in some trouble with my class and that the kids were really on top of me and the situation was out of control.' The teacher further noted that, as the situation deteriorated, parents of individual children started to approach him to say that their child was 'unhappy' at school. 'It was at this point that I realised that apart from the children I was "unhappy" as well.' The situation was exacerbated by a lack of support from a number of colleagues. It was at this point that Tom called upon the services of the education consultant.

As the teacher emphasised to the consultant, 'I know every child needs to experience success but it's hard to focus on this essential idea with the kids all over the place.' The consultant attended first to the physical environment of the classroom. The point is that when students first enter a classroom, they receive powerful messages about the organisation, order and expectations of the classroom. The adviser used the writings of Evertson (1987) to emphasise three important factors associated with the physical environment that influence classroom management, including:

1 Accessibility – that is, the extent to which students can safely move around the room and have ready access to materials and resources.
2 Distractibility – where consideration is given to aspects of the classroom environment that compete for the teacher's attention, e.g. distractions within and outside the classroom and seating arrangements.
3 Visibility – here account should be taken of student visibility of key teaching aids such as the whiteboard, overhead projector and blackboard.

As Tom noted, 'I had not paid much attention to the layout or appearance of the classroom and I had just been overwhelmed by the kids.' He went on to note, 'I looked around to see what I could do and I simply began by picking up a few papers and tidying the shelves.' Other changes that were made by the teacher to the classroom included clearly labelling equipment, providing stickers for bookshelves and generally making the room more accessible to the students. For example, each student was provided with a cardboard box with their name on it in which they were to place their diaries and work-books in the morning and in which notices could be placed at the end of the day for them to take home.

In relation to distractibility Tom noted that, following the consultant's suggestion, one of the most significant changes he made that affected class-room discipline involved the seating arrangements of the students. As suggested by the consultant, in relation to his floorwork, he used coloured masking tape to identify an octagonal space within which the students would sit during floorwork, and used crosses within the identified space where individual students were asked to sit. That is, the teacher considered the advisability of placing distracting and easily distractible students in proximity to each other because, as Tom noted, 'it was quite clear that some kids who were easily distractible were setting others off'.

The consultant further emphasised that the class layout of desks will influence the level of teacher control and class dynamics. Rows of student desks present a means for high teacher control with low student communi-cation and a high level of teacher communication, whereas desks arranged in groups allow for a high level of student–student communication with a low level of teacher control. Most importantly, the maturity of the class group and the range of activities provided by the teacher will determine the most appropriate arrangement for the class. As the consultant suggested to Tom, some discussion of classroom layout with the students accords with the basic DECS principle of encouraging students to accept responsibility for their own behaviour.

Finally, the teacher needs to consider the visual impact of the classroom. and student visibility in key teaching areas. Here considerations include whether:

• the room is visually stimulating – perhaps overstimulating to some students

- the students can readily sight the key teaching aids, e.g. blackboard
- the students' work is prominently displayed.

As the teacher noted after making some of these alterations to the physical environment of the classroom: 'What a change – the students were starting to sit and listen. This was a good start and now I could give more thought to the learning programme for the students.'

The learning programme

As Tom said, 'It was really gratifying to see the kids beginning to enjoy learning.' Along with the assistance of the educational consultant, the teacher could begin to consider that the students who are 'switched on' to learning will be more actively engaged in the learning tasks of the classroom and have a higher rate of participation and thus minimal opportunities for misbehaviour. The consultant encouraged the teacher to consider the following 'pointers for practice' in developing a learning programme that helps to 'switch on' the students to learning:

- What is the approximate developmental stage of the students?
- What ability levels exist within the class?
- How does my learning style match with the students in my class?
- Do I use a variety of teaching methodologies to engage students
- Do I vary the size and nature of the children's learning groups?
- Do I provide opportunities for peer tutoring?
- Am I aware of the common interests of the students?
- Do the activities I use provide for student involvement?
- Is there a balance of teacher-directed learning and experiential activities?

The preceding questions take into account a number of the shared principles underpinning DECS policy including respect for individual students, providing opportunities to experience consequences and allowing students to select and meet their own needs.

The consultant encouraged Tom to consider how, in the future, he could foster a success orientation in relation to the learning programme because students are then more likely to show a high level of interest and to understand the purpose of the content and associated tasks. To achieve this, the following checklist may stimulate some thinking:

- How have the students negotiated and contracted the curriculum?
- Do the students find the curriculum stimulating?
- Are the learning tasks worthwhile and meaningful?
- Are the learning outcomes available for all students?
- Are the learning outcomes and success indicators explicit?

- Are there opportunities for students to evaluate their own and others' work?
- Do the students receive feedback on their work?

Student responsibility

Tom noted to the consultant that, along with the development of a more positive classroom environment based around a success orientation, the students were beginning to take more responsibility for helping in the classroom and in renegotiating rules and routines. For example, Tom established five 'learning teams', with team leaders who were chosen initially because of their particular need for some control or power. The team leaders helped by leading the students in from recess and by performing tasks such as holding the big book while the teacher read from it or by posting notices in the students' mail boxes. Tom observed that 'As my confidence grew, I rotated team leaders.'

Rules and routines

In relation to rules and routines, discussion between the consultant and the teacher centred on how a well-managed classroom is one that maintains the balance between individual rights and social responsibilities. Successful teachers make expectations clear and provide secure, explicit parameters for students to operate within. These are encapsulated in class rules. Students should be afforded the opportunity to learn socially desirable attitudes and behaviour and provided with the experience of participation in, and contribution to, the affairs of the class and school community. As Tom noted, 'giving students responsibility for certain tasks not only helped them, but reduced my stress'. In conjunction with the consultant Tom considered the qualities of effective rules and they are presented here as further 'pointers for practice':

- Have the rules been negotiated with the students so as to better ensure their commitment to them?
- Are the rules clearly defined and few in number so as to state the expected behaviours and to ensure that they are enforceable? Are they positively stated?
- Has a large poster of the class rules been displayed prominently in class?

Rules by themselves have little effect upon children's behaviour. They need to be followed up and constantly reinforced by the teacher. They must be backed up consistently by appropriate consequences. Behaviours to keep in mind include whether:

- the teacher is constantly noticing and reinforcing specific rule-keeping behaviour

- the teacher has a systematic method of recording incidents of rule-breaking and inappropriate behaviour
- the teacher reinforces positive rule-keeping behaviours more often than sanctioning inappropriate behaviour.

In the case of Tom, he developed a procedure for placing a cross alongside each student's name for each incident so that, for example, one cross was a 'reminder', two crosses was a 'sit-out'. In relation to reinforcing positive behaviour, Tom adopted the procedure of establishing a class goal, e.g. hands up to answer a question and with ten ticks on the board for this behaviour the whole class would get a reward. Another procedure was to cut out a picture, e.g. an Easter egg, into a jig-saw and with each positive behaviour a piece would be added until the picture was complete and the whole class could share a reward.

The educational consultant encouraged the teacher to consider the consequences for irresponsible behaviour as described here (Adelaide South Behaviour Support Unit, 1995: 13):

1 Do I apply consequences for irresponsible behaviour consistently?
2 Do I apply the consequences immediately?
3 Do some of my consequences not seem to affect some children?
4 Do I remain calm when I respond to misbehaviour?
5 Do I focus on a child's misbehaviour rather than his or her personality when I respond to misbehaviour?
6 Do I act rather than talk when irresponsible behaviour occurs?
7 Do I make a special effort to catch a previously misbehaving child being 'good'?
8 Have I developed a sequence of consequences to deal with different forms of irresponsible behaviour?
9 Were these consequences discussed with my students?
10 Are these consequences publicly displayed in the classroom?
11 Do I adhere to my consequence system?

Just as established rules and consistently backing them up with appropriate consequences are essential to developing a harmonious and productive learning community, so too is the development of classroom routines. Establishing simple, obvious routines and adhering to them will also help significantly in preserving teachers' wellbeing. In conjunction with the consultant, the teacher considered the following 'pointers for practice':

- As a teacher, are you always in class ahead of time?
- Are you well prepared for the lesson?
- Do you begin and end the day positively and systematically, e.g. by warmly greeting and farewelling students?
- Do you structure some formality around the business that needs to be attended to at the beginning and end of each day?

- Do you have a rotating student job roster organised and posted?
- Have you explained exactly how students should enter and leave your classroom?
- Do you have a short settling task ready for the students to do upon arrival in your classroom?
- Have you established how the students can gain your attention, e.g. hands up?
- Have you a routine for distributing and collecting books and equipment?
- Do you expect students to keep their trays and desks tidy?

Standard procedures for students also need to be clearly explained, discussed and rehearsed. Tom adopted the procedure of modelling the desired behaviour, e.g. asking politely for the scissors instead of snatching them, and then had the student practise the response with appropriate verbal and non-verbal behaviour. Teachers should supervise student performance, particularly in the establishment phase, and reinforce and encourage good performance. In the event of unsatisfactory performance, further practice is required in students' own time. In establishing rules and routines, students are provided with an opportunity to negotiate conditions to meet their own needs and experience making choices and receiving consequences.

Consistent practice

In relation to the strategy of consistent practice, Tom commented to the education consultant that 'I realise the more consistent and predictable I am, the better the behaviour and learning outcomes for the children'. At this point consideration was given to the types of teacher skills that contribute to good behaviour management.

What do effective teachers do that contributes to behaviour management?

The consultant referred to the research of Kampwirth (1988) who summarised the classroom practice of teachers considered by their principals to be best at managing behaviour and using preventative measures in the classroom. These teachers

- maintained an attractive, organised classroom
- developed a set of classroom rules and established clear consequences for following them
- organised well-prepared lessons
- had a continuum of responses for misbehaviour
- developed high expectations of good behaviour
- planned appropriate instructions around the learning styles of the students
- ensured that all students understood the rules and consequences

- managed the group effectively during teaching time
- emphasised success, not failure
- modelled appropriate behaviour
- communicated with students in a positive, sensitive and assertive manner.

Personal qualities of teachers that contribute to sound classroom management

In relation to the personal qualities and traits of teachers that facilitate class-room management, the consultant used the writing of Walker and Shea (1991) in conversation with Tom. Such teachers

- have chosen to work with school students
- are confident, realistic and honest with students
- accept students for who they are
- understand behaviour and can empathise with students
- are willing to examine their own teaching behaviour critically
- are patient with the students
- are flexible in the face of changing circumstances
- when analysing problems, will evaluate the setting, their own behaviour and the students' behaviour.

The manner in which teachers interact with students has a significant impact on the students' behaviour and learning. Highly effective teachers are able to maintain harmony and cooperation by way of their management styles, pedagogy and the manner in which they convey affirmation and affection toward the students.

In analysing personal style, the consultant encouraged Tom to consider the following 'pointers for practice':

- Am I maintaining a healthy balance between respecting my students' rights and my own needs?
- Do I feel that I am in control in my classroom?
- Do I over-control my students to the detriment of a positive learning environment and the development of social responsibility?
- Do I offer structure and set limits so as to protect and promote the welfare of my class members?

Most students respond best when teachers offer them the predictability and security of establishing behavioural parameters and when they are able to employ assertive teacher behaviours consistently. Assertive teachers are extremely effective, for example, when they are employing their repertoire of strategies for conveying messages of care and affection to students because the students are more likely to cooperate when they feel cared about. This forms the basis for productive and mutually respectful relationships. In consistently striving for ways to interact positively, the consultant utilised the following points in discussion with Tom.

- Do you try to begin and end each day on a positive note?
- Do you greet and farewell students individually – offering them eye contact, smiles, humour?
- Do you provide them with meaningful opportunities to make a contribution to the affairs of the classroom by way of class meetings, entrusting them with tasks, roles and responsibilities?
- Do you truly listen to what it is the students have to say and follow up on their questions?
- Do you make time to explore with them their personal issues and respond to them, e.g. watch their TV programmes?
- Do you intersperse their day with short class games to engender fun and laughter?
- Do you write letters or notes to individual students – send good news home to care-givers?

Partnerships

As Tom noted to the consultant, 'now that I'm feeling more in control and better about my teaching, I have the energy to think about how to involve others in my classroom practice'. Along with the consultant Tom began to plan for the future in thinking about relationships with the whole school community, with the emphasis on the following:

- open communication
- mutual respect
- outcomes to achieve
- dealing with conflict and problem-solving.

In developing partnerships with the broader school community, the consultant presented the following points to consider:

- Have you thought of an acquaintance night for the parents where issues to be discussed could include

  - the role of the parents in the children's learning programme?
  - the role of the parents in the development of the behaviour programme?

- What thought has been given to the development of some regular contact with parents by such means as

  - class newsletters home to the parents?
  - regular telephone contact to convey positive news about the student?
  - special awards to be sent home with students regarding their behaviour and learning?

SUMMARY

As a sequel to this case study, the teacher, in reflecting on his year-long experience, noted that 'It is important to teach behaviour – it just does not happen.' To facilitate such an outlook the systemic process of developing and establishing a school discipline policy engages people at all levels of the system. At the classroom level, it requires of teachers a willingness to entertain new and different ideas. At the school level, collegiate support is required in accepting that every student in school belongs to the 'whole school'. Such an ethos means that any discipline problem with a particular student is the responsibility of the whole school. At the administrative level, support is important in terms of clarifying expectations and procedures. Discipline then is incorporated as part of effective behaviour management which in turn is embedded in the overall curriculum.

ACKNOWLEDGEMENT

The authors are particularly grateful to 'Tom' for the time, effort and insight that he put into providing the case-study material for this chapter.

REFERENCES

Adelaide South Behaviour Support Unit (1995) *Classroom Management Book*, Adelaide: Adelaide South Behaviour Support Unit.

Adey, K., Oswald, M. and Johnson, B. (1991) 'Discipline in schools: a survey of teachers. Survey number 1: Teachers in Metropolitan Adelaide', unpublished study.

Australian Government (1994) *Sticks and Stones: Report on Violence in Australian Schools*, Canberra: Australian Government Publishing Service.

Browne, R. and Richard, F. (eds) (1995) *Boys in Schools*, Sydney: Finch Publishing.

Burke, C., Jarman, K. and Whitmore, L. (1994) 'Disruptive and anti-social behaviour in primary schooling: foci for professional development and community education', *The Journal of Teaching Practice* 14: 1–17.

Department for Education and Children's Services (1996) 'School discipline: behaviour codes in schools', draft, January, Adelaide.

Dinkmeyer, D., McKay, G. and Dinkmeyer, D. (1980) *Systematic Training for Effective Teaching*, Minnesota: American Guidance Service.

Dreikurs, R. and Cassell, P. (eds) (1990) *Discipline without Tears*, New York: Dutton.

Egan, G. (1995) *The Skilled Helper: A Problem Management Approach to Helping*, California: Brooks/Cole.

Evertson, C. (1987) 'Managing classrooms: a framework for teachers', in D. Berliner and B. Rosenshine (eds) *Talk to Teachers*, New York: Random House.

Fitzclarence, L. (1995) 'Education's shadow? Towards an understanding of violence in schools', *Australian Journal of Education* 39: 22–40.

Glasser, W. (1986) *Control Theory in the Classroom*, New York: Harper Row.

Gordon, T. (1974) *Teacher Effectiveness Training*, New York: Peter H. Wyden.

—— (1991) *Teaching Children Self-Discipline at Home and at School*, Sydney: Random House.

Kampwirth, T.J. (1988) 'Behaviour management in the classroom: a self-assessment guide for teachers', *Education and Treatment of Children* 11, 286–93.

Porter, L. (1996) *Student Behaviour:Theory and Practice for the Teacher*, Sydney: Allen & Unwin.

Rogers, B. (1995) *Behaviour Management: A Whole School Approach*, Gosford: Ashton Scholastic.

Rogers, C. (1983) *Freedom to Learn for the 80's*, Columbus OH: Merrill.

Slee, R. (ed.) (1988) *Discipline and Schools: A Curriculum Perspective*, Melbourne: Macmillan.

Slee, R. (1992) *Discipline in Australian Public Education: Changing Policy and Practice*, Melbourne: ACER.

Slee, R. and Knight, T. (1992) 'Recent changes in discipline policies and implications for the future', in R. Slee (ed.) *Discipline in Australian Public Education:Changing Policy and Practice*, Melbourne: ACER.

Walker, J.E. and Shea, T.M. (1991) *Behaviour Management: A Practical Approach for Educators*, New York: Macmillan.

Chapter 14

Learning partnerships
The role of teachers in a community of learners

Peter Renshaw and Raymond A.J. Brown

In this chapter we examine the core activity of schools – learning and teaching. In the first section of the chapter, we argue that learning should be considered within the frame of partnerships and relationships, rather than examined as the achievement of individuals disconnected from their social and cultural contexts. Our view is based on contemporary theories that emphasise the centrality of processes of communication and language in student learning. In looking back at our own history of teaching, we note the continuity from the 1970s through to the present of certain key ideas regarding learning – notions such as the importance of student talk, small group interaction, learning how to learn, and developing inquiry strategies and skills. However, we also note that the dominant learning theories of the early 1970s underpinned classroom reforms that were short-lived. We argue that attention to the complementary and active roles of teachers and students in learning partnerships will produce reforms that are more effective in transforming classrooms. The product of our own partnership is summarised in the second section of the chapter. Working with ideas derived from a sociocultural model of learning (Renshaw, 1995), and from a model of classroom interaction called 'collective argumentation' (R.A.J. Brown, 1994), we draw out the central roles that teachers need to play in order to build effective learning partnerships with students. These roles include providing space in the classroom for the voice of students, supporting students to communicate their ideas in their own words and forms of representation, providing social scaffolds to engage children in exploratory talk about key concepts, challenging students to move towards more abstract and general representations, and providing the conditions where students can enact values that sustain a collaborative classroom community.

CONTINUITY AND CHANGE IN THEORIES OF LEARNING

A generation ago . . .

We began our teaching careers as primary school teachers in the early 1970s, just at the time in Australia when teachers were being recognised as key players in educational reform.[1] Innovation at the local level was being supported by increased government funding, and teachers were being encouraged to adopt what were seen as progressive practices such as opening up classrooms, using inquiry activities, setting up small group problem-solving, and teaching in teams. The Karmel Report (1973) drew the attention of governments and educators to social disadvantage, but at the same time there was considerable optimism that endemic educational problems might be tackled and solved. A generation later, we see less certainty and optimism, and both unexpected continuity and significant change. Fenley (1970) published the forecasts of a group of educators regarding changes that they predicted would occur in the 1970s and 1980s. High on their list of anticipated changes was the increasing influence of technology – media and computer technology – on classroom learning. The present generation of forecasters echoes this theme, with the classroom of the twenty-first century commonly being described as a virtual space created by computer and media technologies that will enable students and teachers from all over the world to communicate with each other and gain access to diverse local and international databases. Later in this chapter we refer to the CSILE project (Scardamalia et al., 1994) which has begun to explore the possibilities and pitfalls in that vision.

We also found considerable continuity in the key proposals for reforming classroom learning. Key ideas in 1969 included the following: (i) the need to reduce the dominance of teacher talk and increase the opportunities for students to adopt an inquiry mode where student discussion would lead to deeper understanding; (ii) the importance of developing children's thinking strategies, problem-solving skills and processes of learning how to learn; and (iii) the importance of understanding students' conceptual structure and cognitive processes in designing teaching episodes. The theorists who provided justification for such ideas included Bruner, Ausubel, Piaget and Britton. Bruner's work on the process of inquiry and discovery learning found expression, for example, in the social studies curriculum package MACOS (*Man: A Course of Study*) (Curriculum Development Associates, 1970). Britton's (1970) examination of the centrality of language in school learning found expression in the renewed emphasis on small group learning contexts in classrooms, for example, in the work of Barnes and Todd (1977) on classroom oral language. Piaget's constructivist theory of development was used more broadly to justify curriculum changes and teaching practices that emphasised *process* and defined the teacher's role as facilitating the learner's own activity. Ausubel highlighted the centrality of the learners' existing knowledge structures in curriculum design.

In diverse ways each of these theorists challenged the assumption in traditional models of schooling that knowledge was gained most effectively when students listened attentively to teachers giving clear explanations and appropriate examples of concepts and procedures. The reformers of the early 1970s viewed children as active agents in their own development, even in traditional classrooms. Rather than simply absorbing the knowledge presented by teachers, children were shown to transform and reinterpret the teachers' words and explanations according to their existing knowledge and experiences – leading at times to unexpected outcomes (Donaldson, 1978). By ignoring the transformational activity of the learner, it was argued that the traditional transmission methods of telling and demonstrating could produce only surface knowledge rather than the deep understanding envisaged by the teacher.

Few primary school classrooms in the early 1970s provided working models of effective practices based on the reformist agenda. For such models, we remember being referred to early childhood settings. The typical early childhood setting gave greater scope to the active participation of the learner through the provision of group and individual activities. Usually the activities were open to a variety of approaches, and children were able to experiment with materials in an open-ended manner. The adequacy of their ideas and experiments were able to be tested against those of other group members or actual first-hand experiences, rather than relying on the teachers' authority. In the ideal situation, challenges by students to the ideas of others were open to discussion, so that the search for verification occurred within the context of the peer group.

The reformist vision, however, had little impact on the whole system of primary school education. Many teachers felt that they were losing control of the educational enterprise; that curriculum content and assessment were not as orderly and predictable as previously; and that their role as facilitators was ill-defined. In reflecting on his own experience in primary schools during the swing back to traditional practices, Ray Brown remembers finding himself in a more orderly and predictable self-contained classroom. Lesson content rather than thinking processes were again the focus of teaching, and those children who were unable to progress at the desired rate were sent to a remedial teacher to catch up.

Individualistic versus partnership focus of learning theories

The re-emergence of traditional practices could be rationalised as part of the general turn to more conservative political and social agendas in the early 1980s. However, in retrospect, we believe that the theory of learning itself was incomplete and unbalanced in its overemphasis on the constructive activity of individual learners. The assumption that learners would be able to construct knowledge of the physical and social world assisted by experts standing at arm's length, was difficult for teachers to accept when their professional responsibility was to ensure that all children developed certain basic competencies and came to share certain widely used forms of thinking and acting in a particular society. It also implied that the guidance provided by teachers through language and action could have only a minor role in the development of understanding. We do not deny that children are active, operative and constructive in their own development. Rather, we want to open the aperture, include the whole picture, in order to recognise that individual competence develops in partnership with others – adults and peers. Learners are co-operative, co-active and co-constructive, and we need to focus not on individuals but relationships and partnerships in the teaching learning process (Renshaw, 1992). It has been the advances in learning theory since the 1970s that have enabled such a view to be sustained. The change can be seen in the subtle rephrasing employed by Bruner (1986) to combine his original emphasis on individual inquiry with a new emphasis on social support and community. He now characterises most learning as a communal activity, a sharing of the culture, and he views learning as occurring in the company of others belonging to a particular culture. In drawing together his current view he writes: 'it is this that leads me to emphasise not only discovery and invention but the importance of negotiating and sharing – in a word of joint culture – creating as an object of schooling' (Bruner, 1986: 127).

Contemporary views of classroom learning

The dual emphasis on individual endeavour and social support within particular cultural contexts can also be discerned in the list of effective teaching and learning strategies recently compiled by Biggs (1994):

1 High cognitive demand, but non-threatening assessment.
2 Interaction with others – both peer and adult scaffolded.
3 High level of learner activity – both task-related and self-related.
4 A positive motivational climate – a felt need to know and understand.
5 A developing knowledge base that has both depth and breadth.
6 Embedded teaching – mentor/mentee relationship – so that knowledge is seen as relevant.
7 Content-specific focus but involving collaborative and socially shared intellectual work, for example, where learners teach each other, or collaborate spontaneously, or cooperate on joint tasks.

So how do contemporary writers describe effective teaching and learning? First, active engagement is required by both teachers and learners. Teachers set cognitively challenging tasks but provide scaffolded assistance in a positive climate that legitimates many forms of learner collaboration and interaction. Learners are active both in monitoring their own learning, establishing collaborative arrangements with other learners, tutoring each other and participating with the teacher in scaffolded teaching episodes.

To summarise, the advances in learning theory that we discern are, first, the articulation of how active and complementary roles can be assigned to teachers and learners in the classroom. Below we illustrate how the concepts – *scaffolding, cognitive apprenticeship* and the *zone of proximal development* – have provided the necessary theoretical tools to describe the way that learning and teaching are inextricably linked. Second, we see greater attention in contemporary theories of learning to the communal and cultural embeddedness of knowledge – the situatedness of knowing. There is greater recognition now that children in schools are not just acquiring abstract knowledge, but are learning to participate in ongoing and evolving practices of various communities. That is, rather than saying that a child is learning mathematics, we would say that the child is learning to speak and engage in certain mental and practical activities that are characteristic of the community of mathematicians. It may appear awkward and unnecessary to translate as we did above. Our purpose is to signal that classrooms need to be considered as sites where two processes are occurring simultaneously. Children are learning to talk, act and think in ways characteristic of particular communities, and at the same time their identities are being formed as they become (or resist becoming) progressively more self-regulating participants in those communities.

Contemporary classroom practices

The extensively researched and implemented programme Reciprocal Teaching (Palincsar and Brown, 1984; Rosenshine and Meister, 1994), illustrates how the dual focus on teacher and student activity might be achieved, as well as the notions of *scaffolding* and *cognitive apprenticeship*. The Reciprocal Teaching procedure for teaching reading comprehension strategies begins with the teacher explicitly labelling and modelling comprehension strategies (predicting, summarising, questioning and clarifying) while reading and interpreting a text. The teacher stops at times to reflect aloud about ambiguities in the text, or on personal questions that arise for further reflection or investigation. The teacher models how informed predictions (based on background knowledge) can be made using hints in the text title, or the genre of the text. The activation of such background knowledge is shown to be productive in foreshadowing aspects of the text, and at times the teacher tries to summarise what has been learned from reading the text. Students are incorporated into the process of using the comprehension strategies by being placed in the role of the teacher. They take the lead in reading sections of the text and enact the strategies previously modelled by the teacher. Here the teacher supports and scaffolds their enactments by reminding the student in the teacher's role to engage periodically in the various comprehension monitoring strategies. The central task of this cognitive apprenticeship style of teaching is to provide opportunities for learners to play roles that require them to be more reflective and aware of the processes of expert performance. Peer tutoring, collaborative activities with other learners and playing the teacher's role are the social contexts in which learners are forced to be more conscious of the elements and processes of expertise. Active involvement is required by the teachers in enacting and demonstrating expertise, and by the students as they take over the role of the teacher in guiding and monitoring their own learning activities and that of other students in the class.

As we noted above, there is now a greater emphasis on the cultural and community context of learning. In the company of other learners, students are guided by the teacher to adopt the speech, forms of representation, attitudes and values that characterise particular knowledge communities (writers, readers, mathematicians, and so on). However, this is not a simple matter of the teacher transmitting the language, behaviours and values of the particular community to the student. Learners need to be able to anchor their understanding of the practices of the community in more personal and local forms of language and representation. Teaching is the social process that creates the connections between two of these domains – the domain of the personal, local and experiential, and the domain of the general, abstract and more formal. Progress in learning is marked by greater participation in and understanding of the shared assumptions and values of those communities, their forms of language usage and sets of procedures for testing and consensually validating knowledge claims.

The recent school-based research of Ann Brown (1994) on Community of Learners (COL) is one attempt to give realistic expression to the community and cultural context of learning. Typical teaching strategies in Brown's classroom include the following:

1 *Jigsaw*, where units of study are divided between learners as a way of sharing the responsibility for both learning and teaching the unit to each other. Each member of the jigsaw has to contribute to the learning of the other members by researching their aspect of the topic and teaching it to the other group members.
2 *Majoring*, which is a term coined by Brown to refer to distributed expertise in any group of learners. Distributed knowledge and expertise is valued and used in COL classrooms to place learners in the role of tutors for particular activities.
3 *Performance* refers to the process of displaying what has been learned during an activity. Performance highlights the social nature of knowledge construction and verification. In the process of conveying knowledge to an audience, students are socially constrained to be more coherent, clear and conscious of their evidence than in solitary activities. *Performance* provides a strategy, therefore, of pushing learners to deeper understandings.

The Computer Supported Intentional Learning Environments (CSILE) project uses computer-based technology to create a community of learners in the classroom that draws on and is connected to other classes and knowledge production sites via the Internet (Scardamalia *et al.*, 1994). Originally conceived to focus on self-regulated and goal-directed learning, the CSILE project shifted its focus to emphasise the social dimension of knowledge construction. The project uses classroom-based networked computers as a database and memory bank for the inquiries of students. The students establish problems for group consideration, suggest strategies for finding solutions, contest and elaborate other students' contributions which are stored on the computer memory, and constantly evaluate the adequacy of the group knowledge construction that is occurring with the technical assistance of the computer.

There is a significant shift here in the way that knowledge itself is being conceptualised. Knowledge is seen as socially achieved, and able to be progressively modified as more information and evidence is found and accepted by the community according to publicly accepted criteria. Knowledge is not a set of facts to be accepted on the authority of the expert, but rather is a process that begins with questions and curiosity about social and physical phenomena, and involves the gathering of evidence that satisfies certain public criteria for coherence and logic. In such a classroom students perceive themselves as contributing to knowledge within certain communities of practice, rather than being recipients of knowledge. This shift is captured by a comment from a student in a CSILE classroom that was investigating why offspring resemble each of their parents in some respects – a question initially posed by Karen but taken up by other members in the class. After weeks of working on the problem, one student wrote, 'Mendel worked on Karen's problem'. This student's comment reveals the crucial yet subtle transformation that occurs when students move from a transmission model of teaching to a model that places them in a community of inquiry. They begin to see themselves as active contributors to an ongoing process.

PARTNERSHIP IN CLASSROOM RESEARCH

We began our research partnership in 1992 when each of us was beginning to develop ideas concerning the co-construction of learning and its situatedness in local communities of practice. Our partnership has enabled us to reach a diverse audience of researchers, teacher educators and classroom practitioners that would have been impossible individually. Renshaw (1992, 1995) has been concerned primarily with exploring the implications of a sociocultural model of teaching and learning for practitioners. R.A.J. Brown (1994; Brown and Renshaw, 1995, 1996) has been developing a model of classroom interaction called 'collective argumentation' that provides the context for exploratory talk by students, and teacher scaffolding of advances in student thinking. In particular he has been investigating collective argumentation in the context of teaching mathematics to upper primary school groups of students. Below we have specified the key roles for the teacher that we discern arising from our work.

Providing space for the voice of students: representation and language in the mathematics classroom

We came to view teaching as the social process that creates connections between the domain of the personal, local and experiential, and the domain of the general, abstract and more formal. Central to this view is the notion that forms of representation and language are the tools that mediate movement across these two domains. Lampert (1990) enabled children to make the transition from the local to the general by associating mathematically appropriate activities with words such as 'know, think, revise, explain, problem and answer'. By encouraging the use of such language and representation, Lampert provided children with a communicative space in which they could draw on both personal experience and the language of mathematics. Our own research provides examples of children's voices operating within such spaces. In the example below, two students (Damien and Lauren) are presenting their thinking about a problem to the class – 'Jack can clean a room in 10 minutes and Jane can clean the same room in 15 minutes. What fraction of the room will be cleaned in 1 minute if both Jack and Jane work together?' The children had drawn two representations of the problem on the blackboard. Damien had organised the problem information into boxes; Lauren had drawn a room, complete with bed, window, wardrobe and door. In the transcript Lauren has just presented her group's ideas by referring to the room diagram.

TEACHER   (*to class*) Does talking about wardrobes, clothes and beds help us to work out a solution to the problem? Are there other people who would like to say something?

STUDENT   What fraction of the problem did you get?

DAMIEN   Well, we are not working with fractions, sort of.

STUDENT   Why did you set the information in the problem up like that [referring to the representation of problem information] and not use it?

DAMIEN   What?

TEACHER   Why did you set the information in the problem up like that if you didn't use it?

DAMIEN   Well, we did. We are.

TEACHER   Would anyone like to add to the reasoning process? Damien and Lauren have taken us so far. Is there anyone who can take us the next step forward? The next step forward to a solution.

GREG   You would probably divide the room up into five.

Although it was the teacher who initially cast doubt over the effectiveness of Damien and Lauren's thinking, it was a student who took up this invitation and directed the discussion to the topic of fractions by requesting an answer. Dissatisfied with Damien's answer, again it was a student who directed attention back to the problem information, as represented by Damien, by requesting an answer. The teacher supported this direction by restating the question when Damien sought an explanation. Taking up the teacher's invitation, Greg suggested how the room diagram could be viewed in terms of fractions, although he uses the everyday terms of 'dividing it into five'. This episode began with a non-mathematical representation of the problem – a simple drawing of the room that a child might produce in an art lesson. With the assistance of the teacher, the students move to a more mathematical representation, and the use of more abstract language such as 'fraction', 'information in the problem', 'divide into five'.

The key-word structure: a social scaffold

It was heartening for us to see that when space was made available to children in regular classrooms, they could give voice effectively to their ideas. The diversity of the levels of representation, and the interest that children demonstrated in each others' drawings, diagrams and equations, encouraged us to devise a *key-word structure* to give direction to their collaboration. In our view it is insufficient to simply give children the opportunity to express their ideas. They need to compare their ideas with others, to examine the similarities and differences in the diversity of views, to evaluate the consistency and adequacy of multiple representations of problems and concepts, and to move towards more objective and general forms of representation. To ensure that this happened on a regular basis, we devised and taught the children the following key-word structure: *represent* the problem (diagram, drawing, equation), *compare* representations with your partner, *explain* your representation to your partner, *justify* your views to your partner when there are disagreements, *agree* on a joint representation of the problem that seems the most adequate following discussion, and *validate* your conclusions by reporting your representation to the whole group. The key-word structure acts as a social scaffold, that is, it directs children to engage in certain types of communicative activities (representing and talking about problems) that can lead to advances in thinking. The teacher also can intervene in the key-word structure to challenge children's ideas and assist their use of more mathematical forms of representation and language.

Challenging dyads: from local to general utterances

Teacher participation in the key word structure involves an on-line assessment of group work with challenges being issued to children to engage in and demonstrate higher levels of: (a) representation, (b) cogent explanation, (c) objective justification, and (d) rational consensus. It is during this phase of the learning process that the utterances of individual children can be integrated with the voice of mathematics. The teacher may do this by asking questions about the representations, adding to the representations, noting similarities and differences in representations, redirecting children to problem information, providing a personal representation to challenge children's ideas, seeking explanations or justifications, challenging children to provide more abstract or general justifications for their ideas.

The agent of collective memory

The teacher's role extends beyond working with particular dyads, to becoming an agent for the collective memory of the class. The classroom community is not created simply by placing thirty children in a physical space. It is the shared experiences of the class over time, and the means that they employ to record and remember their experiences that create the local classroom culture. The teacher is strategically placed to be the agent for the collective memory of the class. Specifically, what we have in mind here is the way that the teacher orchestrates the communication of the small group activities to the whole class. The teacher already knows what the groups have been doing, but in managing the reporting process the teacher is able to rephrase, paraphrase and re-represent the contributions of particular groups, draw connections between contributions, refer to previous problems and the way that similar situations were approached. In this way, the teacher can create for the class a sense of continuity in their work, and ensure that the mathematics that is emerging in the local classroom is an effective bridge for the children to eventually participate in the conversation of the broader community of mathematicians.

Linking local and general cultures: the value connection

Mathematical discourse is driven by commitments which privilege certain ways of thinking and acting. These commitments are implicit within the discourse of the classroom at a number of levels. First, at the group level, children's discourse is guided by commitments to: (a) represent ideas, (b) examine ideas in the light of rational argument, and (c) revise ideas when there is sound reason to do so. These commitments are implicit in the social scaffold provided by the key-word structure and lay the foundation for classroom discourse. Second, at the class level, children's discourse is guided by commitments to: (a) frame ideas so that evidence may be brought to bear, (b) subject ideas to constructive criticism, (c) expand the collective ideas of the classroom community, and (d) work towards a common understanding. These commitments are implicit in the utterances of the teacher as he or she orchestrates classroom discourse away from the local and the personal culture of the classroom toward the general and objective culture of mathematics.

Learning in the classroom is not just the accumulation of cold factual information. Rather, as we have argued in this chapter, learning occurs in partnerships and relationships with others, and as such it carries certain value imperatives for how to behave towards one another. So another way of considering the issues of values is in terms of the social virtues of engagement, courage, humility, honesty, restraint, persistence and affirmation. To participate in the collaborative classroom that we have described, children require the courage to state their ideas and opinions to others, the humility to accept that their ideas may not always be adequate, the honesty to give accurate feedback and reports, the restraint necessary to maintain social cohesion, the persistence to pursue ideas and views in the face of opposition, and the generosity to affirm the achievements of others.

CONCLUSION

Teaching and learning are the core tasks of schools, and to ensure the effective achievement of these tasks, teachers need to see themselves as a professional community that neither blames the students and parents for educational problems, nor adopts a helpless attitude in the face of challenges. In this chapter, we have provided an outline of our own approach to empowering teachers and learners in the classroom. In our ideal classroom, teachers set challenging tasks for students and provide the scaffolded assistance required to support engagement in learning activities. Tasks are arranged so that students work in various collaborative arrangements with each other and the teacher. Where possible, the students are placed in roles requiring them to act as tutors, teachers and sources of expertise to other members of the class. A community of learners is fostered by methods such as jigsaw, where tasks and teaching responsibilities are divided between students, and, drawing on our own research, by social scaffolds such as collective argumentation. Teachers do not abrogate their role as experts in these student-centred procedures – they play a pivotal role in linking the actions, language and representations of students with forms used by the knowledge communities of mathematicians, historians, scientists, writers and so on. The features of our ideal classroom reflect also a commitment to a particular type of community – a community based on social virtues that are basic to a democratic and socially just society, namely social engagement, courage, humility, honesty, restraint, persistence and affirmation. Such virtues and values commitments arise, in our view, as a consequence of the types of learning relationships and partnerships that the teacher is able to facilitate in the classroom. Given the enormous challenges that face us in securing a more harmonious society for today's children, we hope that this generation of teachers will be more successful than the cohort of our youth.

NOTE

1 Our careers took different paths – Renshaw entered the university sector in 1975, while Brown continued in his role as a primary school teacher. Since 1992 we have conducted an ongoing dialogue about theory and practice, and collaborated in applied projects on classroom learning and teaching.

REFERENCES

Barnes, D. and Todd, F. (1977) *Communication and Learning in Small Groups*, London: Routledge & Kegan Paul.

Biggs, J. (1994) 'What are effective schools? Lessons from east and west', *Australian Educational Researcher* 21, 1: 19–40.

Britton, J. (1970) *Language and Learning*, Harmondsworth: Penguin Books.

Brown, A. (1994) 'The advancement of learning', *Educational Researcher* 23, 8: 4–12.

Brown, R.A.J. (1994) 'Collective mathematical thinking in the primary classroom: a conceptual and empirical analysis within a sociocultural framework', unpublished B.Ed. (Hons) thesis, University of Queensland.

Brown, R.A.J. and Renshaw, P. D. (1995) 'Developing collective mathematical thinking within the primary classroom', in B. Atweh and S. Flavell (eds) *Proceedings of the Eighteenth Annual Conference of the Mathematics Education Research Group of Australasia*, Darwin: MERGA, pp. 128–34.

—— (1996) 'Collective argumentation in the primary mathematics classroom: towards a community of practice', paper submitted to the Nineteenth Annual Conference of the Mathematics Education Research Group of Australasia, Melbourne.

Bruner, J. (1986) *Actual Minds, Possible Worlds*, Cambridge, MA: Harvard University Press.

Curriculum Development Associates (1970) *Man: A Course of Study*, Cambridge, MA: Education Development Centre Inc.

Donaldson, M. (1978) *Children's Minds*, Glasgow: Collins/Fontana.

Fenley, W.J. (1970) *Education in the 1970s and 1980s: Continuity and Change in Australian Education*, Sydney: Hicks Smith.

Karmel Report, Interim Committee of the Schools Commission (1973) *Schools in Australia*, Canberra: Australian Government Printing Service.

Lampert, M.L. (1990) 'When the problem is not the question and the solution is not the answer: mathematical knowing and teaching', *American Educational Research Journal* 27: 29–63.

Palincsar, A.S. and Brown, A.L. (1984) 'Reciprocal teaching of comprehension-fostering and monitoring activities', *Cognition and Instruction* 1, 2: 117–75.

Renshaw, P.D. (1992) 'The psychology of small group work', in R. Maclean (ed.) *Classroom Oral Language: Reader*, Deakin: Deakin University Press, pp. 90–4.

—— (1995) 'Excellence in teaching and learning', in B. Lingard and F. Rizvi (eds) *External Environmental Scan*, Brisbane: Department of Education, pp. 27–33.

Rosenshine, B. and Meister, C. (1994) 'Reciprocal teaching: a review of the research', *Review of Educational Research* 64: 479–531.

Scardamalia, M., Bereiter, C. and Lamon, M. (1994) 'The CSILE project: trying to bring the classroom into World 3', in K. McGilly (ed.) *Classroom Lessons: Integrating Cognitive Theory and Classroom Practice*, Cambridge, MA: MIT Press, pp. 201–28.

Chapter 15

Alternative ways of grouping pupils for learning

Christine Ure and Kathy Stewart

GOALS OF SCHOOLING

Reviews of education have frequently commented on the need for schools to demonstrate greater recognition of the diverse learning needs of pupils. The Plowden Report (1967), written thirty years ago in Britain, heralded a shift from an authoritarian perspective on schooling towards a philosophy of education that included consideration of individual differences, the need for first-hand experiences and opportunities for creative work. The classroom was acknowledged as being more than a place for learning, it was an important part of pupils' lives and it provided the opportunity for them to acquire attitudes and values.

Lack of an educational rationale and concerns about limitations inherent in the traditional single-aged classroom have lead many educators to seek alternative strategies for curriculum design and classroom groupings. Many educators are now committed to creating classroom environments that are designed to influence the development of the 'whole child' and are sensitive to individual differences in learning styles and rates of progress. Continuity in children's learning is valued and failures in performance are not used for purposes of grading or retention but are used for the purpose of planning further learning objectives (Burchfield and Burchfield, 1992). These changes towards treating children as individuals are multi-faceted and require changes in the relationships that teachers have with children, the instructional methods they use and the assessment strategies employed as well as the actual groupings used.

RIGIDITY VS. FLEXIBILITY

The Schools Council, in a recent review of the compulsory years of schooling in Australia (National Board of Employment, Education and Training, 1993), concluded that rigid approaches to education have limited the scope of pupils to progress and develop at their own rate. The Council recommended there should be greater documentation of examples of schools where alternative and more flexible class groupings have resulted in freeing pupils from the lock-step progress determined by the traditional age-grade structure.

In an earlier publication (National Board of Employment, Education and Training, 1992) the Schools Council defined rigid classrooms as those in which class groupings were determined by age and grade, where a predetermined curriculum fostered dependency by pupils on the teacher and where quantitatively based assessment and lock-step progression were used to determine progress of pupils. Flexible classrooms were characterised as ones in which pupils were encouraged to be enterprising and take initiative in their learning, where assessment was based on qualitative accounts of interest and achievement and where class groupings were multi-levelled and progression individually determined.

It is important that when alternative groupings are implemented by schools, the goals of the grouping strategy are made clear. Many schools, for example, use alternative groupings without an explicit educational rationale. Multi-aged classroom groupings that are designed to free pupils from the rigid model of schooling, will be based on a model of a collaboratively based learning environment where children of mixed ages and mixed abilities learn together. This form of grouping is a deliberate attempt to provide a flexible school programme that facilitates the development of all pupils. The curriculum is also designed to foster academic, social and emotional development, and progression of pupils will be based on individual needs. On the other hand, composite class groupings are often implemented to solve student:staff ratio problems. Composite classes typically comprise two groups of pupils from two year levels and the curriculum will be based on year-level expectations. Progression of pupils will be determined by the year level they are in and there is rarely an option for pupils to work across the curriculum of the two year levels in the class. Some schools use mixed-age groupings as a form of streaming and attempt to match the ability levels of pupils across the mixed-age range. These approaches to alternative groupings may address the short-term needs of the school, or some part of an educational ideology; however, they do not wholly address issues concerning the goals of schooling for all pupils in attendance.

TERMINOLOGY

The terminology used to describe alternative classroom groupings should also be clearly defined. A class using 'multi-age groupings', for instance, is one where students of mixed ages and mixed abilities are grouped together. This type of classroom may also be described by the terms 'vertical age grouping' and 'family grouping'. The term 'non-graded classroom' has also been used although this term was used initially to describe a type of vertical grouping that was based on streaming (Goodlad and Anderson, 1963). More recent literature has used this term synonymously with 'multi-age grouping'

(Pavan, 1992). Composite classes are ones where children are grouped according to age and grade. These classes have two different groupings of students working in parallel under the direction of a single classroom teacher. Open classrooms group children of two or more classes together with two or more teachers working collaboratively. This form of grouping may be based on a single age-grade structure or a multi-age-grade structure.

MULTI-AGE CLASSES: AN AUSTRALIAN VIEW

State departments of education in Australia have recently shown considerable interest in multi-age groupings of pupils. Projects involving multi-age classes have been established in Western Australia, South Australia, Northern Territory and Victoria. For example, in 1993 the Victorian government introduced a pilot project, in which the first three years of schooling were ungraded, in order to investigate more flexible arrangements for the early years of schooling. Thirty-six schools representing both state and Catholic primary schools have been selected into the pilot project. The project was an outcome of the Victorian Ministerial Review of School Entry Age, conducted in 1991–2. The Ministerial Committee argued for greater flexibility in the early years of schooling to meet the individual needs of children entering school and to provide greater continuity in their early school experience. An extensive report on this pilot project is expected to be published in 1998.

MILL PARK PRIMARY SCHOOL: A CASE STUDY OF A PILOT PROJECT SCHOOL

Mill Park Primary School, in Victoria, commenced its multi-age program in 1989, prior to the Victorian Ministerial Review, and presented a case for multi-age grouping to the Review Committee. This section describes how the teachers at Mill Park became committed to changing the organisation of the classrooms in their school and the steps they took to implement these changes. The impact of these changes on the school community are also presented.

Mill Park Primary School is an example of a school that has successfully implemented alternative classroom groupings for its pupils over the past seven years. The school has developed a multi-age structure for the entire pupil population. The school is involved in the Victorian Pilot Project for the First Three Years of Schooling and grades for the first three years are referred to collectively as the Junior Primary Unit.

The school is located in the northern suburbs of Melbourne in a residential area that was established about sixteen years ago. The school population is made up of a diverse range of multi-cultural families, with a minority from non-English-speaking backgrounds. In many instances both parents work and a high percentage of parents are employed in professional positions.

- Pupils are individuals and must be catered for in all aspects of school life according to individual abilities and needs.

- Pupils' learning occurs in developmental stages and that teachers recognise these stages.

- Evaluation is based upon the effectiveness and the impact of curriculum programs on each pupil's progress.

- A whole range of effective evaluation techniques are utilised for the dual purposes of making accurate assessments of pupil progress and providing realistic comprehensive reports to parents.

- Expectations for each pupil are measured solely against potential and ability of the individual.

- Recognition of the importance of the family in each pupil's continued learning ensures that every effort is made to involve, inform and include parents in a supportive and effective manner.

- Age and year level are NOT the criteria used for learning expectations of assessment of pupils.

- The multi-age structure is a deliberate philosophy designed to enhance individual learning through the stages of developmental curriculum.

- The multi-age structure complements the school's curriculum delivery strategies and that such classes heighten teacher awareness of individuality in pupils.

- It is more important for the 'school to be ready for the pupil' than attempt to judge readiness in every pupil.

- Thorough preparation of both pupils and parents will facilitate the orientation of the school beginner and assist to overcome any perceived lack of readiness.

- A delayed start to school may impact negatively on learning. Pupils are more likely to benefit from immersion in the stimulation of an active and exciting classroom.

- From the time they begin school, pupils need to be included as active participants in learning activities and programs.

- The youngest pupils in multi-age groups should not be seen as 'less capable' because of age or year level.

- A regular program throughout the school of parent information and involvement facilitates support of the school's teaching and learning program and its philosophy.

- Over the 7 year period of primary school, curriculum delivery is continuous, consistent, comprehensive, co-ordinated and made available to all pupils.

- Teaching approaches continue to make use of the best information about how pupils learn best.

- Co-operative and sensitive attitudes by all are conducive to the creation of an effective learning and working environment.

- Over a period of time, reference to pupils in year/grade levels, arranging activities in year/grade levels, and naming of classes in year/grade levels will be minimised.

Figure 15.1 Statement of understandings about teaching and learning developed by teachers at Mill Park Primary School.

In 1989, prior to the Victorian Ministerial Review, and under the leadership principal Neil McLean, teachers at Mill Park reached a decision to implement multi-age classes at their school. This decision was taken following an internal review by staff of their attitudes and beliefs concerning teaching and learning. A statement of understandings concerning their philosophy of teaching and learning was generated. The statement (Figure 15.1) expressed a philosophical belief in a needs-based approach to education which featured understanding, appreciation and sensitivity towards each child's development and learning. This statement provided both the impetus and framework for the move to a multi-aged programme. Changes were made in the way that the school grouped pupils in the classroom and in the way that the curriculum was implemented.

The school has worked consistently over a number of years to develop a curriculum and organisational structure that provides opportunities for each of its pupils to maximise their potential and achieve feelings of success and competence in their learning. All planning and changes have been aimed at improving the quality of school life for all pupils, i.e. to ensure academic success, social competence and positive attitude towards themselves as learners.

The success of the programme at Mill Park has resulted in a great deal of interest from parents, teachers and other professionals. Numerous requests have been met by the school for visits from groups wishing to observe at first hand the day-to-day running of the school.

The first step: making the change

The first step for teachers at Mill Park was to thoroughly explore and become familiar with a developmental approach to teaching and learning. This step was assisted through use of the *Frameworks* document, published by the Ministry of Education in Victoria in 1987–8. The *Frameworks* document supported the development of a curriculum that encouraged an individualised approach to teaching and learning and recognised that

- all pupils can learn
- there should be provision of access and success for all
- there should be mixed ability groupings
- cooperative learning techniques should be developed
- there should be greater flexibility in the curriculum
- the school structure should complement a more flexible curriculum.

The adoption and implementation of these principles instilled in the school community a belief that its pupils were offered the best opportunities for educational and social development. The goals of the school community reflected a desire to provide a learning environment where pupils would develop a more realistic view of themselves. The implementation of multi-age groupings would lead to a greater range of development within the class and this would assist pupils to develop a greater appreciation of the talents, skills and abilities of their classmates. The multi-age class grouping was also believed to represent more closely the life situations in which children normally find themselves. School was one of few situations in which children were grouped by age level.

At Mill Park the school community recognised that

- learning is not directly related to chronological age
- pupils learn at different rates
- learning is facilitated by considering the whole child, i.e. social, moral, emotional, physical, cognitive and creative areas of development should all be taken into account when planning learning outcomes.

As a result, classroom organisation and practice was designed to foster social competence (McGrath and Noble, 1993) as well as positive attitudes to learning and academic competence .

School organisation

Between 1988 and 1990 Mill Park Primary School comprised approximately 600 students. The structure consisted of:

- five groups of P/1 classes
- five groups of 1/2 classes
- six groups of 3/4 classes
- six groups of 5/6 classes.

In 1991 Mill Park developed a junior school unit in which all ten classes from the Prep to Year 2 levels were reorganised into multi-age groupings. Each class consisted of children from the three year levels.

In 1992 the ten P/1/2 classes were formed into two units.

The school structure consisted of:

Junior School

- Unit 1: four groups of P/1/2
- Unit 2: six groups of P/1/2

Middle School

- Unit 3: six groups of 3/4

Senior School

- Unit 4: six groups of 5/6

The specialist staff (library, music, art and craft, and physical education) comprised Unit 5.

In 1996 the structure of the Junior School comprised four groups in Unit 1 and five groups in Unit 2. The other units remain unchanged.

The school community

Before implementing any changes the staff agreed on the importance of adequate preparation time for sharing information with parents and staff. Over the course of two years a considerable amount of time was provided for parents to hear about teaching and learning, developmental curriculum strategies and changes in current teaching practice. Regular newsletters were sent home, several information evenings were held for parents, and teachers undertook extensive professional development. During this time a great deal of trust and goodwill was established between the staff and the parents of the school community. Parent involvement in the school directly benefited the whole school community and allowed new initiatives and projects to be approached in a relaxed and collaborative manner. Parent support within classrooms provided teachers with more time to observe group activities and to give more individual help to pupils.

School management

The responsibility for ensuring that there was adequate support for implementing these changes rested with the school principal. The principal provided educational leadership, sought information for parents and teachers, and supported teachers in the changes that they were implementing. The school community was able to identify the principal as a confident leader who provided a strong link between all its members. The principal acted as a 'sounding board' for staff, monitored the success of the programme and initiated changes when they were needed. The principal listened to issues and concerns raised by parents. Teachers also worked cooperatively with the school council to ensure that they understood what the changes meant for the children and the school community. Over a period of time the school, as a whole, developed an understanding of what a multi-age classroom was and how it worked.

Staff relationships and curriculum planning: the foundation of team work

Flexibility for schools to organise their staff, within given staffing ratios, in a manner that suits their own situation, is important if schools are to able to establish more flexible class groupings. At Mill Park, the school organisation permits teachers to work in units of 4–6 people. The physical layout of the school with its double classroom buildings ensures that each teacher has the opportunity to work in a team teaching situation. There is an expectation that each member will contribute to all planning, resourcing and activities of the team. The school administration, for example, takes responsibility for ensuring that there are periods of time that permit effective planning by teams within the weekly timetable. At Mill Park it was found that cooperative planning reduced overall planning time, and allowed the staff to work in other areas such as policy development. As well as allowing for more effective and efficient development of curriculum by utilising each team member's strengths, interests and expertise, it also provided teachers with more opportunities for exchanging information on strategies, assessment techniques and future directions.

Curriculum planning has been based upon an understanding of child development and stresses the importance of individual learning needs, talents and interests and the need to provide active 'hands on' learning experiences. It has been acknowledged that effective learning takes place

- within a supportive environment
- through demonstration and modelling
- through direct experiences
- by doing, by 'having a go' and taking risks
- by engaging in purposeful activities

- when learning is of importance to the learner
- when quality relationships are formed through involvement in activities
- at individual rates.

Because no pupil is ever at exactly the same stage of development as any other, the staff at Mill Park strive to offer programmes that respond directly to the developmental capacities of each pupil. The programmes reflect a great deal of planning, observing and evaluation.

An integrated curriculum approach has been implemented to promote understanding, and to make each learning experience more relevant and meaningful for pupils by actively involving them in their learning. Close links between the key curriculum areas have been established in order to foster understanding. The integrated learning experiences have also produced a more cooperative learning environment and have helped pupils to establish a wider range of social skills, necessary for leadership and nego-tiation. The multi-age programme has also required the teachers to develop a more diverse range of instructional strategies. These have included strate-gies that provide for

- a whole-language approach for learning
- use of Cambourne's conditions for learning
- collaborative learning techniques for teachers and pupils
- teaching across all developmental areas
- opportunities for learning through play
- shared reading/maths experiences
- specific teacher modelling/demonstration techniques
- pupil-selected strategies/activities
- small group activity sessions
- peer tutoring activities
- open-ended and problem-solving activities
- explicit instruction.

The teacher has multiple roles to play (Politano and Davies, 1994). The primary role is to establish and maintain interaction between the pupil, the teacher and the learning process. In addition, the teacher must be able to use a range of flexible teaching strategies. In a multi-age classroom the teacher will need to move from being an instructor to a facilitator and at times will be an equal partner when working with pupils engaged in small group experiences.

CLASSROOM MANAGEMENT: A CASE STUDY REPORTED BY KATHY STEWART

Kathy Stewart has recently taken a new teaching position at Meadowglen Primary School where she is currently teaching a Year 1/2 multi-age class.

Table 15.1   Sample week timetable: integrated study – *Water*

DAY 1	Assembly News-telling Diary writing	Vocab. developments: words to do with water. Brainstorm list, classify.	Undirected play with water and a variety of containers. Shared work response: to list findings.	Shared readings: *There's a Sea in* *My Bedroom* by Margaret Wild. –reading response –sequencing: beginning, middle, end.
DAY 2	PMP Poem: Water Word study: focus -er words.	PHYS. ED. MUSIC	Brainstorm, as group, the ways we use water. Magazine search for pictures of water.	Silent reading. Parts of a book: discuss then label on chart. Cut and paste activity: matching labels to parts.
DAY 3	News telling Handwriting Story writing	Clinics Conferences, as required. Share time	LIBRARY	ART Serial reading Focus: Characters. Predict story.
DAY 4	PMP News telling Handwriting skills session	Estimate then check the capacity of a variety of containers. Maths stories using language 'full', 'empty', etc.	Explore the properties of water. Demonstrate how water can change state. Relate to poem. Write about findings. Partners	MUSIC Word find activity: -er words. Serial reading
DAY 5	News telling Story writing	Story writing PHYS. ED.	How does a tap work: in pairs, take apart and reassemble taps. Record findings.	Serial reading: developing character profiles. Work in small groups.

Note: PHYS. ED., MUSIC, LIBRARY and ART classes are conducted in specialist areas.

The tables in Kathy's classroom are organised into four groups with seating for 4–8 pupils in each group. Each pupil has a name card which is kept in a container at the front of the room and these cards are used to randomly create working groups for activities as needed. At times specific groups are deliberately structured for instructional purposes. Random groupings like this are used to ensure that all pupils are included in activities, to avoid exclusion, and to give pupils the opportunity to model and learn from a wide range of peers. For individual work, each pupil has been designated their own seat in order to foster a sense of belonging. The curriculum uses an integrated design and Table 15.1 presents a sample of a weekly timetable in which the learning experiences in each of the key learning areas have been integrated through a study on the topic of water.

Group work

Groups may be formed according to the skill focus, pupil choice, or randomly using name cards. Groups are changed several times during the day, depending on the learning situation, to give pupils the opportunity to work with a wide range of class members. Groups are sometimes formed on a social or friendship basis to allow for a secure working situation in which pupils may feel more comfortable with each other. Also groups that are established on the basis of a shared interest may have greater team work and show motivation to persist at a task. At times this structure may be the appropriate choice. The timetable shown in Table 15.1 provides for a variety of small group experiences in addition to paired and individual activities.

Behaviour

At the beginning of the year, through class discussion, pupils are encouraged to form their own code of behaviour within the room. Ownership of the rules leads to greater compliance and greater self-discipline. The classroom environment is designed to allow pupils freedom to play, to explore, to experiment, to practise, and above all, to think. It is expected that all pupils are capable of responding to high expectations, of working effectively with others, of accepting responsibility for their learning and of expressing themselves in creative ways. Pupils who are occupied and interested in the classroom display few behavioural problems. Positive classroom behaviours are established over time as pupils adjust to the routines, self-discipline and self-assessment required in a multi-age class. Many of the learning experiences during the first term of the year are designed to foster the communication and social skills necessary for small group work. Collaborative experiences are used to help pupils to identify and articulate those interactions that lead to group interdependence and productivity.

Assessment

Assessment strategies are selected to ensure that the individual needs of pupils are met through more specific use of instructional techniques. Assessment is integrated with plans for curriculum and instruction and is used to provide greater continuity for each pupil's learning. Profiles are developed for each pupil in order to get to know them well. This is essential in order to be able to provide learning experiences that are purposeful, relevant, interesting and challenging for all the different ability levels shown by members of the class. Information is also collected to assist in working with each pupil to set realistic and achievable goals. Assessment is an ongoing practice that is undertaken in both a formal and informal way. A wide range of assessment strategies and instruments are used to build up a profile of each pupil. Strategies based on observation using prepared checklists help to demonstrate evidence of new and emerging competencies during normal classroom activities. Assessment is also used to provide information on each of the major developmental domains in addition to each of the Key Learning Areas. Self-assessment by pupils is also encouraged to assist them to become more reflective about their learning, and to identify their own learning needs and strengths. Self-assessment is implemented through strategies that include teacher–pupil discussions or through pupils recording their own learning outcomes, expectations and performance on a prepared checklist or comment sheet.

The value in multi-age classes is in the learning that takes place and assessment strategies should be selected and developed to assist in the evaluation of a range of abilities, stages of development and levels of understanding. Information about the development, interests and abilities of the pupils is used to select more appropriate experiences and strategies to enhance their learning. At Meadowglen, Kathy Stewart uses a range of assessment activities that, like the learning experiences, allow for and encourage a range of responses. The methods of assessment include:

- end outcomes, e.g. a piece of work
- skill or content checklists
- student folders for various curriculum areas
- observation
- discussion, e.g. conferences, informal chats
- teacher-designed tests
- interviews
- anecdotal records
- questionnaires
- self-assessment
- peer appraisal.

Table 15.2 Sample assessment

LANGUAGE (READING)		NAME: Mary
Date	Comments / skills / behaviours	Context
4/2	Displays an interest in books and reading	Free reading activity
20/2	Understands vocabulary associated with books (i.e. book, cover, author, illustrator, etc.)	Shared reading session
15/3	Joins in reading of familiar and repetitive stories	Shared reading session
21/5	Beginning to use picture cues to help reading	Oral reading (one to one)
30/5	Able to retell a story in own words. Writes in response to a story	Reading response activity
11/7	Able to sequence events of a story fairly accurately. Able to talk about the characters in a story and answer questions from the text	Reading response activity
3/8	Can choose a book they would like to read. Able to say whether or not they like a book and say why or why not	Selection of books for home reading

Criteria relating to the quality of the work expected, how students are going about their work and the end product are also included. Table 15.2 illustrates a qualitative account of the reading skills of a child in the Year 1/2 class at Meadowglen. The context in which observations were made are normal classroom situations.

CHALLENGES AND SAFEGUARDS

This chapter has described challenges faced in setting up an alternative method for grouping pupils. At Mill Park Primary School the challenge commenced with an examination, by the teachers, of the philosophy that defined their attitudes and beliefs about how pupils learn and develop. The school community then developed a set of goals and implemented a wide array of changes, while maintaining cohesion between staff, parents and pupils. Safeguards were established for all participants through communication at all levels of the school's administration and school community. The resulting changes in grouping strategies influenced all aspects of classroom functioning, including how the curriculum was implemented and how pupils were assessed and monitored. The case study of the Year 1/2 multi-age class at Meadowglen has demonstrated how these changes are implemented in a cohesive manner. These case studies illustrate the need for schools to examine the rationale for the class groupings that they use and to ensure that where alternative groupings are used, classroom practice is consistent with the desired outcomes.

REFERENCES

Alessi, L., Hoyne, P., Stewart, K., Ure, C. and Walker, K. (1994) *Teaming Up*, Melbourne: Dellasta Publishers.

Burchfield, D.W. and Burchfield, B.C. (1992) *Two Primary Teachers Learn and Discover Through a Process of Change*, in S. Bredekamp and T. Rosegrant (eds) *Reaching Potentials: Appropriate Curriculum and Assessment for Young Children*, Vol. 1, Washington, DC: National Association for the Education of Young Children.

Department of School Education (1992) *Ministerial Review of School Entry Age*, Victoria: Department of School Education.

Department of Education (1995) *The Multi-Age Group Project*, Western Australia: Department of Education.

Goodlad, J.I. and Anderson, R.H. (1963) *The Non Graded Elementary School*, New York: Harcourt Brace & World Publishers.

McGrath, H. and Noble, T. (1993) *Different Kids: Same Classroom*, Melbourne: Longman Cheshire.

Ministry of Education (Schools Division) (1988) *Frameworks*, Victoria: Government Printer.

National Board of Employment, Education and Training (1992) *Developing Flexible Strategies in the Early Years of School: Purposes and Possibilities*, Canberra: The Australian Government Printing Service (AGPS).

—— (1993) *Five to Fifteen: Reviewing the Compulsory Year's of Schooling*, Canberra: The Australian Government Printing Service (AGPS).

Pavan, B. (1992) *School Effectiveness and Non-Graded Schools*, AREA ERIC Document No. 346608.

Plowden Report (1967) *Children and Their Primary Schools*, London: Central Advisory Council for Education.

Politano, C. and Davies, A. (1994) *Multi-age and More*, Winnipeg: Peguis Publishers.

Ruminations

Chapter 16

Building professional community and supporting teachers as learners
The potential of case methods

Lawrence Ingvarson and Merrin Marett

Much of what happens in the name of in-service education falls well short of conditions necessary for significant changes in teaching practice or the implementation of policy. This chapter is directed to teachers looking for something more satisfying than the usual short course mode of in-service education where teachers play the role of passive audience to someone else's agenda for change. We want to share some of our recent experiences in using cases and case methods for professional development. These experiences indicate that case methods can provide a valuable means for building the kind of professional communities and networks that many now identify as essential to effective professional development (Fullan, 1994, 1995; Lieberman, 1988, 1992).

THE POLICY CONTEXT

The policy context for this chapter is the Victorian Curriculum and Standards Framework (CSF), a local adaptation of the national curriculum statements launched in controversial circumstances a few years ago. By 1995, most Victorian teachers had attended short 'familiarisation' sessions about the CSF presented by Board of Studies personnel. As part of the implementation process, schools were also expected to conduct curriculum 'audits' to 'clarify the extent to which existing practice matched the curriculum framework outlined in the CSF'.[1] Audit meetings, according to the teachers we worked with, often turned out to be brief because staff readily convinced one another that the CSF outcomes were covered in current courses and therefore the CSF had few implications for change in their practice. This meant that the CSF ran the risk of becoming another example of 'innovation without change', a common phenomenon in the history of curriculum reform (Fullan, 1991). Full implementation of the CSF, according to the DSE memorandum, will involve two more steps:

- the development of sequential teaching and learning programs in each key learning area to reflect the strands, modes and levels of the CSF
- development and implementation of procedures and practices for assessment and reporting of student achievement in relation to the levels, strands, modes and learning outcomes within the CSF.

(Executive Memorandum No. 96/021: 3)

The memorandum goes on to state that by the end of 1996 'it is expected that schools . . . will have established an appropriate implementation plan which would include professional development activities for teachers'. Support and course advice materials have been written for schools, and a 'district-based CSF teacher network strategy' has been put in place to 'provide collegiate support for teachers as they implement the CSF'.

We were interested in the role that case methods could play in bringing teachers together around issues related to the CSF, not as passive implementers of the framework but as 'shapers, promoters, and well-informed critics' of the reform (Little, 1993: 130). The CSF, in effect, was what teachers who had studied the reform and attempted to put it into practice were doing. Case methods were a means for teachers to document their learning about what it meant to implement the CSF and to help each other to develop new knowledge and understanding about how it might be implemented in ways that were educationally fruitful and justifiable.

CASES AND CASE METHODS

As used here, cases are candid stories that teachers have written about particular events that have arisen from their own teaching. They are usually brief, first-hand accounts (1–3 pages) of their experiences in teaching particular topics or ideas, often including rough and ready evidence of what students have said, done or written in class. Teachers come together in case methods groups to read one another's cases, or cases that other teachers have written. In developing our approach, we were influenced by the valuable research on case methods conducted by Barnett and Tyson (1993) and Judy Shulman *et al.* (1990) at the Far West Laboratory for Educational Research and Development in San Francisco.

Case methods include individual case writing and group discussion of cases with a facilitator. As we use them, cases are written to stimulate collaborative reflection through discussion. They are a means for teachers to share insights and reflections, to identify dilemmas and problems, and to find support and challenge in a professional environment. Cases provide teachers with windows into each others' pedagogical reasoning and practice. Most importantly, they come to see their own experiences and assumptions through the eyes of respected others, a critical prerequisite for change in beliefs, or 'seeing anew' as Jenny Nias puts it (1987).

Case methods have a long history of use in professional fields such as law, business studies and medicine. Over the past ten years or so there has been a renewed interest in their potential for initial and in-service teacher education. Excellent reviews of these developments can be found in Merseth (1996), Sykes and Bird (1992) and L. Shulman (1992). There is no one case method, but case methods have a common aim of helping to build more effective bridges between theory and practice than usually exists in professional education.

A CASE METHODS GROUP AT WORK

The best thing to do at this point in the chapter is to take the reader inside case methods groups with which we have worked over the past two years at Monash University, in conjunction with the Science Teachers Association of Victoria (STAV). The project, called 'Getting down to cases', was funded by the National Professional Development Program (NPDP).

Although the teachers in our groups were teaching science at the junior secondary level, primary teachers will find the case methods described readily applicable to their situation. The cases groups were formed by sending a general invitation to teachers of science who were interested in exploring innovatory professional development methods in relation to the implementation of the CSF.

Mark Trofimiuk and Libby Parkinson, whose cases are discussed below, are members of the group. They have been writing cases about issues and questions that have arisen for them in teaching toward student learning outcomes delineated in the CSF. They have also been learning how to facilitate effective discussion of their cases using methods developed by Barnett *et al.* (1994a, b), J. Shulman (1992) and others (Merseth, 1996). The group met weekly after school at Monash from 4.30 p.m. to 7.30 p.m. for about four months.

The leaders of this 1995 group were three teacher members of a similar NPDP-funded group in the previous year who were keen to further their experience with case methods. It was part of the strategy that teachers in each cases group would gain sufficient understanding and skills to use case methods themselves in their schools and other professional development settings in a kind of pyramid effect. Most did. Our aim was to strengthen the professional networks among science teachers and to build a tradition of case writing methods, in this case among science teachers, but the approach could have been used for any group with a common teaching interest.

Mark's case

Mark has brought copies of a case he has just written about a recent lesson with a Year 8 high school science class, which he describes as somewhat 'difficult'. His aim was to help the class to 'recognise that plants and animals are made up of cells and describe the major features of cells'. This is one of the learning outcomes set down in the 'Life and living' strand of the Victorian Curriculum and Standards Framework. Mark's case describes briefly the context, what he is aiming to do in the lesson, how the lesson works out, how the students respond, and a problem or dilemma that he begins to perceive as a result of reflecting on the lesson.

Mark's case begins as follows:

'In 1665 Robert Hooke looked at "cells" in cork, and in 1670 Antoni van Leeuwenhoek used a microscope to . . . '

NO! I can't do that to the poor kids! There must be a better way of getting the concept of cells across to the students.

That night, while watching a program about Japan, one of the segments caught my attention and ideas began to flow. The segment was about a car manufacturing plant – its setup and operation.

What if we thought of a cell as a factory or manufacturing plant and we brainstormed the idea on the board? Let's see . . . what would you need to set up and run a factory?

I started to jot down some ideas and the analogy seemed to work OK, but would it be as clear to the students when we try it group discussion? . . . 'There is only one way to find out!'

The Year 8 class next day was one of the better ones and, as it happened, they seemed to be quite settled and attentive right from the start. I introduced the topic very briefly and asked the class to arrange themselves into groups of three or four.

'The cell can be thought of as a manufacturing plant or a factory and what I would like you to do is to write down as many things as possible that you would need to build and set up to run a factory. We will list them on the board after you have worked on it for about ten minutes.'

At first the class comes up with things related to structures, such as walls, buildings and machines. Later, after some discussion and probing questions, the group starts to come up with necessary functions such as administration and management, storage, waste disposal, a source of power and a source of water. When Mark is satisfied with the list he puts up an overhead transparency of a detailed and labelled cell and asks the students to identify those parts of the cell that they think would represent the factory walls, the administration, assembly lines, storage areas, etc.

Toward the end of his case Mark says that he felt that the lesson had gone well and that the majority of students were able to understand the analogy and had a better idea of what a cell was and how it functioned. He then raises a dilemma that he now faces in assessing this CSF outcome.

> Now the problem is how I am going to assess their understanding. What level of detail will they need to remember mitochondria? endoplasmic reticulum? Golgi apparatus? What sorts of activities or tests will show me that they have a good idea of what a cell is and what it does?

In the last paragraph Mark briefly describes how in a later lesson, he asked students to plan how they make a model of a cell using any materials to hand as a way of gaining some insight into their current level of understanding of cells.

Mark passes copies of his case around to members of the group and they spend the next hour and a half absorbed in lively discussion about the particulars of the case, the pedagogy used and alternatives that they have tried, the advantages and disadvantages of using analogies like this, and what the CSF outcome actually means that students should know and be able to do.

Facilitating case discussion

The discussion of Mark's case is facilitated by another group member who follows a set of steps carefully designed to engage the whole group and to draw out the full range of different perceptions of the case and the issues and questions it raises. This is a critical feature of effective case discussions if they are to lead to learning and change in group members. Issues and questions raised are carefully recorded over the first twenty minutes or so with little comment and discussion permitted. Group members are often surprised at how extensive the list of questions and issues usually is. Case writers are also surprised by the range of different perceptions that readers have of their case.

When the list seems to have exhausted members' questions, the facilitator asks the group to review the list, to look for commonalities among the questions, and to decide on those they would like to discuss in greater depth. At this stage the facilitator will often be asking group members to identify what they think the case is a case of. This is equivalent to asking the group to identify more general, deeper or theoretical issues underlying the case. Although cases are deeply personal as reconstructions of experience, they can also be objective when they help teachers to identify common situations and dilemmas that they face in their own teaching. Good cases are cases of something of wider or theoretical significance; they are instances of a general class of experience.

We developed a rule that case writers were not expected to talk during this period or to answer questions, and we believe that this strategy worked well. It leads group members to focus on their perceptions of the case and the questions it raises, not to an interrogation of the writer. It helps to separate the person from the case of teaching in question. It is also invaluable feedback to the case writer about how others perceive their case and its intentions.

As the case discussion winds down, the writers begin to talk about their intentions in writing the case. At this point the writers have usually identified ways in which they want to revise their case to add to its effectiveness in leading to good discussion. Members of the group are asked to offer suggestions on how the case might be redrafted or refined, often in order to enhance the likelihood that the case will raise questions of general or theoretical significance. This stage of rewriting was important for us because we wanted to build up a set of cases, or a 'casebook', that could be used in other professional development settings.

Libby's case

Libby, a head of science in her high school, presents a case that she has just written, called 'Planning for learning', about the problems that she is experiencing in teaching toward another CSF outcome. Here are some extracts:

> In this time of transition from the established curriculum to the 'new' CSF, I am constantly confronted with the problem of what depth and breadth is expected in a particular outcome, as well as the even more compounding problem of how to assess the achievement of the actual outcome . . .

> Last night I sat down with three Year 8 text books that I regard as useful, to look at alternatives that could be applied to cover the learning outcome, 'Explain how plants and animals obtain, transport and store nutrients' (Level 5, Life and Living Strand). I ended up closing the books and trying to write a unit from scratch so I could include a variety of much activity work and focus on the outcome without spending too much time on peripheral matters.

> I have taught a unit on food in previous years but it does not really address the whole of that outcome. Maybe I should be writing a textbook for CSF!

> On studying the examples of how to check evidence of satisfying the outcome I started listing areas of work that could be covered: digestive system; circulatory system; diffusion (active and passive), photosynthesis in plants as well as xylem and phloem, leaf and root structure and function. Okay, maybe I should take a different tack. How long do I want to spend on this outcome? Should I plan this first and then design the unit to fit? What other outcomes can I incorporate to 'kill two birds with one stone'?

My planning of lessons usually 'just flows'.

I am finding myself taking an enormous amount of time and effort to plan ahead a single unit of work. Maybe I am overdoing it. I have always thought that teaching the CSF would require minor adjustment and really wanted to convince other science teachers of this by example. Why then am I finding this so difficult?

Libby's case generates some of the most profound debate that the group has about the nature and purpose of CSF. Her case has somehow managed to capture an unease or uncertainty that most members of the group have experienced, but have not yet been able to articulate. Why does she find it so difficult to plan units around something so obvious as learning outcomes for students? Old debates from the 1960s resurface about the limitations of behavioural objectives as a focus for curriculum planning. Do the same criticisms then apply now to outcomes-based curriculum planning? What does it mean to learn science – to do science – to think scientifically? How do these aims now fit in with the CSF idea of outcomes-focused curriculum planning? Does learning science mean the same as reaching predictable outcomes?

The discussion rages on and it is clear that, although no definite answers have been arrived at, the group has pooled a lot of experience and clarified the nature of the problem, which is usually 90 per cent of finding workable solutions. Some feel that they were misled by the CSF into believing that outcomes should be the focus for their course planning when that was not the intention at all. Others take the view that the CSF should be seen as a legitimate device for setting out some areas that all students, in passing, should have an opportunity to learn – an accountability device – not the 'North Star' that guides all the reasons for doing science. Others again express concern about the negative consequences and 'dumbing down' effects which can follow when 'high stakes' assessment is only a pale reflection of what it means to learn and do science.

Later Libby commented on the value of the case discussion:

I just wrote the case, and it wasn't until after the group discussed it that I understood what the heck I was saying and I think it made me realise a lot about my teaching . . . that I hadn't verbalised . . . that other people were pointing it out to me through my writing, and that was really helpful.

CASE METHODS AND PROFESSIONAL COMMUNITY

For some years the research literature on in-service education has been pointing to the need for new principles for professional development that match the increasingly complex demands placed on teachers for reforms in curriculum and school organisation. Little (1993) reviews this research and provides a set of such principles. In summarising these principles she states:

> The most promising forms of professional development engage teachers in the pursuit of genuine questions, problems and curiosities, over time, in ways that leave a mark on perspectives, policy and practice. They communicate a view of teachers not only as classroom expert, but also as productive and responsible members of a broader professional community and as persons embarked on a career that may span 30 years or more.
>
> (Little, 1993: 133)

But what does it mean to build professional community? Kruse, Louis and Bryk (1994) provide a valuable synthesis from their research of the critical elements of professional communities.

> Professional communities are strong when the teachers in a school demonstrate five critical elements:
>
> 1 Reflective Dialogue.
> 2 De-Privatisation of Practice.
> 3 Collective Focus on Student Learning.
> 4 Collaboration.
> 5 Shared Norms and Values.
>
> (Kruse *et al.*, 1994: 4)

Case methods aim directly to strengthen these critical elements of teacher interaction within schools and through various district networks and teacher/subject associations. In terms of the above list, Mark and Libby certainly exemplify what it means to be members of a professional community. Through 'de-privatising' their practice, teachers in the case methods groups have become far more accountable than many teacher appraisal and performance management schemes can ever hope to achieve. In the processes of discussing and analysing cases, teachers come to frame their aims and problems anew, and to increase their opportunities to learn from each other's experience.

Case methods provided a context of trust and support in which they were able to engage in stimulating, non-threatening collegial dialogue around the details of their teaching and learning. As Libby says in her reflections on joining the case methods group: 'Here I was of equal importance. I did not have to impress, or to make an impression, I could be myself.'

McLaughlin (1994) argues that we have to move beyond the mentality of the in-service 'course' to building new structures or contexts that support regular and sustained teacher interaction with colleagues over matters directly connected with their teaching, their students and what they are learning. The importance of context is captured well in this statement from McLaughlin who studied a variety of long-standing networks (Lieberman and McLaughlin, 1992) and collaboratives that teachers had set up to meet their own professional development needs:

My analysis is based on the view that teachers' professional development of the most meaningful sort takes place not in a workshop or in discrete, bounded convocations but in the context of professional communities – discourse communities, learning communities. Further, I show that teachers can and typically do belong to multiple professional communities, each of which functions somewhat differently as a strategic site for professional growth. Thus the argument is made that enabling professional development is, at root, about enabling professional community.

(Lieberman and McLaughlin, 1992: 31)

Case methods provide one means of establishing the professional 'discourse communities' or 'networks' that McLaughlin refers to. There is a lot of glib talk, however, about 'professional community', 'learning community' and 'collegiality' within the workplace that reflects little understanding of how the entrenched culture and norms of privacy, territoriality and hierarchy can inhibit trust and risk-taking in the workplace. Our experience suggests that it may be more fruitful in some circumstances to aim first at building professional networks of teachers from different schools, in order to build up confidence and numbers. We are not saying that genuine collegiality, or 'joint work' (Little, 1990), is a hopeless cause, but participants, in our cases groups, all believed that there would have been considerable difficulties in starting case methods from within their school science departments, even though opportunities for such discussion of classroom practice were badly needed. Marianne, a science coordinator in a Catholic regional girls college, took one of the cases into her science department meeting. Her experience was echoed by other participants:

There was a whole lot more stuff to contend with than here [in the case methods group]. First of all they don't want to be there . . . they think that discussion is a waste of time . . . you have to deal with a tremendous interplay of personalities who feel they have the power in the place – and they can totally undermine the discussion (as they did). I had younger teachers coming up to me and telling me, 'I really thought there were terrific issues in that case and I wanted to say something further, but I was too scared because so and so had put the death knell on it from the very first sentence onwards.' You would need a full day with that particular staff to break down all the barriers and start them looking at the issues and not play personalities with each other all the time. Here, when you come from different schools, everyone is starting on a level plane – and that's one less barrier you have to break down.

CASE METHODS AND PROFESSIONAL DEVELOPMENT

Reference was made earlier to Little's statement that 'one test of a teacher's professional development is its capacity to equip teachers individually and collectively to act as shapers, promoters and well-informed critics of reforms' (Little, 1993: 130). Case methods certainly met this criterion, as the cases above illustrate. These teachers have been evaluating the potential of case methods for professional development. It is also clear from these extracts that they are adding to knowledge and deepening understanding about issues involved in 'implementing' the CSF. They are in a rather different situation from that which usually prevails when teachers are being 'in-serviced' about yet another curriculum reform. They have moved well beyond merely implementing the CSF.

The cases above indicate that what the CSF is, as in any curriculum reform, is problematic. Libby says at the end of the cases course, 'When I first came to the cases group I thought I had a good understanding of the CSF. By the second week I thought, I don't know much about the CSF at all! By the end I thought that I had a much broader under-standing.'

What the CSF is in practice depends, of course, on what it *means* to each and every teacher. One of our first cases, written in 1994 by Marianne, was in response to a talk given to the cases group by a visitor to the group from the Board of Studies. It was called 'Angry with the CSF' and begins this way:

> I am so sick of being treated as someone who doesn't know her business and who can't be treated with the common courtesy of being listened to and accepted as a responsible member of a profession. These were the feel-ings generated when it became quite clear that the CSF would in all likelihood be mandated for us.

Marianne goes on to describe a lively and innovative science programme with electives that her teachers have developed over the years, which has been very successful in sustaining girls' interest in science during Years 9–10, when interest usually plummets. More teachers actually want to teach Years 9–10 than there are classes available. She points out that her staff are not scared of change and are very active in various kinds of professional development. She expresses concern about the effects that teaching toward CSF outcomes will have on student and staff interest.

Marianne's perception, and perception is all-important here, is that complying with the CSF will mean that the school will have to dismantle the elective system and return to a system that makes all students do tradi-tional 'science' courses. She feels that the CSF desire to ensure that everyone has a sound science education will result in less student interest and there-fore less real learning of science. She asks:

> How much power do I have to ensure the continued development of valu-able science education? Who are the faceless people who think they know better than I do? When did they last stand in front of a class of Year 10 students, half of whom know they will never continue with chemistry

and so have no interest (and no need) to balance chemical equations correctly? . . .

I believe committed teachers should have a real influence on the design of state-wide curriculum. For this to occur we need consultation before the curriculum is written, not afterwards when it becomes an issue of being seen to consult rather than truly consulting. However, if the [CSF] is not a document whose main aim is to improve education but merely a document which is devised for some political purpose, what can I do? Who can I argue with?

As can be imagined, this case provokes a range of strong responses and enables some central questions to be raised about the purposes of the CSF and the expectations of those who have introduced it.

This case, with others, was fed back to relevant people in the Board of Studies. The less defensive saw it as a valuable insight into the various interpretations that teachers were making of their reforms and the need for rethinking their approaches. We used Marianne's case in other in-service settings and it provided a powerful means for eliciting different perceptions of the CSF and, consequently, a valuable vehicle for discussing and learning about deeper implications of the CSF.

FLOW-ON EFFECTS FROM CASE METHODS

The process of case writing and discussion helped teachers to analyse and share their own practical knowledge, as it relates to making sense of the CSF. Participants also gained more general professional development skills in facilitating case discussions they have used with colleagues in other contexts. They have gone on to run case methods workshops, using the casebook at state and national science teacher conferences, in schools and in district-based CSF network meetings.

Most members of the group took the initiative of using cases in staff meetings back in their own schools, with mixed results, as we saw above. Mark, a head of science in his own school, took the brave step of asking colleagues to read his case on cells (above) in the context of an after-school departmental meeting, not a setting conducive to in-depth discussion about teaching in the best of circumstances. But he did not tell them that it was a case based on his teaching. Twenty minutes was all the time that he could afford to discuss the case. Mark tape-recorded the discussion of the case and presented a transcript of it at the next meeting of the case methods group, which aroused great interest. In fact it became the basis for another case that Mark prepared on the dilemmas he faced in fulfilling his responsibility to provide opportunities for professional development in his department.

It is fascinating to analyse the transcript. At the start, one teacher says,

'What are we supposed to do with this – read it?' as he flicks through it with a look of impatience on his face. Initial comments by teachers are rejecting or dogmatic: 'This would not work with our Year 8s.' Toward the end of the transcript, however, it is clear that the mood shifts and the talk starts to become a more productive exchange of views about pros and cons of the factory analogy and other ways of tapping into the students' experience in relation to cells. This is a common transition as teachers begin realise the potential of case discussions to provide the kind of interaction with colleagues that they value for their professional development.

Merrin used a case as part of the peer appraisal scheme in her school. The scheme means that pairs of teachers have to observe each other's teaching. When a suitable time was eventually found for Merrin to observe her shy and elusive 'peer appraisal' colleague, she found his physics lesson so interesting that she decided to write her observation as a 'case'. In other words, she simply recorded and described the events in the lesson as she saw it and fed it back to the teacher. As Merrin writes:

> The teacher and I actively engaged in a discussion on the lesson. I thought that it was fantastic. We shared comments on a variety of the events and he gave me further insights into why he had done particular things at particular times. He seemed honestly amazed that I was so impressed with the strategies and content of his lesson. I read through the eight pages of notes I had scrawled down during the forty-five minute lesson. We were so rapt in our discussion that we both arrived late for our lunch duties.

Merrin had discovered, paradoxically, that description is a far better basis for appraisal discussions than judgements and opinions. By feeding back to the teacher a non-judgemental mirror on his practice she provided a framework within which the teacher was much more willing to self-evaluate and reflect on his own practice. Merrin thought that other teachers would be very interested in reading the case. She asked if he would mind if she wrote it up and distributed it around the staffroom. He did not mind, so she did and the case aroused considerable staffroom interest and discussion.

CONCLUDING COMMENTS

Case methods have provided us with some of the most exciting and rewarding professional development we have ever experienced. They seem to match well with the preferred learning styles of many teachers. Teachers take enthusiastic control of their own professional development with case methods. We have seen teachers set their own demanding agenda for reform and focus their energy on what really matters to them in meeting their own standards and aspirations to do a better job. Case methods seem to release teachers from the artificial deference, and consequent anger and impatience, frequently induced by traditional in-service courses and workshops. This chapter illustrates how teachers' perceptions of knowledge and authority about practice can shift from formal, external sources to their own internal and collective sources. These teachers began to see themselves as producers of knowledge about teaching, especially producers of the kind of knowledge that is essential if often poorly conceived and inadequately resourced government-initiated policies are to be translated into educationally defensible teaching practices.

A few years ago I asked a large sample of teachers, 'What have been the most important avenues for your professional development?' The avenues that they rated most highly were feedback from students, and the opportunities that they had had to work with colleagues on tasks directly related to their teaching, especially those who taught the same subjects or levels as themselves. It did not seem to matter whether they were teachers from the same school or not. They rated these informal or unintended sources of professional development more highly than planned in-service education activities, no matter whether the latter had been based in their school or somewhere else.

This finding will not surprise anyone, least of all teachers. What is surprising is how infrequently we build on this knowledge in the organisation of teachers' work and professional development planning. If it happens, it is more by accident than design. It is an interesting question why so few in-service education activities are actually designed to capitalise on what teachers say are the most valuable avenues for their professional development. One reason is that these avenues would require radical reorganisation of teachers' work and school management to allow time for teachers to document and evaluate what they are doing in consultation with colleagues, the kind of practice that is assumed to be essential in other professions. Perhaps it has something to do with the fact that teachers have rarely had the opportunity to set the agenda for their own professional development. Most in-service education courses have been based on someone else's agenda, someone else's priorities, someone else's fad. The unfortunate consequence over the years is that many teachers do not feel that they have a right to set the agenda for their own professional development, or they have ceased to think they might have a responsibility to do so.

NOTE

1 Executive memorandum No. 96/201, 'Implementation of the Curriculum and Standards Framework', Directorate of School Education, Victoria.

REFERENCES

Barnett, C., Goldenstein, D. and Jackson, B. (eds) (1994a) *Mathematics Teaching*

Cases: Fractions, Decimals, Ratios and Percents – Hard to Teach and Hard to Learn?, Portsmouth, NH: Heinemann.

—— (eds) (1994b) *Facilitator's Discussion Guide. Mathematics Teaching Cases: Fractions, Decimals, Ratios and Percents – Hard to Teach and Hard to Learn?*, Portsmouth, NH: Heinemann.

Barnett, C. and Ramirez, A. (1996) 'Fostering critical analysis and reflection through mathematics case discussions', in J.A. Colbert, P. Desberg and K. Trimble (eds) *The Case for Education: Contemporary Approaches for Using Case Methods* (pp. 1–13), Boston: Allyn & Bacon.

Barnett, C. and Tyson, P. (1993) 'Mathematics teaching cases as a catalyst for informed strategic enquiry', paper presented at the Annual Meeting of the American Educational Research Association, Atlanta, April.

Colbert, J.A., Desberg, P. and K. Trimble (eds) *The Case for Education: Contemporary Approaches for Using Case Methods*, Boston: Allyn & Bacon.

Fullan, M. (1991) *The New Meaning of Educational Change*, New York: Teachers College Press.

—— (1994) 'Broadening the concept of teacher leadership', in D. Walling (ed.) *Teachers as Leaders* (pp. 241–54), Bloomington, IN.: Phi Delta Kappan.

—— (1995) 'The limits and potential of professional development', in T. Guskey and M. Huberman (eds) *Professional Development in Education: New Paradigms and Practices* (pp. 253–67), New York: Teachers College Press.

Kruse, S., Louis, K.S. and Bryk, A. (1994) 'Building professional community in schools', *Issue Report No. 6* (pp. 3–6), Madison, WI: Center on Organisation and Restructuring of Schools.

Lieberman, A. (ed.) (1988) *Building a Professional Culture in Schools*, New York: Teachers College Press.

—— (ed.) (1992) *The Changing Contexts of Teaching: Ninety-first Yearbook of the Society for the Study of Education, Part 1*, Chicago: University of Chicago Press.

Lieberman, A. and McLaughlin, M.W. (1992) 'Networks for educational change: powerful and problematic', *Phi Delta Kappan*, 73: 673–7.

Little, J.W. (1990) 'The persistence of privacy: autonomy and initiatives in teachers' professional relations', *Teachers College Record* 91, 4: 509–36.

—— (1993) 'Teachers' professional development in a climate of educational reform', *Educational Evaluation and Policy Analysis* 15, 2: 129–52.

McLaughlin, M.W. (1994) 'Strategic sites for teachers' professional development', in P. Grimmett and J. Neufeld (eds) *Teacher Development and the Struggle for Authenticity: Professional Growth and Restructuring in the Context of Change* (pp. 31–51), New York: Teachers College Press.

Merseth, K. (1996) 'Cases and case methods in teacher education', in J. Sikula (ed.) *Handbook of Research on Teacher Education*, 2nd edn (pp. 722–44), New York: Macmillan.

Nias, J. (1987) *Seeing Anew: Teachers' Theories of Action*, Geelong: Deakin University Press.

Schifter, D. and Fosnot, C.T. (1993) *Reconstructing Mathematics Education: Stories of Teachers Meeting the Challenge of Reform*, New York: Teachers College Press.

Shulman, J.H. (ed.) (1992) *Case Methods in Teacher Education*, New York: Teachers College Press.

Shulman, J.H. and Colbert, J.A. (eds) (1987) *The Mentor Teacher Casebook*, San Francisco: Far West Laboratory for Educational Research and Development.

—— (eds) (1988) *The Intern Teacher Casebook*, San Francisco: Far West Laboratory for Educational Research and Development.

Shulman, J.H., Colbert, J.A., Kemper, D. and Dmytriw, L. (1990) 'Case writing as a site for collaboration', *Teacher Education Quarterly* 17, 1: 62–78.

Shulman, J.H. and Mesa-Bains, A. (eds) (1990) *Diversity in the Classroom: A Casebook for Teachers and Teacher Educators*, San Francisco: Research for Better Schools.

Shulman, L. (1992) 'Toward a pedagogy of cases', in J. Shulman (ed.) *Case Methods in Teacher Education*, New York: Teachers College Press.

Silverman, R., Welty, W.M. and Lyon, S. (1992) *Case Studies for Teacher Problem Solving*, New York: McGraw-Hill.

Sykes, G. and Bird, T. (1992) 'Teacher education and the case idea', in G. Grant (ed.) *Review of Research in Education* (Vol. 18, pp. 457–521), Washington, DC: American Educational Research Association.

Wassermann, S. (1993) *Getting Down to Cases: Learning to Teach with Case Studies*, New York: Teachers College Press.

Chapter 17

Musing on the future of primary schooling

Judyth Sachs and Lloyd Logan

The unchallenged wisdom of experience can frequently act as a professional and practical barrier to change. This unchallenged wisdom often provides a justification or excuse for maintaining and continuing the *status quo*. Accordingly it becomes a regressive rather than a progressive force in terms of teachers' school and classroom practice. In this chapter we assert that, given the current economic, social and political conditions facing teachers engaged in primary schooling, it is imperative for them to reach behind that experience in order to develop a more profound understanding of the 'everydayness' and taken-for-granted aspects of their practice as it relates to teaching in primary school classrooms. We argue that by understanding the complexities of the taken-for-granted, teachers can position themselves individually and collectively within their schools to be even more responsive to the increasing challenges and demands that are being placed on them virtually on a daily basis.

In order to be responsive to emerging political agendas, in this chapter we argue also that teachers need to have an understanding of the 'big picture' and the issues that are driving and shaping current educational policy and practice. To this end, we have organised the chapter around two questions: what are the issues currently confronting primary schooling and primary school teachers, and how can primary school teachers respond, both individually and collectively, to these challenges in ways that are in the best interests of children, their parents and the nation? We begin by describing the broader social, political and economic contexts that are currently shaping primary education policy and practice both nationally and internationally. Using examples from primary schools involved in the National Schools Network (NSN),[1] we indicate some ways that teachers in Australian primary schools are responding positively to these challenges by taking the initiative to shape their own professional futures. At the core of our argument is the view that successful primary schools develop as places for teacher learning as well as student learning. This in turn facilitates the development of a learning profession.

THE BROADER SOCIAL, POLITICAL AND ECONOMIC CONTEXT OF PRIMARY SCHOOLING

Teachers in schools are currently being confronted with immense socio-historical transformations. These transformations are occurring across all institutions within modern economies. Hargreaves (1994: 23) argues that the challenges and changes facing teachers and schools are not parochially confined to education but are rooted in a major socio-historical transition from a period of modernity to one of postmodernity. A consequence of this is that schools and teachers are being affected more and more by the demands and contingencies of an increasingly complex and fast-paced, postmodern world. Not surprisingly, there are few elements of public life that have gone unchallenged. Since the 1980s every feature of the public sector in Australia has undergone extensive reform. These reforms are based on the assumption that the application of market theory and private sector management principles, procedures and structures to public sector activity result in higher productivity, improved quality of service and greater accountability.

Public sector reform in Australia occurred in response to the need for governments to respond to increasing social and cultural complexity, rapid change and public demand for 'user-free' government services. Governments of all persuasions have sought to meet this situation by adopting a market orientation towards the provision of services and a managerialist approach to its delivery. Government-initiated changes to schooling are part of these wider public sector reforms and primary schools have not been left out of these social transformations.

The central precepts underlying the application of commercial approaches to the public sector include assumptions that: the traditional structures, procedures and services are inefficient; there is a set of generic skills called 'management'; private enterprise management approaches are superior to other alternatives; managerial and structural reforms guarantee revision to practice that results in increased productivity; government services can be quantified for accountability purposes; and reform is management led. Critics of this position such as Boston (1991) and Ball (1994) argue that significant differences between the public and private sectors 'have crucial implications for the management of the public sector and the exercise of public power' (Boston, 1991: 22). Nevertheless, market and managerial theories are being applied to public sector management and policy in Australia through the imperatives of deregulation, efficiency, effectiveness, decentralisation, performance monitoring, management information systems and devolved accountability to 'executive agencies' (Boston, 1991). One of these 'executive agencies' is the local school. In short, the three Es of 'efficiency, effectiveness and economy' are now the central tenets shaping education policy and practice at the system and individual level.

Within this broader context of public sector management reform an array of political, economic and professional challenges are being directed towards education institutions at all levels; school education, TAFE (technical and further education) and higher education. The pressures of these economically driven imperatives present significant challenges for the teaching profession as a whole and for teachers individually. The outcomes of these political interventions already have significantly reshaped the form and content of primary school education. To some extent this has been done without the consent or intellectual leadership of the teaching profession and the expertise of primary school teachers and administrators. The challenge facing the teaching profession is how to reclaim the education agenda.

In part reclaiming the education agenda requires us to peer into the future and speculate about what all of this means for the structure of schools and the work of teachers? Hargreaves (1994) argues that the response of schools to rapid societal and cultural change is often inappropriate and ineffective – because it leaves intact the systems and structures of the present or retreats to comforting myths of the past. Given this observation, we speculate that schooling, which we define as the learning of stated content, skills, attitudes and values in communal settings, will continue to play a major role in the lives of primary aged children. However, being mindful of Hargreaves' observation, we assert that the process and sites of such learning will go beyond current schooling locations. In particular the increased use of, and access to, information technology will change the form and processes of learning. The temporal dimensions of learning, that is when learning occurs, will be confronted by information technology, as will conventional structures and beliefs about schooling. This in turn has implications for notions such as compulsory attendance, age-graded learning and classrooms themselves. The possibility of virtual classrooms where students log in to information databases will become a reality.

A second area of change will be who provides learning opportunities. We speculate that primary schools in their traditional sense will no longer monopolise the learning market. More alternative providers will enter the school marketplace and the distinction between home learning and school learning will be blurred. However, despite the opportunities for access to information available to each individual, schools will continue to provide a key site for socialising children into becoming a member of Australian society. Social learning, then, will become a more important dimension of the schooling experience of children.

Nevertheless, a significant challenge for schooling still remaining is how to move its focus from socialisation to education, from knowledge dissemination to judgement-making and problem-solving, from teaching the answers to questioning the questions. This changed focus will move the orientation to schooling from teacher-directed and controlled teaching to student-initiated learning. This requires finding new ways to teach children how to access and process knowledge in disciplined and critical ways, and how to work collaboratively rather than individually, as suggested by Renshaw and Brown in Chapter 14.

It is likely that parents, teachers and pupils will emphasise the personalising of schooling, specialised instruction and self-directed learning. Furthermore, they will emphasise greater control and choice over the form, timing and location of their schooling. We assert that diversity of forms and offering will characterise schooling systems as they respond to the demands placed on them by new social, economic and political agendas. There will be a move to counter the 'large is economically efficient' argument which characterised institutional amalgamations in the 1980s. In this scenario schools will be small. Large schools will be divided into sub-schools, which share some common facilities and services in order to capitalise on the social and economic benefits of smallness coupled with economies of scale. This runs counter to recent trends of amalgamations which incorporated smaller elements into larger ones. Evidence of this organisational restructuring within schools is happening in a number of schools associated with the NSN.

Issues regarding what constitutes quality schooling and how to guarantee and measure quality assurance, quality improvement and quality management will become a core part of a school's intellectual and administrative technology. As Highett indicates in Chapter 5, issues of quality will not only be concerned with accountability purposes, even though this will remain a strong focus. Instead, issues of quality improvement and quality management will become even more important as schools strive to respond to rapidly changing social, economic and cultural conditions. Concerns about quality and accountability will be implemented within the context of reconceptualising and questioning the purposes of schooling. Quality will no longer be a tool for government control of schools; indeed, it will provide opportunities for schools to become more responsible for their own development and continual responsiveness to the changing internal and external conditions.

In their responses to broader political, social and economic pressures, primary schools will have to fundamentally rethink their place in the world and reorganise themselves institutionally and administratively. The following are some of the areas where we envisage change occurring:

- Staff will be professionally cosmopolitan, a combination of educational, welfare, health, community, legal and technology professionals supported by technicians, clerical and ancillary staff. In smaller schools these services will be shared.
- Patterns of employment will vary from part-time appointments to service contracts. Services and facilities will be a mix of free and 'user pays', some of which will be available twenty-four hours a day.
- The use of IT in particular will make the 9 a.m.–3.30 p.m. day an

anachronism, an artefact of the post-industrial school rather than the information school.

- Units providing school services will be smaller and more diverse.
- The demand for specialisation and vocational education along with the continuation of a common or general curriculum. This will be more obvious in secondary schools but will become increasingly the case in the later years of primary schooling.
- The call for schools to be more responsive to contemporary events while retaining officially sanctioned core values.
- The need for schools to be 'technology rich' and to provide learning experiences appropriate to an information age. This has to be implemented while operating under tight economic constraints which force teachers and students to continue to use 1960s professional practices and 1980s technology.
- The changing and multi-faceted role of teachers that requires them to be multi-skilled professionals while at the same time de-skilling them and assigning them the role of technician will have to be addressed professionally and industrially.

In responding to the above, teachers and administrators can be strategic in creating and enacting their own visions of what primary schooling ought to be. However, failure to respond to these challenges and paradoxes may well lead to new forms of education provision being established and imposed upon primary schooling without any input from teachers and administrators themselves. This in turn presents challenges for the profession and teachers at both the structural and the individual level.

SOME CURRENT CHALLENGES FACING PRIMARY SCHOOLING

At the structural level the current challenges facing primary schooling and teachers include: pressure of external accountability from a variety of education stakeholders; increased political pressure to direct the processes and provision of school education; the provision of more economically and efficient education; and the preparation of students who are numerate, literate and able to take civic and social responsibility. Finally, politicians and bureaucrats are demanding greater conformity of education offerings.

At the individual level a major challenge for primary teachers is the need to be skilled practitioners who can work both collaboratively and independently, are able to solve complex practical and theoretical problems, are able to reflect on their practice in order to develop quality learning opportunities for their students, and finally, are professionals who are able to cope with rapid social and technological change.

Not surprisingly, these challenges have immense implications for the practice of primary schooling and the development and maintenance of the teaching profession. In order to be professionally responsive, primary school teachers need to improve their own commitment to learning as members of a learning profession. In practice this means that they need to establish and continue to establish a knowledge and skill base that is embedded in practice and has as its central aim the understanding and improvement of their own practice and the theory and beliefs that form it. In many cases to achieve such aims will require a significant reorientation of the conception and implementation of continuing teacher professional development programmes, as indicated by Ingvarson and Marett in Chapter 16.

Importantly, good teaching in primary school classrooms requires a thoughtful, caring teacher committed to the lives of students. The new conditions facing primary teachers requires them to make explicit the foundations upon which they base their practice. It requires them to take moral choices and demands that they be able to justify their choices in public and private arenas. It requires them to reclaim their professional voice and expertise. Good teaching is not a matter of specific techniques or styles, plans or actions.

The paradoxes listed above and the challenges that they generate provide primary teachers with the opportunity to think about what ought to be, what could be and what ought not to be. Being responsive and strategic to the current conditions provides teachers with a legitimate means for taking control of their own professional and personal lives in schools. It means shaping the profession of teaching in ways that suit the profession and are not imposed upon by political dictates.

American educator Maxine Greene suggests that we can achieve this by what she calls 'doing philosophy'. Doing philosophy means being self-aware and highly conscious of the world around us. It means attending again and again to a fundamental teaching question: 'Given what I now know (about the world, about this class, about these students), what should I do?' (Greene, 1973).

Because the rewards of teaching are neither ostentatious nor obvious and are often internal, invisible and of the moment, the achievements of individual teachers are often left unrecognised. Paradoxically, however, these achievements can be deep and long lasting. They can mean making the difference in someone's life. Given that primary schooling establishes the foundations for and dispositions toward learning, primary school teachers are placed in a singularly important position to contribute to rethinking the purposes of schooling. It is on this basis that teachers need to have visions of what ought to be and what can be. They need to be seen in the community as visionaries, as people who can and do make a difference in the lives of a variety of people. Primary school teachers need not and should not take up the role of unthinking technicians or implementers of government policy.

More positively, the emerging social, economic and political conditions will mean that the ethos of our schools and classrooms will be required to change. Within a new context schools and classrooms will have to become concerned with learning rather than teaching. They will be required to become, in popular parlance, learning organisations. This in turn, as indicated above, requires that teaching becomes a learning profession. One of the great paradoxes of teaching, and one not missed by Michael Fullan (1993), is that as a profession we are not a learning profession. While student learning is a goal, often the continuing learning of teachers is overlooked. As teachers we should be concerned with continuous learning and the improvement of our practice. To achieve this we should examine our practice and engage in professional conversations with our colleagues so that we develop a shared language and vocabulary about improvement. As Nias and colleagues, reporting on a project in the United Kingdom, observe:

> seeing colleagues learning was an added encouragement, because individuals realised that they were not alone in their need to learn. Learning was regarded as a means of increasing one's ability, not as a sign of inadequacy; the desire to improve practice also led to a constant quest for good ideas, that is ideas that were relevant to classroom practice.
>
> (Nias *et al.*, 1992: 76)

The experience of working together also enabled teachers to challenge one another's thinking and practice (*ibid.*: 88). These ideas and practices are pivotal to developing a learning profession. National initiatives such as the NSN are working towards such a goal and to resolving the challenges and paradoxes of the broader political context.

RETHINKING THE WORK OF PRIMARY SCHOOL TEACHERS

The National Schools Network is a reform network providing support for over 200 Australian schools which are rethinking their work organisations and teaching and learning in order to improve learning outcomes for students and staff. NSN schools have developed projects that have been concerned with asking teachers to examine and question the link between the organisation of teachers' work and pedagogy. Second, the NSN continually links teacher professional development with ongoing school-based research initiatives. The NSN research framework involves building a research culture among teachers in schools. It promotes and supports collaborative research and collegial reflective practices using critical action research methodologies. Through such an orientation to school practice, teachers in schools are rethinking and revitalising various aspects of their practice.

Two examples will be presented to indicate the diversity of ways that teachers, through their involvement in the NSN, are rethinking their work practices. Teachers at Ascot Vale Primary School in metropolitan Melbourne, for example, have been concerned with reorganising learning across the school through the implementation of 'mini schools'. The 'mini schools' are organisational structures for regular teacher planning and review, professional development and delivery. The school, subscribing to principles of collegiality, have adopted a two-team approach (Mini School One and Two) with a flat team structure. Team organisation, planning and participation are essential elements of the structure and culture of the school.

As part of a dynamic form of work organisation, teachers at Ascot Vale are not only concerned with the practice of teaching itself, that is working with children; they are constantly engaged in collaborative activities to develop team participation and skills at an individual, group and whole-school level. Team structures are organised for the purpose of planning and learning from each other, distributing the workload, so that teachers are able to use their time more efficiently and effectively in order to be in control of their own professional development.

As a result of their affiliation with the NSN and the work associated with this project, staff have refined new and existing teaching and learning strategies such as student-based curriculum planning, student contracts, group and individual inquiry learning, peer and cross-age tutoring that includes observation, shared experiences and reporting (National Schools Network, 1996).

At Ascot Vale Primary School there is evidence to support Beattie's (1995) observation that collaboration, collegiality and conversation provide teachers with a means for professional learning and development within the context of self and community. Through their participation in the NSN, teachers were provided with the skills and opportunities to record their learning so that colleagues in other schools across the country could learn from their experiences. Consequently, as is usually the case, the learning gained from these conversations and deliberations, which is usually restricted to the teachers involved and is not available for scrutiny or sharing, was able to be communicated to a wider audience. By making these learnings and the process of deliberation available to a wider audience and open to more intensive critiques, the worth of the experience for the participants, the school community and the wider profession has been enhanced.

Bellambi Public School in New South Wales is another primary school participating in the NSN which has been struggling with organisational structures. In this school the project took the form of creating both a learning community and a community of leaders. It has achieved this by adopting cooperative learning strategies among staff and expressing them through school decision-making. This links adult learning and student learning (National Schools Network, 1996).

The project undertaken at Bellambi represents a major departure from traditional structures, both administrative and organisational. As a result it has required a significant reculturing of the school and its communities.

Rethinking leadership, so that shared responsibility for decision-making and flatter management structures has provided a significant challenge for the hierarchical and line management ethos of the New South Wales Department of School Education. Collegiality is essential to the working of the school. The new structures that have been developed and the resources to sustain the change are devoted to enabling learning between staff to take place.

Not surprisingly, rethinking management and classroom practices so that the emphasis within the school has been redirected to learning and away from managing and teaching has created some challenges for teachers working in this new environment. Among others, this has meant that teachers have had to reassess the role of traditional teaching and forms of assessment that they have previously used in their classrooms. That this change has confronted much of the conventional wisdom of teaching and firmly held beliefs about what it means to be a teacher is an understatement. Nevertheless, the outcomes of the project, namely flatter management structures, an authentic culture of cooperation, a learning environment that is more productive in terms of student learning, teacher satisfaction and community involvement, all attest to the mutual benefits gained from a project that at its inception was seen as high risk.

The projects described briefly above indicate how teachers and administrators in two states are responding creatively and strategically to reculture and restructure their schools. Through their involvement in the NSN teachers have undergone significant individual and group professional development. Both of these projects and the many others associated with the NSN have demonstrated that the kind of professional development required in the context of reform that is driven by practitioners is highly problematic (Groundwater-Smith, 1996). Rethinking schools and classroom practice is highly demanding. It requires that teachers, administrators and parents confront some of the taken-for-granted assumptions that have guided their professional work for many years. It means that these people take risks about making public their successes, failures, reservations and anxieties. For some this is an activity that has never been undertaken during their professional lives. Nevertheless, evidence gained from teachers involved in the NSN has indicated that this risk-taking has enormous potential for re-enlivening their life and practice in schools.

The experience of the NSN has demonstrated quite clearly the importance of leadership in the endeavour of rethinking schools. Traditional notions of both leadership and education need to be reformulated to accommodate powerful barriers to reform which are embedded in the thinking and the practices of teachers and administrators. As Groundwater-Smith (1996) argues, these include traditional concepts of hierarchical leadership, stereotyped roles of teachers and administrators and dominant curriculum and assessment regimes.

Peters, Dobbins and Johnson (1996) identified the areas for teacher professional development that were essential for school reform. These include: the knowledge, skills and attitudes needed to implement change in ways that improve learning outcomes for all; strategies for coping with the change process; strategies for democratic decision-making; the interpersonal skills needed to work collaboratively; and the skills of critical reflection and collective inquiry.

These skills cannot be developed by one-off in-service events. They require a deliberate attempt by systems and schools to construct teacher professional development opportunities that are contextually embedded and are responsive to the specific needs of a school community as a community of learners.

It is clear that one requisite for job-embedded professional development to be extensive, effective and efficient is for learning to be seen as a major *resource* of the school. As Senge (1990: 3) argues, people in organisations continually expand their capacities to create the results they truly desire, where new expansive patterns of thinking are nurtured, where collective aspiration is set free and where people are continually learning how to learn together (Senge, 1990: 3). He calls such organisations 'learning organisations'. Such organisations empower people, create free space for learning, encourage collaboration and sharing for gains, promote inquiry and provide continuous learning opportunities (Watkins and Marsik, 1993). Conceptualising schools as learning organisations shifts the 'core activity' from teaching to learning and transforms the social roles and relations to staff, parents and students. Everyone is cast as a learner and involved in creating and sharing knowledge and skills. Given the structure and ideologies about learning presented in Chapter 1, primary schools are well placed to become learning organisations.

In primary schools that are learning organisations, both students and teachers are provided with opportunities to learn from each other. Consequently in such schools the social relations between students and staff have been transformed. Both parties are seen to be involved in mutual knowledge creation.

The challenge of creating a learning primary school may be seen as principally how well the students and teachers succeed in creating conditions in which all its people, including parents, take responsibility for the whole business of learning, knowledge creation and consumption.

In developing a learning profession and working in communities of learners, a climate of support and a commitment to learning together is developed. In such a context as Nias *et al.* (1992) discovered, a questioning approach to improvement can be generated and teaching can be a matter of taking more, rather than less, risks. The experience of teachers working in the NSN schools clearly demonstrated the fruits of such an approach.

CONCLUSION

Primary teaching and schooling in the future will require that we find new and different ways of working. We must be able to respond to and manage change and to see change as an integral part of our personal lives. To this end, change should not be seen as frightening but rather as something that we take up as a challenge. At the core of this is the need for teachers to develop the habits and skills of continuous inquiry and learning. As Fullan (1993: 81) suggests, 'we should have as a central tenet of our practice the disposition of always seeking new ideas inside and outside their own settings'. In so doing, teachers and students are positioned to have some agency in creating their own futures.

Primary schooling will be the responsibility of those who have the most at stake: parents, teachers and students. The example of projects such as the NSN and the ways that teachers have begun to rethink their work organisation provide some indication of what is possible if teachers work collaboratively and see reform as a form of problem-solving. The work lives of teachers will be enhanced and student learning outcomes will be improved. These projects provide opportunities for teachers to rethink their professional practice within the context of their schools and their personal beliefs and goals by working with their colleagues in generative and collaborative ways. They provide examples of ways forward for all of us concerned with enhancing the quality of learning and developing through primary schooling.

NOTE

1   The National Schools Network was formed in 1994 to continue the school reform agenda begun by the National Schools Project for the Quality of Teaching and Learning. The NSN is a school reform network, providing support for over 200 Australian schools that are rethinking their work organisation and teaching and learning practices in order to improve learning outcomes for students and teachers.

REFERENCES

Ball, S. (1994) *Educational Reform: A Critical and Post-structural Approach*, Buckingham: Open University Press.

Beattie, M. (1995) 'New prospects for teacher education: narrative ways of knowing teaching and teacher learning', *Education Research* 37,1

Boston, J. (1991) 'The theoretical underpinnings of public sector restructuring in New Zealand', in J. Boston, J. Martin, J. Pallott and P. Walsh (eds) *Reshaping the State: New Zealand's Bureaucratic Revolution*, Auckland: Oxford University Press.

Fullan, M. (1993) *Change Forces*, London: Falmer Press.

Greene, M. (1973) *Teacher as Stranger*, Belmont, CA: Wadsworth.

Groundwater-Smith, S. (1996) *Let's Not Live Yesterday Tomorrow: A Study of*

Curriculum and Assessment Reform in the Context of Reculturing, National Schools Network Research Paper No. 3, Ryde, New South Wales: NSN.

Hargreaves, A. (1994) *Changing Teachers, Changing Times*, New York: Teachers College Press.

National Schools Network (1996) *Ministerial Brief*, Ryde, New South Wales: NSN

Nias, J., Southworth, G. and Campbell, P. (1992) *Whole School Curriculum Development in Primary School*, Lewes: Falmer Press.

Peters, J. Dobbins, R. and Johnson, B. (1996) *Restructuring and Organisational Culture*, National Schools Network Research Paper No. 4, Ryde, New South Wales: NSN.

Senge, P. (1990) *The Fifth Discipline*, New York: Doubleday.

Watkins, K. and Marsik, V. (1993) *Sculpting the Learning Organisation*, San Francisco: Jossey Bass.

Index